Additional Praise for *Global Asset Allocation*

"*Global Asset Allocation* forms a perfect bridge between modern empirical research on financial markets and its practical implementation in global portfolio management. The book will appeal to professionals with prior knowledge of the topic, keeping them abreast of the latest methods and concepts in their field of expertise in a didactically efficient way."

> Professor Bruno Gehrig
> Vice-President of the Governing Board
> Swiss National Bank

"Global asset allocation models have been drastically impacted by the phenomenon of globalization. Correlations and the degree of integration between financial markets in different countries have risen significantly. Recognizing this change, *Global Asset Allocation* focuses on the methodological implications of global asset allocation decisions. The empirical results provided in the book go far beyond what current textbooks on international finance cover."

> Dr. Markus Rudolf
> WHU-Otto Beisheim Graduate School of Management
> Dresdner Bank Endowment Chair of Finance

"Great overview of the most recent literature that is also fun to read."

> Dr. Erwin W. Heri
> Chief Investment Officer
> Credit Suisse Financial Services, Zurich

"Heinz Zimmermann and his coauthors have produced a serious book, of interest to academics and practitioners of the art of asset management alike. Integrating new theoretical and empirical research, to which they have made important contributions during the past few years, they offer unorthodox insights with considerable practical implications for global asset allocation. Anyone interested in the latest thinking on consumption-based portfolio construction, the impact of macroeconomic factors on expected returns, and the emerging issue of the efficiency of diversification using country versus global sector criteria, will find much food for thought in this book. Well-written, comprehensive, and up-to-date!"

> Gunter Dufey
> Professor of Finance, Corporate Strategy and International Business
> The University of Michigan Business School, Ann Arbor
> Adjunct Professor, NBS, Nanyang Technological University, Singapore

Global Asset
Allocation

John Wiley & Sons

Founded in 1807, John Wiley & Sons is the oldest independent publishing company in the United States. With offices in North America, Europe, Australia, and Asia, Wiley is globally committed to developing and marketing print and electronic products and services for our customers' professional and personal knowledge and understanding.

The Wiley Finance series contains books written specifically for finance and investment professionals as well as sophisticated individual investors and their financial advisors. Book topics range from portfolio management to e-commerce, risk management, financial engineering, valuation and financial instrument analysis, as well as much more.

For a list of available titles, please visit our Web site at www.WileyFinance.com.

Global Asset
Allocation

New Methods and Applications

HEINZ ZIMMERMANN
WOLFGANG DROBETZ
PETER OERTMANN

John Wiley & Sons, Inc.

Published by John Wiley & Sons, Inc., Hoboken, New Jersey.
Published simultaneously in Canada.

For general information on our other products and services, or technical support, please contact our Customer Care Department within the United States at 800-762-2974, outside the United States at 317-572-3993 or fax 317-572-4002.

Wiley also publishes its books in a variety of electronic formats. Some content that appears in print may not be available in electronic books.

For more information about Wiley products, visit our Web site at www.wiley.com.

Library of Congress Cataloging-in-Publication Data:

Zimmermann, Heinz.
  Global asset allocation : new methods and applications / Heinz Zimmermann, Wolfgang Drobetz, Peter Oertmann.
    p. cm. — (Wiley finance series)
  ISBN 0-471-26426-1 (cloth : alk. paper)
  1. Asset allocation. 2. Investments, Foreign. 3. Globalization —Economic aspects. I. Drobetz, Wolfgang. II. Oertmann, Peter. III. Title. IV. Series.
  HG4529.5.Z56 2003
  332.67'3—dc21   2002009972

Printed in the United States of America.

10 9 8 7 6 5 4 3 2 1

This book is about global asset allocation decisions. The benefits of international asset allocation have been recognized for a long time. H. Grubel, H. Levy, M. Sarnat, and B. Solnik demonstrated the benefits of international diversification more than 25 years ago, when only a small number of global investment opportunities were available. This picture has drastically changed. Most institutional investors, such as pension plans or insurance companies, invest a substantial part of their assets in foreign markets, sectors, and currencies, and mutual funds offer a wide range of global investment products at reasonable cost. The globalization of the economy has progressed dramatically in this time period, which is particularly true for the internationalization of the financial system, including the banking sector. Financial services have become a truly global business.

Many excellent books have been published on these topics over the past years, for example, Frankel (1994), Ledermann and Klein (1994), Giddy (1994), Jorion and Khoury (1995), Solnik (2000), Smith and Walter (2000), to mention just a few. The distinguishing feature of this book is its attempt to incorporate recent methodological advances in the treatment of the various topics. Much progress has been made in the statistical modeling of time-varying risk and return characteristics of financial markets. These tools make it possible to shed new light on the time-varying relationship between volatility and the correlation between markets and sectors, and to investigate the implications for international asset allocation strategies. This literature also suggests a "dynamic" view of the risk-return trade-off of financial assets: Risk premia are time-varying and predictable based on changing business conditions. Numerous econometric research has tested the time-series and cross-sectional implications of conditional multifactor asset pricing models. This research has major implications for the implementation of dynamic (tactical) asset allocation strategies, as well as the measurement of investment performance. Finally, a substantial part of the recent progress in the asset pricing literature relies on test strategies based on stochastic deflators. This approach is extremely useful to investigate the degree to which markets are integrated or segmented in terms of the pricing of systematic risk across national borders, sectors, or entire asset classes. This has important implications for asset allocation strategies, but also for corporate funding decisions.

This book focuses on the practical applications of these methodological advances for global asset pricing and portfolio decisions. Original empirical work is presented throughout the book.

Most of the chapters were originally presented at two Global Asset Allocation Conferences organized by Peter Oertmann and Heinz Zimmermann in October 1999 and October 2000, respectively, in Zurich, Switzerland. We are grateful to the Swiss Institute of Banking and Finance (s/bf) at the University of St. Gallen for hosting the conferences. The senior author of this book was then a director of the Institute. The presented papers were evaluated by the organizers of the first conference, and a few were refereed by outside reviewers. Earlier versions of Chapters 4 and 10 were published in the *Journal of Financial Markets and Portfolio Management,* where a German version of Chapter 6 was published also. All chapters have been updated and revised from the papers originally presented.

While the three authors of this book bear full responsibility for the content of this volume, we gratefully acknowledge the contribution of David Rey, the author of Chapter 4, who did an excellent job in preparing the final version of the entire manuscript; and of Viola Markert, co-author of Chapter 8. We also acknowledge the motivating comments and suggestions by the participants of the conferences, as well as by our students and colleagues. We hope that this volume will stimulate further research in this area.

HEINZ ZIMMERMANN
WOLFGANG DROBETZ
PETER OERTMANN

Basel and St. Gallen, Switzerland
October 2002

contents

Global Asset
Allocation

CHAPTER 1

The Global Economy and Investment Management

EXECUTIVE SUMMARY

- Globalization, or more precisely, integration of financial markets implies the convergence of risk premiums between national markets, sectors, and other market segments. In integrated financial markets, risk is priced consistently across national markets and currencies.
- The most important reason for increased integration is the liberalization and deregulation of capital markets, with relaxed investment restrictions, free cross-border capital flows, and significantly lower transaction costs.
- Globalization affects expected risk premiums through three main channels: the profitability of firms, the structure of the market portfolio, and the pricing of global risk.
- Whether markets are integrated or (at least partially) segmented has important implications for the design of asset allocation strategies as well as the cost of capital of firms.

This chapter gives a brief overview of the material covered in this book.

MOTIVATION

Financial markets have become increasingly globalized over the past two decades for a number of reasons, including:

- The globalization of the economies themselves.
- The broader recognition of the benefits of international diversification.
- The decreasing role of purchasing power and foreign exchange risk in Western economies.
- The progress and internationalization of information technology and communication systems.
- The emergence of global trading systems.
- The decrease of information and transactions costs for international trades.
- The institutionalization of investors such as pension funds, mutual funds, and hedge funds, with a broad focus on international investments.

The trend toward international investments is a natural consequence of the overall globalization of the economies and the international financial system. However, the question remains: How exactly are portfolio diversification strategies affected by the general trend toward globalization?

GLOBALIZATION AND RISK

Neglecting transaction costs and capital market imperfections, global portfolio decisions are determined by the risks and expected returns on national markets as well as global sectors. A first observation, well documented in numerous empirical studies, is that country-by-country correlations between global stock and bond market returns have substantially increased over the past decades. Alan Greenspan and Wall Street seem to be the leading indicators for what happens on the exchanges across the rest of the world (see Oertmann, 1997, for an interesting empirical study on this subject). This increase in correlations has dramatic effects on the risk of globally diversified portfolios. Global systematic risk has increased substantially. This implies that the international diversification benefits reported in the early studies by Grubel (1968), Levy and Sarnat (1970), and Solnik (1974c) have largely disappeared in recent years. From a practical standpoint, what are the investment implications: staying at home, taking a different asset allocation approach (e.g., a sector approach), or investing in nontraditional asset classes such as hedge funds, private equity, commodities, or emerging markets?

GLOBALIZATION AND EXPECTED RETURNS

We cannot derive investment implications without taking expected returns into account. Asset allocation decisions always reflect a tradeoff between risk and expected returns. Globalization affects expected returns through three main channels: the profitability of firms, the structure of the market portfolio, and the pricing of global risk. The first effect is immediately obvious: Globalization is a major force for the competitive power of firms, sectors, and countries; it determines their profitability, growth potential and, finally, expected returns. Second, globalization has a substantial effect on the industrial structure of national economies (or international sectors), and consequently also affects the composition of the major stock market indices. Even ignoring the growth of alternative investments and mutual funds, the investment universe has changed substantially over the past decade (e.g., due to numerous initial public offerings, or IPOs, and the associated growth of the information technology and communication sectors). This has had a substantial effect on the composition of the relevant market (or benchmark) portfolio, which in turn affects equilibrium expected returns on individual assets. Third, globalization affects the pricing of market risk (i.e., the unit price of nondiversifiable risk in the economy). The next section discusses this third channel in depth.

GLOBALIZATION AND THE MARKET PRICE OF RISK

In the development of the financial sector, new products (e.g., funds), markets, and financial instruments (e.g., derivatives) that have been introduced to transfer economic and financial risks could potentially affect the size of the risk premiums demanded by investors. In addition, the emergence of institutional investors—acting under different constraints than private investors—has probably changed the aggregate risk tolerance of the market and, therefore, the magnitude and the temporal behavior of market risk premiums.

But most important, the liberalization and deregulation of capital markets with relaxed investment restrictions, free cross-border capital flows, and significantly lower transaction costs has led to an increased integration of markets. In integrated markets, risk is priced consistently across national markets and currencies. Whether markets are integrated or (at least partially) segmented has important implications for asset allocation strategies. In integrated markets, there should be less room for tactical asset allocation strategies than in segmented markets—investors diversify their portfolios to reach their desired level of expected return. If markets are (partially) segmented, investors use active return bets to improve portfolio performance by over-weighting markets where they perceive attractive risk-return tradeoffs.

However, to determine whether markets are integrated or segmented requires a joint test of integration and market equilibrium. Integration is conceptually related to the consistency of expected returns across markets or sectors, but expected returns must be derived from an underlying asset pricing model. The results of empirical tests for integration are notoriously hard to interpret because one cannot distinguish which of the two underlying hypotheses fails.

TACTICAL ASSET ALLOCATION AND ESTIMATION RISK

Portfolio optimization tools and simulation techniques are widely used to investigate the impact of alternative market assumptions and parameter specifications on the optimal asset allocation. If investors would fully agree on estimated returns, volatilities, and correlations of the relevant asset classes, they would passively hold the market portfolio. But most investors have individual views and opinions about markets and sectors, and thus over- and underweight selected asset categories relative to the market. In the aggregate, however, these categories must add up to the market portfolio. Thus, as investors, we must ask: How can we incorporate the level and confidence of our individual estimates and forecasts to portfolio strategies consistent with capital market equilibrium?

ABOUT THIS BOOK

Chapter 2 contains an overview of international asset allocation and asset pricing models, including a discussion on currency hedging. It grew out of a series of lecture notes used by Peter Oertmann and Heinz Zimmermann in their international finance classes. Chapters 3 and 4 cover the observation that stock market volatility and correlation are substantially different in up and down markets. The two chapters contain detailed analyses of this empirical observation and discuss the implications for diversification strategies and risk management.

Chapter 5 describes an empirical methodology that is useful in implementing global asset allocation strategies. It empirically explores common economic determinants of returns (volatility drivers) as well as expected returns (value drivers) across international stock and bond markets. The empirical results lead to the conclusion that multiple sources of global economic risk affect both the variability of returns and the valuation on international stock and bond markets. To control the variance and measure the performance of an internationally diversified portfolio including both stock and bond positions, a framework with multiple global risk factors is preferable to the single-factor model specified in the international Capital Asset Pricing Model (CAPM).

Chapter 6 presents an econometric test on the integration of stock markets. As mentioned, whether markets are integrated is important not only for tactical asset allocation strategies but also for corporations in optimizing their financial structure. The same methodology can be used to test whether new investment opportunities expand the risk-return menu from existing investments in an economically meaningful sense. Chapter 7 investigates whether emerging stock markets can be seen as integrated parts of the developed worldwide stock markets.

Chapter 8 addresses whether global sector diversification strategies produce risk-return patterns different from asset allocation rules defined in terms of national markets. This question is important not only for portfolio managers, but also for financial analysts. In Chapter 9, strategies exploiting a specific investment style-value and growth characteristics of stocks are analyzed in a global asset pricing framework by implementing active style rotation strategies.

Finally, Chapter 10 shows how the approach originally developed in the Black-Litterman (1992) model can improve global asset allocation decisions. The approach combines a passive (market equilibrium) approach with an investor's subjective view of markets, based on his or her confidence in the forecasts. This is a useful methodology because it allows investors to take an intermediate view about the informational efficiency of markets.

CHAPTER 2

International Asset Pricing, Portfolio Selection, and Currency Hedging

An Overview

EXECUTIVE SUMMARY

■ International asset pricing models differ from domestic asset pricing models because currency risk and institutional barriers to international diversification such as investment restrictions or transaction costs, capital controls, and political risk (to mention just the most important) must be considered.

■ This chapter focuses on currency risk or, more specifically, on purchasing power risk and its role in efficient diversification strategies, hedging decisions, and asset pricing.

■ If purchasing power parity (PPP) holds, there is no currency risk, no currency hedging, and no currency risk premium—the simple Capital Asset Pricing Model (CAPM) can be extended to an international setting.

■ If exchange rates are correlated with stock market returns, exchange rate risk is not fully diversifiable, and investors hedge against exchange rate risk.

■ Different models have been developed to demonstrate the diversification, valuation, and hedging effects of exchange rate risk. In this chapter, the classical models of Solnik (1974a), Sercu (1980), Stulz (1981a), Adler and Dumas (1983), and Black (1989) are presented in an integrative survey.

■ The currency hedging decision is part of the overall diversification strategy and it cannot be separated from the asset allocation across markets. Currencies are best regarded as separate asset classes.

■ This casts serious doubts on the adequacy of "overlay" currency hedging strategies often implemented in practice.

■ In general, currency risk is associated with a positive risk premium, implying that currency hedging is not a free lunch and full hedging is not optimal.

■ A partial equilibrium model of international asset pricing can be constructed postulating a CAPM-like relationship conditional on a minimum-variance currency hedge implemented by investors.

■ However, a general equilibrium model (including equilibrium on currency forward markets) is much more difficult and relies on unobservable variables.

■ Universal—noninvestor-specific—currency hedge funds as postulated by Black (1989, 1990) only exist under special circumstances.

INTRODUCTION

International asset pricing models are similar in structure to the valuation concepts developed in the closed-economy setting. The mainstream theories of beta pricing, the single-beta Capital Asset Pricing Model (CAPM), the Arbitrage Pricing Theory (APT), and the multibeta IntCAPM can be extended to international pricing relationships in principle. However, such extensions require assumptions on the behavior of exchange rates, on consumption, and on the investment opportunity sets in different countries. Some of these assumptions are quite restrictive. Country-specific consumption and investment opportunities imply that investors from different countries perceive asset returns differently. A central factor in international valuation theory is the examination of how these differences affect the investors' portfolio holdings and expected returns in a certain numéraire currency. Two strands of theory development can be identified. First, some models start with presumptions on individual portfolio choice in different countries and obtain pricing relationships via aggregation and market clearing conditions. Solnik (1974a) and Sercu (1980) show the derivation of partial equilibrium models for international capital markets. The models are developed in a continuous-time mean-variance framework and yield portfolio separation theorems and a CAPM-like pricing restriction. More general equilibrium theories of international asset pricing were introduced by Stulz (1981a) and Adler and Dumas (1983). The second strand of valuation concepts in an international setting was originated by Solnik (1983b) and elaborated by Ikeda (1991). The authors successfully show that the APT can be applied to an international framework as long as exchange rates obey the same factor structure as stock returns.

The next section, which provides a brief discussion on the fundamental problems of asset pricing in an international framework, introduces the differences between domestic and international valuation models. In the third section, the structure of international asset pricing models is discussed in a setting without deviations from Purchasing Power Parity (PPP), that is, without real exchange rate risk. Then in the fourth section, portfolio selection and equilibrium pricing implications in the presence of PPP deviations are analyzed. In particular, the Solnik-Sercu, the Adler-Dumas, and the Stulz versions of the International CAPM (IntCAPM) are discussed. In the fifth section, the focus is on equilibrium currency hedging policies. The final section discusses the Arbitrage Pricing Theory (APT) in the international context.

VALUATION IN AN INTERNATIONAL SETTING: BASIC FACTS

As briefly mentioned, standard separation, aggregation, and asset pricing results developed in a domestic setting cannot be easily extended to an international framework by simply including foreign investments in the feasible investment opportunity set. International valuation theories have to reflect that investors evaluate returns from the same asset differently in different countries. This heterogeneity in the investors' perception of risk and return is primarily caused by deviations from PPP between countries.

Purchasing Power Relationships

The concept of Purchasing Power Parity goes back to Cassel (1916) and, according to Adler and Dumas (1983), simply measures the similarity of consumption opportunities in different countries. Stulz (1981a) defines the consumption opportunity set of an investor as "[...] the set of goods available for his consumption, the current prices, and the distribution of the future prices of those goods [...]" (p. 384). Hence, the major causes of PPP deviations are differences in the composition of national consumption baskets, the relative prices of goods in different countries, and the time-evolution of those prices. In international finance, two versions of PPP are distinguished: absolute PPP and relative PPP.

Absolute PPP and Commodity Price Parity (CPP): Absolute Purchasing Power Parity asserts that the exchange rate between the currencies of two countries should be equal to the ratio of the average price levels in the two countries. That is, at any instant, the following relation is assumed to hold:

$$\sum_{g=1}^{G^d} w_g^d \cdot P_g^d = S_f^d \cdot \sum_{g=1}^{G^f} w_g^f \cdot P_g^f \tag{2.1}$$

where P_g^d denotes the price of the gth good in the domestic country, and w_g^d stands for the weight of that good in the domestic consumption basket. P_g^f and w_g^f are the gth good's price and its weight in the foreign country, respectively. G^d is the number of domestic goods, and G^f is the number of goods in the foreign country. Finally, S_f^d is the spot price of the foreign currency in terms of domestic currency units, the exchange rate. Equation 2.1 establishes a relationship between average price levels. This absolute PPP relation must be distinguished from Commodity Price Parity (CPP), also known as the "law of one price." CPP states that the real price of any individual good is the same irrespective of the country, implying the subsequent relation for any good g that is available in both the domestic and the foreign country:

$$P_g^d = S_f^d \cdot P_g^f \tag{2.2}$$

CPP can thus be characterized as an instantaneous arbitrage condition that holds in the absence of trade barriers between countries. This relation generally holds for homogeneous goods traded on organized auction markets such as commodities exchanges—the best examples are gold or other precious metals.[1] On the other hand, because absolute PPP is defined on the basis of a weighted average of individual prices, it is, at least to some extent, an "average version" of the law of one price. But PPP can be violated between two countries even if CPP holds for each individual good. In such a case, the weighting schemes of the goods in the national consumption baskets differ. Differences of that kind are likely to emerge because of the heterogeneity of national consumption tastes. In accordance with the review of empirical work provided by Adler and Dumas (1983), violations of CPP are the rule rather than the exception. Thus, there may be two sources of deviations from absolute PPP—differences in national consumption baskets and deviations from CPP, respectively.

Relative PPP: Relative purchasing power parity focuses on the relationship between inflation rates in two countries and the change of the exchange rate for the countries' currencies over a certain period. The inflation rate in a country is usually calculated on the basis of a consumer price index (CPI), which is the price of a representative basket of consumer goods. In general, the composition of a CPI should reflect the consumption opportunities as well as the preferences of the citizens in a country. Then, the rate of inflation can be determined from the change of the CPI over the relevant time period.[2] Relative PPP claims that any inflation differential between two countries is exactly compensated by respective movements in the spot exchange rate between the countries' currencies. Using the CPIs of the domestic and a foreign country as valid representations of the average price levels, and taking the ratio of the absolute PPP written at the start and at the end of a certain time period, leads to the following representation of relative PPP:

$$s_f^d = \frac{S_{f,t}^d}{S_{f,t-1}^d} = \frac{1 + \pi_t^d}{1 + \pi_t^f} \qquad (2.3)$$

where $S_{f,t}^d$ is the spot exchange rate at time t (at the end of period t), and $S_{f,t-1}^d$ is the spot exchange rate at time $t - 1$ (at the beginning of period t). π_t^d denotes the domestic inflation rate for period t and π_t^f is the foreign inflation rate for the same time period, respectively. Evidently, if relative PPP holds, exchange rate shifts perfectly mirror inflation differentials and thus do not influence the valuation of financial assets in real terms.

The Core Problem of International Asset Pricing

Deviations from absolute and relative PPP can be observed at almost all times and between almost all countries. However, it is widely accepted that PPP serves as a reliable hypothesis for long-run considerations. Not surprisingly, empirical work, such as that summarized in Adler and Dumas (1983), shows that the average deviation tends to zero over long periods. Nevertheless, the fact that PPP may fail in the short run introduces an additional dimension to international valuation theories which does not exist in domestic asset pricing models. The obstacle associated with PPP violations stems from the way real asset returns are determined. Because nominal returns gained in a foreign currency are first translated into domestic currency units and then the domestic CPI is used to deflate this income, deviations from PPP imply that investors in different countries have different notions of the real return for the same asset. Consequently, the heterogeneity of national consumption tastes is the core problem of international valuation models.

Most asset pricing theories define a "country" as a subset of investors who use the same CPI to deflate asset returns. The feasible consumption opportunity set serves as a criterion to distinguish between nations. Alternatively, the feasible investment opportunity set can be used to define a country. According to Stulz (1995), the "[...] investment opportunity set is described by the distributions of wealth available [...] for each future date" (p. 1). In an international setting, market imperfections such as taxes, transaction costs, and border controls, tend to segment capital markets. It is even possible that some investors are completely restricted from buying foreign assets. Of course, such investment barriers influence expected returns as well. Summing up, the structure of any international asset pricing model must include assumptions about both the consumption opportunity set and/or the investment opportunity set.

PORTFOLIO SELECTION AND ASSET PRICING I

Utility-Based Asset Pricing Models—Overview

Basically, pricing restrictions with a similar structure as the widely accepted domestic CAPM or the Intertemporal CAPM (ICAPM) can also be developed in an international context. The theories that imply this result are based on the "classical" set of assumptions on individual portfolio choice, aggregation, and market clearing. However, pricing restrictions derived this way differ in the additional presumptions made on the consumption and investment opportunity sets across countries. Consistent with the classification of Stulz (1995), three major classes of utility-based international valuation models can be identified:

1. Models that assume equal consumption and investment opportunity sets across countries.
2. Theories that explicitly consider differences in the national consumption opportunity sets.

3. Models that identify the impact of barriers to international investment.

The first class of international valuation theories yields a CAPM-like pricing restriction in terms of real returns, which is often used as a baseline case for more general frameworks. Stulz (1984, 1995) provides a derivation of this model together with a broad discussion of its implications.

The second class of models uses different approaches to model differences between consumption opportunities across countries. Solnik (1974a) suggests a model in which the investors' consumption is limited to their home country and local inflation is zero. Refinements of this model are suggested by Sercu (1980). Grauer, Litzenberger, and Stehle (1976) and Fama and Farber (1979) derive a pricing restriction similar to the International CAPM of Stulz (1984, 1995) in a world where consumption opportunity sets differ and PPP holds. Explicit deviations from PPP are considered in the more general settings of Stulz (1981a) and Adler and Dumas (1983). Whereas Stulz (1981a) presents a consumption-based valuation model for international asset returns, Adler and Dumas (1983) derive a multifactor model including premiums for market risk as well as exchange rate risk.

The third class of models comprises the work of Black (1974) and Stulz (1981b), among others. Although these approaches certainly provide additional dimensions to the international pricing problem, they are not discussed in the following text. Stulz (1995) and Frankel (1994b) give up-to-date surveys of the most important findings in this area.

The Basic International Capital Asset Pricing Model (IntCAPM) without Deviations from PPP

Assuming that the simple pricing relation of the domestic CAPM can be applied in an international context lacks any intuitive reasoning. As the domestic CAPM is stated in terms of nominal returns, the heterogeneity in the investors' perception of risk and return caused by PPP deviations is not an issue. Stulz (1984, 1995) derives an international single-beta pricing model in terms of real returns, which is sometimes called International Capital Asset Pricing Model (IntCAPM).[3] For this model, a world is assumed in which there are no differences in consumption and investment opportunity sets among countries. It is presumed that all investors consume the same single consumption good, which is available in every country and freely traded across borders. The real price of the good in any currency is always the same in all countries: CPP holds all the time.[4] In addition, markets are perfect and frictionless, and there are no barriers to international investment. Finally, it is assumed that the investors are risk-averse, maximize end-of-period consumption, and use the consumption good as the numéraire to calculate real returns.

Portfolio Separation and the IntCAPM in Real Terms

If investors located in different countries determine real returns in terms of the same consumption good and CPP is satisfied all the time, expected real returns of assets are the same for all investors. With the additional assumption that investors can lend and borrow in units of the consumption good at a given real rate, the existence of multiple countries can be completely ignored. All investors identify the same input parameters for portfolio optimization. Hence, the results of standard mean-variance portfolio theory apply. Any investor desires a combination of (1) the risk-free asset and (2) a portfolio of risky assets that is common to all investors across the countries. This must be the world market portfolio. Then, a representative investor can be introduced and a restriction on expected real returns can be derived from the first-order condition of his or her portfolio optimization problem:[5]

$$E\left[r_i^c\right] = \beta_{iwm}^c \cdot E\left[r_{wm}^c\right] \text{ with } \beta_{iwm}^c = \frac{Cov\left[r_i^c, r_{wm}^c\right]}{Var\left[r_{wm}^c\right]} \qquad (2.4)$$

r_i^c denotes the one-period real return of the ith asset in excess of the risk-free rate and r_{wm}^c is the contemporaneous excess real return on the world market portfolio. Finally, β^c_{iwm} stands for the sensitivity of the real return of the ith asset to the real return of the world market portfolio (the real world market beta). Excess real returns are measured in units of the consumption good in the following way:

$$r^c_i = \frac{\dfrac{P_{it}}{P_{gt}}}{\dfrac{P_{i,t-1}}{P_{g,t-1}}} - 1 - R^c_f \quad \text{and} \quad r^c_{wm} = \frac{\dfrac{P_{wt}}{P_{gt}}}{\dfrac{P_{w,t-1}}{P_{g,t-1}}} - 1 - R^c_f \qquad (2.5)$$

respectively, where P_{it} is the price of the ith asset at the end of period t and P_{wt} is the price of the world market portfolio at that time. P_{gt} is the corresponding price of the consumption good. The prices at the beginning of the period are denoted with the subscript $t - 1$. R^c_f is the risk-free rate given in units of the consumption good, quoted at the beginning of the period.

Equation 2.4 constitutes the pricing restriction of the IntCAPM. Just as with the domestic CAPM, a single-beta pricing relationship is implied in the international context. However, this relation is stated in terms of real returns measured in units of a single consumption good common for all international investors. Consistently, the expected real excess returns implied by the IntCAPM have no "country index."

The IntCAPM in Nominal Terms

The expected real excess returns implied by the preceding model are different from those given by the domestic CAPM applied to nominal asset returns after conversion to a domestic currency. If it is assumed, however, that (1) in a certain country an asset with a risk-free return exists denominated in the country's currency as well as a zero world market beta in real terms, and (2) the inflation rate in that country, which is equal to the growth rate of the price of the consumption good, is uncorrelated with nominal asset returns, then a nominal version of the IntCAPM can be derived.[6] To demonstrate this, Equation 2.4 can be rewritten as follows:

$$E\left[\frac{r_i^d}{1+\pi^d}\right] = \beta_{iwm}^d \cdot E\left[\frac{r_{wm}^d}{1+\pi^d}\right], \text{ where } \beta_{iwm}^d = \frac{Cov\left[\dfrac{r_i^d}{1+\pi^d}, \dfrac{r_{wm}^d}{1+\pi^d}\right]}{Var\left[\dfrac{r_{wm}^d}{1+\pi^d}\right]} \quad (2.6)$$

and r_i^d is the nominal one-period excess return of the ith asset, calculated in units of the domestic currency as follows: $r_i^d = R_i^d - R_i^f$, where R_i^f stands for the nominal domestic risk-free rate. r_{wm}^d is the nominal excess return on the world market portfolio. Finally, π^d denotes the domestic inflation rate in the period considered. Further transformation of Equation 2.6 yields:

$$Cov\left[\frac{1}{1+\pi^d}, r_i^d\right] + E\left[\frac{1}{1+\pi^d}\right] \cdot E\left[r_i^d\right] = \beta_{iwm}^d$$
$$\cdot \left\{ Cov\left[\frac{1}{1+\pi^d}, r_{wm}^d\right] + E\left[\frac{1}{1+\pi^d}\right] \cdot E\left[r_{wm}^d\right] \right\} \quad (2.7)$$

So it becomes evident that the pricing statement depends on the covariance between nominal excess returns in domestic currency and the domestic rate of inflation. If conditions (1) and (2) are satisfied, the latter equation reduces to the subsequent model:

$$E\left[r_i^d\right] = \beta_{iwm}^d \cdot E\left[r_{wm}^d\right], \text{ where } \beta_{iwm}^d = \frac{Cov\left[r_i^d, r_{wm}^d\right]}{Var\left[r_{wm}^d\right]} \quad (2.8)$$

The second condition guarantees that the covariances within Equation 2.7 are equal to zero. The first condition implies that the betas computed based on nominal excess returns are equal to those computed using real excess returns. Equation 2.8 establishes the IntCAPM in terms of returns denominated in a certain country's currency. As long as the law of one price is presumed to hold, the currency in any country can be used to express returns.

The nominal IntCAPM assumes that inflation does not represent a source of systematic risk influencing the cross-section of expected returns in a country. If the covariance between the inflation rate and the nominal return on assets is small in magnitude, then Equation 2.8 may be used to approximate the original IntCAPM in real terms as given by Equation 2.4. However, the empirical evidence regarding the relationship between shifts of domestic inflation and returns on stocks is inconclusive across different countries. Most of the studies on international stock markets document a negative correlation between nominal stock returns and both expected and unexpected inflation (see, e.g., Solnik, 1983b, or Gultekin, 1983). Overall, we cannot derive a general statement about the potential error when using the nominal IntCAPM as an approximation to the real IntCAPM.

PORTFOLIO SELECTION AND ASSET PRICING II

Accounting for PPP Deviations and "Real" Exchange Rate Risk

The IntCAPM, as discussed in the previous section, presumes a world in which there are no real differences between investors. It is assumed that all investors have the same tastes, face the same set of consumption opportunities, and PPP holds all the time. Of course, such a world does not represent the real world, and investors do not have the same preferences over consumption across countries. In addition, transportation costs, taxes, tariffs, and the like, usually cause differences in the structure of relative prices across countries. Moreover, the structure of relative prices changes differently over time in different countries. As a result, the representative consumption baskets differ in a time-varying fashion across countries and there is no reason for PPP to hold.

Because consumption opportunity sets evolve differently among countries, investors face exchange rate risk. In accordance with Solnik (1974a), exchange rate risk stems from unforeseen deviations from PPP. A sudden shift in the parity relation affects the perception of the risk-return characteristics of internationally traded assets differently for investors from different countries (see, e.g., Solnik, 1974a). As a consequence, the hedging property of the same asset concerning changes in the costs of consumption depends on which country's perspective is taken. Because investors are always willing to hedge against unanticipated changes in the price of their consumption baskets, exchange rate risk causes a different asset demand across countries and thus different expected returns. Consequently, investors in different countries choose among different sets of efficient portfolios. Although in such a setting investors still care about the distribution of real returns, the covariance of the real return of an asset with the real return of the world market portfolio, as formulated by the IntCAPM in the previous section, no longer sufficiently describes expected returns.

The Solnik-Sercu International Asset Pricing Model

Solnik (1974a) is among the first authors to analyze portfolio separation as well as asset pricing in an international model based on a constant investment opportunity set while allowing for differences in the consumption opportunity sets across countries. His model is developed in the intertemporal, continuous-time framework of Merton (1973). In addition to standard assumptions on perfect world capital markets and homogeneous expectations, Solnik (1974a) considers unconstrained international capital flows with perfect exchange markets. For the national investors' consumption opportunities, it is presumed that there is a single consumption good in each country. The price of each country-specific good is constant over time in the respective country's currency, and any investor's consumption is limited to the good in his or her home country. By assuming zero local inflation in each country, exchange rate changes purely mirror changes in the relative prices of the national consumption baskets; exchange rate shifts represent pure deviations from PPP. Moreover, a strict segmentation of the product markets is postulated, implying partial equilibrium. Nevertheless, the model preserves the core of the valuation problem arising from exchange rate risk. The exclusion of international trade in goods simplifies the analysis because the effect of an exchange rate shift on the return of a foreign investment is the same for all investors in a country. Finally, it is assumed that exchange rates are uncorrelated with stock returns in domestic currency, and in each country a risk-free asset exists.

Portfolio Selection and Currency Hedging in the Solnik-Sercu Model　Within this model setting, Solnik (1974a) derives a statement on the portfolio strategy of a utility-maximizing investor. The domestic risk-free asset, domestic common stocks, foreign risk-free assets, and foreign common stocks are considered as investment opportunities. Then, all investors hold a combination of (1) the world market portfolio hedged against exchange rate risk, (2) a portfolio of the risk-free assets of all countries, and (3) the risk-free asset of their home country.[7] The first portfolio, the world market portfolio, is hedged against exchange rate risk by going short in the respective local risk-free asset. Actually, this is a zero-investment fund. The second portfolio is made up of foreign risk-free assets and does not contain any market risk—it purely mirrors exchange rate speculation. Whereas these two funds are entirely held by all investors across all countries, the third fund depends on the investor's country of residence.[8] Any investor irrespective of nationality obtains a desired level of risk by investing in two mutual funds, one representing pure market risk, the other just exchange rate risk. Then, the investment proportions among these funds portray the investor's willingness to hedge the stock investment against exchange rate risk. The model includes a dimension of portfolio choice that is irrelevant in a domestic setting: a hedge portfolio for exchange rate risk.

In the following, based on Jorion and Khoury (1995), we highlight the main features and implications of the model. To start, we take up the remark of Adler and Dumas (1983) and do not differentiate between foreign stocks (fund 1) and foreign risk-free assets (fund 2) in the characterization of the risky part of portfolio $\underline{w}$. The vector of expected excess returns in domestic[9] currency is denoted by μ and the variance-covariance matrix of the domestic excess returns is $\underline{\underline{V}}$. λ is the coefficient of relative risk tolerance. Applying a standard mean-variance portfolio selection problem gives the vector of optimal portfolio weights as $\underline{w} = \lambda \underline{\underline{V}}^{-1} \mu$. The fraction of wealth that is invested in the domestic risk-free deposit is then

$$w_{N+1} = 1 - \sum_{i=1}^{N} w_i = 1 - \lambda \, \underline{1}' \underline{\underline{V}}^{-1} \underline{\mu} = \lambda \left[1 - \underline{1}' \underline{\underline{V}}^{-1} \underline{\mu} \right] + \left[1 - \lambda \right] \quad (2.9a)$$

such that the portfolio demand of the investor in a specific country can be summarized by

$$\begin{pmatrix} \underline{w} \\ w_{N+1} \end{pmatrix} = \lambda \begin{bmatrix} \underline{\underline{V}}^{-1} \underline{\mu} \\ 1 - \underline{1}' \underline{\underline{V}}^{-1} \underline{\mu} \end{bmatrix} + (1 - \lambda) \begin{bmatrix} \underline{0} \\ 1 \end{bmatrix} \quad (2.9b)$$

This highlights our previous characterization. The portfolio demand can be separated into a common risky portfolio (fund) and the domestic risk-free asset. The risky assets are held in the same proportion by all investors. Because investors with a logarithmic utility function (which exhibits a relative risk tolerance of one) would optimally invest all their wealth in this risky fund, the portfolio is sometimes called the *log-portfolio*. The disadvantage of this characterization is that it does not reveal the currency hedging decision followed by the investors. The optimal currency positions are part of the log-portfolio, but it would be more natural to characterize the optimal currency exposures in terms of the demand and supply of currency forward contracts. Note that the covered interest rate parity in logarithmic form is $r_t - r_t^* = f_t - s_t$, which can be written as

$$\left[r_t^* + (s_{t+1} - s_t) \right] - r_t = s_{t+1} - f_t \quad (2.10)$$

and states that the excess return of foreign deposits, expressed in domestic currency, is equal to the payoff of a long forward contract. Thus, the elements of the portfolio vector $\underline{w}$ related to foreign deposits can be interpreted as positions in currency forward contracts. To make these positions explicit, we can partition the respective vectors and matrices accordingly. The vector of expected returns and the variance-covariance matrix become

$$\underline{\mu} = \begin{pmatrix} \underline{\mu}_S \\ \underline{\mu}_F \end{pmatrix} \text{ and } \underline{\underline{V}} = \begin{pmatrix} \underline{\underline{V}}_{SS} & \underline{\underline{V}}_{SF} \\ \underline{\underline{V}}_{FS} & \underline{\underline{V}}_{FF} \end{pmatrix} \quad (2.11)$$

respectively, where $\underline{\mu}_S$ is the vector of expected stock returns and $\underline{\mu}_F$ is the vector of expected returns on the currency forward contracts. $\underline{\underline{V}}_{SS}$ is the variance-covariance matrix of stock returns, $\underline{\underline{V}}_{SF}$ the matrix of covariances between stock and currency forward returns, and, consequently, $\underline{\underline{V}}_{FF}$ the variance-covariance matrix of currency forward returns. This partition makes it possible to write the portfolio vector as

$$\underline{w} = \lambda \begin{pmatrix} \underline{w}_S \\ \underline{w}_F \end{pmatrix} = \lambda \begin{pmatrix} \underline{\underline{V}}^{-1}_{S\bullet F}\underline{\mu}_S - \underline{\underline{V}}^{-1}_{S\bullet F}\underline{\underline{\beta}}'_{SF}\underline{\mu}_F \\ \underline{\underline{V}}^{-1}_{FF}\underline{\mu}_F - \underline{\underline{\beta}}_{SF}\underline{w}_S \end{pmatrix} \qquad (2.12)$$

now separating the demand for risky stocks and the demand for currency forward contracts. However, before we can give this equation economic content, a few technical comments are necessary. First, consider the matrix of betas,

$$\underline{\underline{\beta}}_{SF} \equiv \underline{\underline{V}}^{-1}_{FF} \underline{\underline{V}}_{SF} \qquad (2.13a)$$

which represents the coefficients of a linear regression of excess stock returns (in domestic currency) on excess returns on the risk-free deposit (in domestic currency), or, equivalently, the payoffs of the currency forward contracts. Taking currency forward positions according to this matrix produces a minimum-variance currency hedge. Next, the matrix

$$\underline{\underline{V}}_{S\bullet F} = \underline{\underline{V}}_{SS} - \underline{\underline{\beta}}'_{SF} \underline{\underline{V}}_{FF} \underline{\underline{\beta}}_{SF} \qquad (2.13b)$$

is a residual variance-covariance matrix of stock returns. On the one hand, from an economic point of view, this matrix represents stock market risk after implementing a perfect currency hedge. On the other hand, from a statistical point of view, it represents the stock market variances and covariances conditional on a minimum-variance currency hedge, represented by the beta-matrix given in Equation 2.13a.

We are ready to analyze the optimal stock market and currency allocation implied by Equation 2.12. Consider the optimal demand for currency forward contracts, $\underline{w}_F$, first. The second part of the demand, $\underline{\underline{\beta}}_{SF}\underline{w}_S$, represents a minimum-variance hedge strategy. Given the optimal stock market allocation $\underline{w}_S$, investors sell forward contracts implied by the beta-matrix. However, this hedge strategy is complemented by a speculative position of $\underline{\underline{V}}_{FF}\underline{\mu}_F$, which is determined by the expected excess returns on the forward contracts, $\underline{\mu}_F$. If forward rates are considered to be unbiased predictors of future spot rates, then these excess returns are zero and no speculation occurs.

We now turn to the optimal stock market portfolio, $\underline{w}_S$. This portfolio has two parts, a market fund and a currency fund, which are determined by the respective vectors of excess returns, $\underline{\mu}_S$ and $\underline{\mu}_F$. The structure of the two funds is similar to the mean-variance case, $\underline{\underline{V}}^{-1}\underline{\mu}$, except that the inverse of the variance-covariance matrix is replaced by the inverse of the residual (or conditional) stock market matrix, $\underline{\underline{V}}_{S \bullet F}^{-1}$, which reflects the minimum-variance currency hedge. Thus, without knowing the appropriate minimum-variance hedge, the optimal stock portfolio cannot be determined. But the reverse is also true. Without knowing the optimal stock portfolio, the minimum-variance hedge cannot be determined either. Therefore, only a joint solution leads to an efficient portfolio. This is an important result. In practice, it is common to separate market and currency management in portfolio decisions and to delegate the task to two separate teams or asset managers. The preceding analysis shows that, in general, this does not lead to an overall efficient portfolio. Thus, overlay currency hedges (e.g., general hedging rules that are independent of the structure of the underlying stock portfolio) are not justified theoretically. The intuition of this result is immediate in our current setting. Currencies (or equivalently, foreign risk-free assets) just represent a specific asset class, and optimizing the stock market allocation without simultaneously optimizing the currency decision would waste part of the information contained in $\underline{\mu}$ and $\underline{V}$. This insight is also important for evaluating the feasibility of overlay currency hedging strategies introduced later in this chapter.

The Solnik-Sercu Pricing Restriction   The portfolio selection just described leads directly to the pricing relation valid in equilibrium. We assume that the aggregate optimum stock holdings correspond to the market portfolio weights represented by the vector $\underline{w}_M$:

$$\sum_i W^i \lambda^i \underline{w}_S = M \underline{w}_M \qquad (2.14)$$

where W^i is the wealth of the ith individual and M is the stock market capitalization. The key insight is that the structure of the log-portfolio, $\underline{w}_S$, is independent of the benchmark currency, which implies

$$\underline{w}_S \underbrace{\sum_i W^i \lambda^i}_{W\lambda} = \underline{w}_S W\lambda = M \underline{w}_M \qquad (2.15)$$

From the partitioned version of the log-portfolio,

$$\underline{w} = \lambda \begin{pmatrix} \underline{w}_S \\ \underline{w}_F \end{pmatrix} = \lambda \begin{pmatrix} \underline{V}_{S\bullet F}^{-1} \underline{\mu}_S - \underline{V}_{S\bullet F}^{-1} \underline{\beta}'_{SF} \underline{\mu}_F \\ \underline{V}_{FF}^{-1} \underline{\mu}_F - \underline{\beta}_{SF} \underline{w}_S \end{pmatrix} = \lambda \begin{pmatrix} \underline{V}_{S\bullet F}^{-1} \left[\underline{\mu}_S - \underline{\beta}'_{SF} \underline{\mu}_F \right] \\ \vdots \end{pmatrix}$$

we have

$$\underline{w}_S = \underline{V}_{S\bullet F}^{-1} \left[\underline{\mu}_S - \underline{\beta}'_{SF} \underline{\mu}_F \right] \qquad (2.16)$$

which can be substituted into Equation 2.15 resulting in

$$\underline{w}_S W\lambda = \left\{ \underline{V}_{S\bullet F}^{-1} \left[\underline{\mu}_S - \underline{\beta}'_{SF} \underline{\mu}_F \right] \right\} W\lambda = M \underline{w}_M \qquad (2.17)$$

This, in turn, can be solved for

$$\left[\underline{\mu}_S - \underline{\beta}'_{SF}\, \underline{\mu}_F\right] = \frac{M}{W}\frac{1}{\lambda}\underline{V}_{S\bullet F}\,\underline{w}_M$$

$$= \frac{M}{W}\frac{1}{\lambda}\sigma^2_{S\bullet F}\,\underbrace{\frac{\underline{V}_{S\bullet F}\,\underline{w}_M}{\sigma^2_{S\bullet F}}}_{\equiv\underline{\beta}_{S\bullet F}} \qquad (2.18)$$

where $\sigma^2_{S\bullet F} = \underline{w}'_M\, \underline{V}_{S\bullet F}\,\underline{w}_M$ denotes the variance of the currency hedged market portfolio, which is perfectly hedged against currency risk (minimum-variance hedge). $\underline{\beta}_{S\bullet F}$ represents the beta vector—the betas of the currency hedged stock returns with respect to currency hedged market returns. Multiplying both sides of Equation 2.18 with $\underline{w}'_M$ implies

$$\left[\underbrace{\underline{w}'_M\,\underline{\mu}_S - \underline{w}'_M\,\underline{\beta}'_{SF}\,\underline{\mu}_F}_{=\mu_M}\right] = \frac{M}{W}\frac{1}{\lambda}\underbrace{\underline{w}'_M\,\underline{V}_{S\bullet F}\,\underline{w}_M}_{\sigma^2_{S\bullet F}}$$

where μ_M is the expected excess return of the market. We thus finally get

$$\left[\underline{\mu}_S - \underline{\beta}'_{SF}\,\underline{\mu}_F\right] = \frac{M}{W}\frac{1}{\lambda}\sigma^2_{S\bullet F}\underline{\beta}_{S\bullet F} = \left[\underline{\mu}_M - \underline{w}'_M\,\underline{\beta}'_{SF}\,\underline{\mu}_F\right]\underline{\beta}_{S\bullet F} \qquad (2.19)$$

which is a CAPM-like relationship. On the lefthand side, we have expected excess stock returns conditional on a perfect hedge against currency risk. Thus, the expression $\underline{\beta}'_{SF}\,\underline{m}_F$ represents the economic costs of a perfect currency hedge. The same interpretation applies for expected excess returns on the market portfolio on the right-hand side. The expression $-\underline{w}'_M\,\underline{\beta}'_{SF}\,\underline{\mu}_F$ again represents the expected costs of hedging the market perfectly against currency risks. The expected cost of hedging is equal to the expected return on a basket of forward contracts constructed with the intention to eliminate stock return-exchange rate covariances. Finally, the traditional betas are replaced by regression coefficients calculated from currency hedged stock and market returns. Thus, the CAPM holds in a fully (currency risk) hedged version. Because it rests on the assumption that individuals try to hedge their stock positions fully against currency risk, it can be regarded as a "conditional" asset pricing model.

The conclusion of this section is that the linear CAPM-relationship between beta and expected return prevails even when there are deviations from PPP because the composition of the log-portfolio is independent of the benchmark currency and thus allows separation. However, no equilibrium condition has been imposed so far on currency hedging (on the demand and supply of currency forward contracts) or equivalently, on the demand and supply of risk-free deposits. Therefore, Equation 2.19 is only valid as a partial equilibrium relationship.

Solnik (1974a) derives Equation 2.19 for the special case where stock returns are uncorrelated with currency returns. In this event, the covariance and beta terms vanish. This leads to a simplified CAPM-relationship given by

$$\underline{\mu}_S = \mu_M \underline{\beta}_{S \bullet F} = \mu_M \underline{\beta}_S \qquad (2.20a)$$

where $\underline{\beta}_S$ is the vector of simple market betas. In the notation of the equilibrium relationships introduced previously, Equation 2.20a reads as follows:[10]

$$E\left[R_i^d - R_f^d\right] = \beta_{iwm}^{dl} \cdot E\left[R_{wm}^l - R_f^l\right] \text{ with } \beta_{iwm}^{dl} = \frac{Cov\left[R_i^d, R_{wm}^l\right]}{Var\left[R_{wm}^l\right]} \qquad (2.20b)$$

where R_i^d is the return on asset i measured in domestic currency and R_f^d stands for the domestic risk-free rate. R_{wm}^l is equal to the return on the aggregated world market portfolio, where each component is expressed in the respective local currency. Similarly, R_f^l is the (world) market value weighted average of the countries' risk-free rates (an average international risk-free rate). Finally, β_{iwn}^{dl} is the beta of the return on the ith asset denominated in domestic currency with respect to the return on the world market portfolio calculated in local currencies. In Solnik's (1974a) simplified framework, world stock investments do not carry any exchange rate risk and no potential for hedging exchange rate risk. Protection against exchange rate risk is attainable solely by investing a part of wealth in foreign currency deposits.

Another version of Equation 2.19 was first derived by Sercu (1980).[11] He shows that the linear pricing result of Solnik (1974a) maintains even when the assumption of independence between stock returns and exchange rate shifts is relaxed.

The asset pricing framework developed by Solnik (1974a) and Sercu (1980) is often referred to as the "Solnik-Sercu International Asset Pricing Model" (SS-IAPM). The SS-IAPM supports the notion that investors can always completely hedge against exchange rate risk by either going short in the respective foreign bonds or buying forwards. The pricing relation implied by the model includes either expected returns in excess of the corresponding interest rate or expected returns adjusted by hedging costs. Consistent with results of standard domestic valuation theory, unsystematic risks that can be eliminated are not relevant for pricing in an international context. However, a clear difference between the SS-IAPM and versions of the IntCAPM arises because the risk-free rate on the left-hand side of Equation 2.20b is generally not equal to the average risk-free rate given on the same equation's right-hand side.[12] Moreover, SS-IAPM excess returns are based on zero-investment portfolios hedged against exchange rate risk rather than on a common numéraire currency.

From Partial to General Equilibrium

A fundamental drawback of the equilibrium model is that no equilibrium condition was imposed on the demand and supply of risk-free assets, or, alternatively, on the currency forward contracts. Of course, these assets are all in zero net supply. This restriction should be explicitly taken into account in modeling capital market equilibrium.

The implications of this generalization are illustrated using the model developed in the previous sections.

The Equilibrium Condition for Risk-Free Assets   Solnik (1993a) explicitly mentions that risk-free assets serve two fundamentally different functions: First, seen as foreign investments, they are risky assets and thus part of the overall log-portfolio. This is the "return enhancement" function. Second, seen as domestic investments, they represent a hedge against the log-portfolio. Therefore, deposits in currency j are part of the common log-portfolio of the universe of those investors with reference currency i ($\neq j$) and a share of w_F^j independent of the reference currency. The risk tolerance of the investors in currency i is l^i and their aggregate wealth is W^i. The aggregate demand for the deposits derived from the log-portfolios is therefore

$$\sum_i W^i \lambda^i w_F^j = w_F^j W \lambda \tag{2.21}$$

where W and λ are the respective aggregated values. Investors with benchmark currency j hold deposits as risk-free assets in the fraction of $(1 - \lambda^j)$ of their wealth generating an additional demand of $(1 - l^j)W^i$. Thus, the total demand for deposits in currency j is

$$w_F^j W \lambda + \left(1 - \lambda^j\right)W^i \tag{2.22}$$

which must be zero in equilibrium. This condition must hold for the universe of deposits. Solving for w_F^j implies

$$w_F^j = -\frac{\left(1 - \lambda^j\right)W^i}{W\lambda} = -\frac{\left(1 - \lambda^j\right)}{\lambda}\frac{W^i}{W} \tag{2.23}$$

which must be the relative share of the deposits of currency j in the log-portfolio. This is the fundamental equilibrium condition for risk-free assets in the presence of real currency risk.

Equilibrium Expected Return on Currency Forward Contracts What is the expected return on risk-free deposits to support the equilibrium given in Equation 2.23? After some tedious manipulations, we have

$$\underline{\mu}_F = \frac{1}{\lambda}\underline{V}_{FM} + \underline{V}_{FF}\underline{w}_F \qquad (2.24a)$$

or, for a specific currency j,

$$\mu_F^j = \frac{1}{\lambda}Cov(F^j, M) - \left\{ \sum_i Cov(F^j, F^i)\frac{(1-\lambda^j)W^i}{\lambda W} \right\} \qquad (2.24b)$$

where M denotes the market portfolio return. Let us define

$$w_H^i \equiv \frac{(1-\lambda^i)W^i}{(1-\lambda)W} \qquad (2.24c)$$

as the jth component of a yet unknown hedge portfolio with return H^j. Later in this chapter (in the section on equilibrium currency hedging), it is shown that this portfolio provides a minimum-variance hedge against global currency risk. But it is apparent that—in sharp contrast to the market portfolio—the composition of this portfolio is unknown.[13] Both risk tolerance and aggregate wealth (λ^j and W^j) cannot be observed directly. Nevertheless, the following equilibrium relation results:

$$\mu_F^j = \frac{1}{\lambda}Cov(F^j, M) - \frac{(1-\lambda)}{\lambda}\underbrace{\left\{ \sum_i Cov(F^j, F^i)w_H^i \right\}}_{\equiv Cov(F^j, H^j)} \qquad (2.25)$$

The first term is the market risk premium corresponding to the CAPM. The second term is the additional risk premium related to currency risk. As noted, the currency hedge portfolio cannot be observed—therefore Equation 2.25 is of limited empirical content. In an analogous way, equilibrium expected returns can be derived for stocks markets.

Equilibrium Expected Stock Returns   We can deduct equilibrium expected returns for stocks in a similar way. From the structure of the log-portfolio we get

$$\underline{\mu}_S = \frac{1}{\lambda}\underline{V}_{SM} + \underline{V}_{FS}\underline{w}_F \qquad (2.26)$$

where the similarity to Equation 2.24a is obvious: $\underline{V}_{FM}$ is replaced by $\underline{V}_{SM}$, and $\underline{V}_{FF}$ is replaced by $\underline{V}_{FS}$ (currency forward returns are replaced by stock returns). For the stocks in currency j, the following equilibrium relation holds:

$$\mu_F^j = \frac{1}{\lambda}Cov\left(S^j,M\right) - \frac{(1-\lambda)}{\lambda}\underbrace{\left\{\sum_i Cov\left(F^i,S^j\right)w_H^i\right\}}_{\equiv Cov\left(S^j,H^j\right)} \qquad (2.27)$$

The interpretation is the same as before. In contrast to the CAPM, there is an additional—although unobservable and reference currency specific—currency hedge component.

General Models Accounting for Domestic Inflation

The IntCAPM is developed in a world in which there are no cross-country differences between investment and consumption opportunity sets. The SS-IAPM considers differences in consumption baskets across countries but assumes zero domestic inflation and identical tastes within each country. In this case, international asset returns expressed in domestic currency units are regarded as real returns, and the investment in domestic bonds is risk-free in real terms. In such a model setting, the investors' purchasing power is affected solely by unexpected shifts in exchange rates. Yet, in reality, the investors' purchasing power is also influenced by changes in consumption good prices. Stulz (1981a) and Adler and Dumas (1983) develop an international valuation theory, often referred to as the International Asset Pricing Model (IntAPM), that explicitly considers differences among the country-specific consumption baskets as well as stochastic inflation in each country. In such a model, domestic bond investing is generally not safe in real terms and the correlations between returns on risky assets and changes in the rate of inflation affect the variance of real returns. Nevertheless, investors can reduce the purchasing power risks stemming from nominal risk-free as well as risky investments by investing in those assets positively correlated with the evolution of the purchasing power of their reference currency. In accordance with Stulz (1984), a portfolio consisting of risky assets with returns perfectly correlated with changes in the purchasing power of the domestic currency is called a *domestic purchasing power hedge portfolio*.

Portfolio Selection and Currency Hedging in the General Model In this framework, portfolio separation is closely related to the notion that investors across all countries take positions in such hedge portfolios to achieve lower variances of real wealth. Adler and Dumas (1983) demonstrate that in such a world the optimal portfolio of any risk-averse investor with logarithmic utility consists of two components: (1) a universal portfolio of risky assets, and (2) an individual portfolio that provides the best possible hedge against domestic inflation.[14] The universal portfolio of risky assets is the same for all investors, irrespective of the country of residence because prices of consumption goods do not affect the objective function of a logarithmic investor. The second component represents investors' personalized global minimum-variance portfolios in real terms. These are the portfolios with nominal returns most highly correlated with the inflation rates of the price of the consumption baskets specific to the investors. As long as investors have divergent consumption baskets and hence divergent perceptions of inflation across countries, the respective minimum-variance hedge portfolios differ in their composition across investors. Consequently, investors do not hold the same portfolio of risky assets, and the tangency portfolio is not a priori observable in this setting. When domestic bond investing can be considered risk-free in real terms (as with the SS-IAPM), then this hedge portfolio collapses to the domestic risk-free asset.[15] In general, the introduction of mutual fund portfolios for hedging state variable risk is consistent with Merton's (1971, 1973) work on the domestic ICAPM.

Formally, these results can be easily derived from our previous framework. However, it is now easier to include the domestic nominal risk-free asset in the risky portfolio, which is denoted by $\underline{\omega}$ and contains $N + 1$ assets with weights summing up to unity. The objective function in real terms is

$$\max_{\underline{\omega}} \quad V = \mu_{PR} - \frac{1}{2}\frac{1}{\lambda}\sigma_{PR}^2 \qquad (2.28)$$

where μ_{PR} is the expected real excess return of the portfolio given by $\mu_{PR} = \underline{\omega}'\underline{\mu} - \mu_\pi - \underline{\omega}'\underline{V}_{s\pi}$, and σ_{PR}^2 is the real portfolio variance given by $\sigma_{PR}^2 = \underline{\omega}'\underline{V} - 2\underline{\omega}'\underline{V}_{s\pi} = \sigma_\pi^2$. The first order condition implies

$$\underline{\omega} = \lambda\left(\underline{\mu} - \underline{V}_{s\pi}\right)\underline{V}^{-1} + \underline{V}^{-1}\underline{V}_{s\pi} \qquad (2.29a)$$

which shows that, although no real risk-free asset exists, the portfolio selection problem can be decomposed into two components. Investors with zero risk tolerance hold a portfolio characterized by $\underline{V}^{-1}\underline{V}_{s\pi}$. This is a portfolio with the lowest possible risk in real terms: the global real minimum-variance portfolio. It thus provides the best possible—but not perfect—protection against domestic inflation. Technically, it represents the vector of linear regression coefficients of the nominal stock returns on the unexpected inflation rates, or, alternatively, on PPP deviations. Equation 2.29a can be written as

$$\underline{\omega} = \lambda\underline{V}^{-1}\underline{\mu} + (1-\lambda)\underline{V}^{-1}\underline{V}_{s\pi} \qquad (2.29b)$$

which reveals that the weighting between the nominal efficient portfolio, $\underline{\underline{V}}^{-1}\underline{\mu}$, and the "new" inflation-hedge portfolio, $\underline{\underline{V}}^{-1}\underline{V}_{S\pi}$, occurs with the risk tolerance factor. The amount invested in the nominal risk-free asset, that is, asset $N + 1$ in vector $\underline{\omega}$, follows from

$$w_{N+1} = 1 - \sum_{i=1}^{N} \omega_i$$

which can be transformed into

$$w_{N+1} = \lambda\left[1 - \underline{1}'\underline{\underline{V}}^{-1}\underline{\mu}\right] + (1-\lambda)\left[1 - \underline{1}'\underline{\underline{V}}^{-1}\underline{V}_{S\pi}\right] \qquad (2.30)$$

which can be aggregated further using Equation 2.29b, such that

$$\underline{\omega} = \begin{pmatrix} \underline{w} \\ w_{N+1} \end{pmatrix} = \lambda\begin{bmatrix} \underline{\underline{V}}^{-1}\underline{\mu} \\ 1 - \underline{1}'\underline{\underline{V}}^{-1}\underline{\mu} \end{bmatrix} + (1-\lambda)\begin{bmatrix} \underline{\underline{V}}^{-1}\underline{V}_{S\pi} \\ 1 - \underline{1}'\underline{\underline{V}}^{-1}\underline{V}_{S\pi} \end{bmatrix} \qquad (2.31)$$

This equation is first derived by Adler and Dumas (1983). Note that $\underline{\omega}$ is a $N + 1$ vector, whereas $\underline{w}$ contains N elements. In contrast to the Solnik-Sercu solution given in Equation 2.19, the nominal risk-free asset (the second fund besides the log-portfolio) is substituted by the real hedge portfolio. Investors still hold the nominal risk-free asset, but not as a separate fund anymore. Whereas in the previous case investors with zero risk tolerance invest their entire wealth in the risk-free asset, they invest only a fraction here—the remaining part is allocated to the real hedge portfolio.

The Adler-Dumas Multi-Beta IntCAPM   In a world in which investors desire to hedge against purchasing power risks caused by unexpected inflation, the holdings of various hedge portfolios affect expected returns. Stated differently, the expected return of an asset depends on its usefulness to hedge purchasing power risks as well as on its world market risk. Thus, in equilibrium, expected returns must be consistent with the assets' hedging potential in each country and the investors' willingness to pay for hedging in each country. Assuming that investors hold a combination of the universal portfolio of risky assets and a personalized inflation hedge portfolio, Adler and Dumas (1983) develop the following condition for the expected return on any asset i in a world with L countries:[16]

$$E\left[R_i^d\right] = R_f^d + \sum_{j=1}^{L} \lambda_{\pi j} \cdot Cov\left[R_i^d, \pi^{\,j}\right] + \lambda_{wm} \cdot Cov\left[R_i^d, R_{wm}^d\right] \quad (2.32)$$

where π^j denotes the rate of inflation in the jth country and $\lambda_{\pi j}$, $j = 1, 2, \ldots, L$, is the premium investors demand for the comovement of the nominal return of the ith asset with the rate of inflation in the jth country. Finally, λ_{wm} denotes the premium for the asset's exposure to world market risk. The remaining variables have already been defined. Thus, the expected return on any asset, denominated in any numéraire currency (here the domestic one), is generated by the covariance of the asset's return with the return on the world market portfolio, denominated in the chosen currency and by the covariances of the asset's return with changes in the price levels in all countries.

Inflation Risk Premiums The pricing restriction in Equation 2.32 is the result of an aggregation over the countries. In addition to the world market premium, the equation contains multiple inflation premiums, one for each country. The argument is as follows. Swiss investors are ready to pay a premium on certain assets that best protect the real purchasing power in Switzerland and Italian investors grant a premium on those assets that best protect the real purchasing power in Italy, and so on. Because investors in different countries view the hedging potential of the same assets differently, separate inflation premiums appear in an aggregated valuation model. These risk premiums are related to the wealth-weighted risk aversion in the respective countries. In sum, the multi-beta IntAPM of Adler and Dumas (1983) provides a general framework to incorporate the effects of PPP deviations in international valuation models. But it is often argued that such a model is difficult to implement empirically because national consumption baskets and prices cannot be measured exactly (see, e.g., Stulz, 1984). However, if a world is assumed in which the countries' local inflation risk is negligible or even zero, a handier pricing relationship for implementation can be obtained. This is the world of Solnik (1974a) and Sercu (1980). There, PPP deviations are precisely mirrored by exchange rate changes. Thus, the covariances with the countries' inflation rates can be substituted by covariances with the exchange rates of the countries' currencies. The most comprehensive empirical study of the pricing of exchange rate risk in the framework of such a model is provided in the paper of Dumas and Solnik (1995).

The Stulz Consumption-Based IntCAPM   In several papers, Stulz (1981a, 1984) suggests a consumption-based equilibrium model to determine expected returns in an international setting. This model may also be seen as a simple alternative to the multi-beta IntAPM of Adler and Dumas (1983). The model documented in Stulz (1981a) is developed in a continuous-time framework and is more general than the model of Adler and Dumas (1983); it is probably the most general model of international asset pricing.[17] Stulz (1984) contains a discrete-time version of the model. In this setting, if an asset exists with real returns uncorrelated with real consumption, then the pricing restriction can be written as follows:[18]

$$E\left[r_i\right] = \beta_{ic} \cdot E\left[r_c\right] \text{ with } \beta_{ic} = \frac{Cov\left[r_i, r_c\right]}{Var\left[r_c\right]} \qquad (2.33)$$

and r_i is the (inflation adjusted) real return on the ith asset in excess of the real rate of return on the asset that is risk-free in terms of real consumption growth. r_c stands for the real excess return on a portfolio whose real return is maximally correlated with the growth rate of real consumption. Finally, β_{ic} is the beta of the real excess return on the ith asset with respect to the real excess return on the consumption proxy portfolio. In principle, thus, this linear pricing model can be implemented using the price index of any country. Hence, it holds for any investor's perspective in the international setting. In addition, the model holds under general assumptions about exchange rate dynamics.

In contrast to all the other international asset pricing models previously discussed, the consumption-based model of Stulz (1981a, 1995) does not require the identification of the world market portfolio. Therefore, the model is not exposed to the general criticism of pricing restrictions incorporating a market aggregate. Instead, systematic risk is purely measured relative to changes in the level of real consumption of a representative domestic investor. Nevertheless, this approach has some drawbacks. From a theoretical point of view, an exact empirical implementation of the model is impossible because real consumption rates are endogenous variables that are solved for in the investors' utility maximizing problems. Furthermore, empirical testing of consumption-based pricing generally suffers from the insufficiencies of imprecisely observed consumption data.

The Home Country Bias Both the IntCAPM and the SS-IAPM predict that investors hold the same portfolio of risky assets, irrespective of their country of residence. Thus, neither model can explain the home country bias in portfolio holdings commonly observed across the capital markets (for a detailed discussion of the home country bias, see, e.g., Frankel, 1994b). The more general IntAPMs of Stulz (1981a) and Adler and Dumas (1983) do not make this prediction. These models, in principle, allow relative stock holdings to differ across countries. Stulz (1995) argues that especially the consumption-beta IntAPM is basically consistent with the generally observed bias in equity holdings. However, Uppal (1993) does not support the view that the preference for domestic assets can be explained by domestic consumption in a conclusive way.[19]

CURRENCY HEDGING

In this section, the equilibrium conditions for currency hedging are analyzed based on the models previously developed.

Equilibrium Currency Hedging

Define the hedge ratio of currency j as short positions in deposits (in currency j) in relation to the long stock position in market j,

$$h^j = -\frac{w_F^j W^j}{w_S^j W^j} = \frac{w_F^j W^j}{M^j} \tag{2.34}$$

If risk aversion is large (λ low), investors will choose a hedge ratio close to one. In contrast, log-investors do not hedge at all. But what currency hedging strategies are consistent with international equilibrium? The equilibrium model previously developed implies the following portfolio holdings for investors with reference currency j:

- An investment of $\lambda^j W^j$ in the global log-portfolio.
- An investment of $(1 - \lambda^j) W^j$ in the domestic risk-free asset.

The deposits in currency j (as well as all other deposits) are in zero net supply in equilibrium. Therefore, the deposits held as domestic risk-free assets by country j investors must have the capitalization of $-(1 - \lambda^j) W^j$ in the log-portfolio. If the value of the market j portfolio is M^j, the equilibrium hedge ratio is

$$h^j = \frac{w_F^j}{w_S^j W^j} = -\frac{-\left(1 - \lambda^j\right) W^j}{M^j} = \frac{\left(1 - \lambda^j\right) W^j}{M^j} \tag{2.35}$$

It is easy to recognize that the equilibrium currency hedge ratio is different between the various benchmark currencies. Moreover, it depends on unobservable parameters, such as the aggregate risk tolerance of country j investors and their wealth in relation to the stock market capitalization. However, under certain restrictive assumptions, Black (1990) is able to show that a unique (universal) currency hedge strategy exists for all investors irrespective of their benchmark currency.

Universal Currency Hedging

Black (1989, 1990) assumes that the risk tolerance of investors is the same across all currencies, $\lambda^j = 2$. Moreover, the stock market capitalization is assumed to be equal to the aggregate net wealth in each country, $W^j = M^j$. Further, there is no public debt and no foreign debt. Under these assumptions, the equilibrium currency hedge collapses to

$$h^j = \frac{(1-\lambda^j)W^j}{M^j} = (1-\lambda) = h \qquad (2.36)$$

Equation 2.36 reveals that the universal risk tolerance directly determines the universal hedge ratio. For example, log-investors with $\lambda = 1$ do not hedge at all. In contrast, if the risk tolerance is zero, a full currency hedge is optimal. A risk tolerance of, say, 0.33 (corresponding to a risk aversion coefficient of 3) implies a universal currency hedge of 66 percent.

Black (1989, 1990) suggests the following universal currency hedge:

$$h = (1-\lambda) = \frac{\mu_M - \sigma_M^2}{\mu_M - \frac{1}{2}\sigma_F^2} \qquad (2.37)$$

where μ_M denotes the expected stock market return, σ_M the market volatility, and σ_F the forex volatility. Note that the preference parameters are replaced by market parameters and are assumed to be the same across all countries. Black (1989, 1990) proposes the following parameter values: $\mu_M = 8\%$, $\sigma_M = 15\%$, and $\sigma_F = 10\%$, which implies a universal hedge ratio of 77 percent. This implies a relative risk aversion of 4.34, which is (empirically) a rather high value.

Black's universal hedge ratio is heavily criticized in the literature, because of both the restrictive and unrealistic assumptions and the conceptional weaknesses. Black relates the main result of his model, the optimality of less than full hedging, to Siegel's paradox. However, Solnik (1993a) demonstrates that the result relies exclusively on the double role of the resk-free deposits in the asset allocation of investors, as risk-free securities for domestic investors and as part of currency hedging decisions for foreign investors. In the same spirit, Adler and Prasad (1990) show that the universality of Black's hedge ratio can be easily derived from the equilibrium models developed in the previous sections. Analyzing the demand for currency forward contracts (see Equation 2.12), we have

$$\underline{w}_F = \underline{\underline{V}}_{FF}^{-1} \underline{\mu}_F - \underline{\underline{\beta}}_{SF} \, \underline{w}_S \qquad (2.38)$$

where the first term is the speculative demand based on expected returns, whereas the second term represents the pure hedging demand. It is obvious that the second part, $-\underline{\underline{\beta}}_{SF} \underline{w}_S$, is completely independent of the reference currency of the investor—it is universal. Adler and Dumas (1983) therefore suggest running multiple regressions of excess stock returns on excess forward currency returns to determine the "universal" hedge ratios $-\underline{\underline{\beta}}_{SF}$. It is then an empirical question whether these regression coefficients prove to be universal with respect to alternative benchmark currencies. Empirical evidence is provided by Adler and Jorion (1992), Brandenberger (1995), and Müller (2000).

Free Lunch and Full Currency Hedging

Perold and Schulman (1988) argue that exchange rate risk can be hedged at zero cost—the expected excess return on currency forward contracts is zero, $\underline{\mu}_F = \underline{0}$. This is a special case of our model and implies that the full foreign stock exposure must be hedged:

$$\underline{w}_F = -\underline{w}_S \qquad (2.39)$$

In the context of our model, this case emerges if the stock returns are uncorrelated with exchange rate changes: the beta-matrix is

$\underline{\underline{\beta}}_{SF} = \underline{\underline{0}}$. However, there is no theoretical and empirical justification for this case.

Overlay Currency Hedges

The overlay hedge is a more general case than the full currency hedges. Overlay strategies define the currency decision in fixed proportions with respect to the optimized asset allocation of the portfolio. For example, a portfolio manager hedges 25 percent of foreign bonds and 50 percent of foreign stocks in his clients' portfolios. Overlay currency hedges often are selected by investors because, for competitive reasons, they choose different asset managers for the currency and asset allocation decisions.

Overlay currency hedges are based on the assumption that the currency decision of a portfolio can be separated from the market allocation. However, Equation 2.12 shows that this is not generally true. The optimal stock market and currency allocation must be jointly determined—currencies are just a specific asset class. The reason is that the information in the covariance matrix $\underline{\underline{V}}_{SF}$ must be fully exploited in finding truly efficient portfolios. An overlay strategy, in contrast, implicitly assumes that stock and currency returns are all uncorrelated:

$$\underline{\underline{V}}_{SF} = \underline{\underline{0}} \qquad (2.40)$$

such that the beta-matrix and variance-covariance matrix become $\underline{\underline{\beta}}_{SF} = \underline{\underline{0}}$ and $\underline{\underline{V}}_{SS} = \underline{\underline{V}}_{S \cdot F}$, respectively, implying an optimal market allocation of

$$\underline{w}_S = \lambda \underline{\underline{V}}_{SS}^{-1} \underline{\mu}_S \qquad (2.41a)$$

and an optimal currency allocation of

$$\underline{w}_F = \lambda \underline{\underline{V}}_{FF}^{-1} \underline{\mu}_F \qquad (2.41b)$$

The two equations imply full separation of market and currency allocation. However, there is no empirical or theoretical justification supporting $\underline{\underline{V}}_{SF} = \underline{0}$, and thus overlay currency hedges do not produce efficient portfolios in general.

INTERNATIONAL ARBITRAGE PRICING THEORY

The pricing restrictions implied by utility-based international asset pricing models strictly depend on the assumptions about consumption and investment opportunity sets in different countries as well as the change of these opportunity sets over time. Although the structure of the pricing restrictions, derived by assuming that all markets are in equilibrium, is similar to standard closed-economy valuation concepts, a prevalent conclusion is that the world market portfolio is not optimal a priori. In an international environment, unexpected changes in exchange rates affect the investors' perception of asset returns differently, inducing a demand for individual purchasing power hedge portfolios. Hence, a well-identified benchmark portfolio of risky assets does not exist in the setting of an IntAPM, which makes the theory burdensome to test empirically. In response to these complications, Solnik (1983b) suggests an international version of the Arbitrage Pricing Theory (IntAPT) as an alternative approach to explain cross-sectional differences between international asset returns. Almost at the same time, Ross and Walsh (1983) provided similar work. But Ikeda (1991) probably presents the most clarifying and straightforward analysis of the IntAPT, together with a generalized version of the model.

The Arbitrage Pricing Theory (APT) exploits the notion that in a large capital market it is possible to construct arbitrage portfolios that do not have any systematic or unsystematic risk in the sense of a factor structure. The cross-section of assets is assumed to be large enough to permit diversification of idiosyncratic risk. In fact, the pricing in the APT framework critically relies on the existence of such risk-free arbitrage portfolios. In the international framework, the fluctuating exchange rates add risk to an internationally diversified portfolio. In accordance with Ikeda (1991), this might also affect arbitrage activities in the capital markets. Hence, an extension of the APT to an international setting is not a trivial exercise. The IntAPT basically requires the following conditions to hold: (1) risk stemming from exchange rate shifts must be diversifiable like any other unsystematic risk, (2) an arbitrage portfolio that is risk-free in any given currency must be risk-free in any other currency as well, and (3) the factor structure must be invariant to the choice of a currency. Whereas conditions (1) and (2) are somewhat technical, condition (3) must be satisfied for the IntAPT to be a viable theory. The brief outline of the IntAPT in this section is consistent with the model setting of Ikeda (1991). The IntAPT of Solnik (1983b) can then easily be recognized as a special case.

Pricing Condition with Currency Risk Adjustment

Consider a world consisting of L countries. To simplify the argument, in each of those countries there exists only one risky asset and one risk-free asset.[20] These assets are traded without restrictions in perfect international capital markets. The number of countries and hence the number of assets is assumed to be large. Similar to the closed-economy APT, the international version of the model starts with the assumption that asset returns denominated in local currency are generated by a linear k-factor model in the following way:

$$R_i^i = E\left[R_i^i\right] + \beta_{i1}^i \cdot \delta_1 + \beta_{i2}^i \cdot \delta_2 + \cdots + \beta_{ik}^i \cdot \delta_k + \varepsilon_i^i \qquad (2.42)$$

for $i = 1, 2, \ldots, L$ (assets/countries), where R_i^i is the one-period return of the risky asset in country i, in terms of the local currency i.[21] The variables δ_j, $j = 1, 2, \ldots, k$, represent changes in the values of the j common factors driving international asset returns. The coefficients β_{ij}^i, $j = 1, 2, \ldots, k$, are the sensitivities of the local-currency return of the ith asset with respect to shifts in the values of the risk factors. Finally, ε_i^i denotes the error term. The variables' moments and correlations are consistent with a standard factor model as discussed in the closed-economy context.

Returns from international investments have to be translated into some specific numéraire currency. Henceforth, the perspective of a certain domestic country is chosen. Without loss of generality, the currency of that country is assumed to be the numéraire. This is denoted by the superscript "d". The following model then describes the dynamics of exchange rates:

$$s_i^d = E\left[s_i^d\right] + \upsilon_i^d \qquad (2.43)$$

for $i = 1, 2, \ldots, L$ (currencies), where s_i^d denotes the rate of change in the price of the ith country's currency calculated in terms of the domestic currency. Then, υ_i^d captures the unexpected part of any exchange rate shift. In addition, it is assumed that the law of one price holds for each internationally traded asset: $P_i^d = s_i^d \cdot P_i^i$, where P_i^d is the price of the ith asset translated into domestic currency, s_i^d denotes the price of country i's currency, and P_i^i is the asset price in terms of the local currency in country i.

To develop the IntAPT in this setting, we assume that the k-factor model in Equation 2.42 holds in continuous time (over any short trading interval). Then, by using Ito's Lemma, the return on any asset i can be expressed in domestic currency units as follows:

$$R_i^d = R_i^i + s_i^d + Cov\left[R_i^i, s_i^d\right] \qquad (2.44)$$

Combined with Equations 2.41 and 2.42, this can be transformed to

$$R_i^d = E\left[R_i^d\right] + \beta_{i1}^i \cdot \delta_1 + \cdots + \beta_{ik}^i \cdot \delta_k + \varepsilon_i^i + \upsilon_i^d$$
$$\text{with } E\left[R_i^d\right] = E\left[R_i^i\right] + E\left[s_i^d\right] + Cov\left[R_i^i, s_i^d\right] \qquad (2.45)$$

This shows that asset returns translated into some numéraire currency, here the domestic currency, incorporate exchange rate risk in addition to the risk components motivated by the original factor structure. This extra source of risk is represented by the unexpected component of the respective exchange rate change, which is the last term on the right-hand side of the preceding equation, v_i^d. Ikeda (1991) demonstrates that it is impossible to construct risk-free arbitrage portfolios according to the usual APT hedging rule in the presence of exchange rate risk.

Nevertheless, the model of Ikeda (1991) demonstrates that expected returns are consistent with APT pricing in the international setting, too, at least as long as returns are adjusted by the cost of exchange rate risk hedging. If any risky investment in a foreign country is fully financed by going short in the respective local risk-free asset, risk-free arbitrage portfolios can be identified; and the usual no-arbitrage argument can be invoked to derive the subsequent condition on expected net asset returns:[22]

$$E\left[R_i^d\right] - \left\{R_{fi}^i + E\left[s_i^d\right]\right\} = \lambda_1^d \cdot \beta_{i1}^i + \lambda_2^d \cdot \beta_{i2}^i + \cdots + \lambda_k^d \cdot \beta_{ik}^i \qquad (2.46)$$

for $i = 1, 2, \ldots, L$ (assets), holding for any currency of denomination: $d = 1, 2, \ldots, L$. R_{fi}^i denotes the interest rate of the risk-free asset in country i, measured in local currency. Then, $\lambda_j^d, j = 1, 2, \ldots, k$, is the premium an investor in country d can expect for a unit exposure of any foreign investment with regard to the jth international source of risk. Notice that the factor exposures, $\beta_{ij}^i, j = 1, 2, \ldots, k$, are generally measured on the basis of local currency returns. The left-hand side of Equation 2.46 denotes the expected return on an investment in country i adjusted by the cost of hedging exchange rate risk, which is given by the term in curly brackets. The right-hand side includes factor prices that are consistent with the expectations of investors in the domestic country d, multiplied by the local factor betas. Thus, the derived pricing statement has a "local character" while satisfying conditions (1) to (3) as stated earlier.

In sum, if a cross-section of international assets is considered with returns fully hedged against exchange rate risk by local borrowing, then the IntAPT provides benchmark returns for any investor irrespective of his or her country of residence. The hedging approach suggested by Ikeda (1991) is similar to the exchange rate risk hedging principles applied in the SS-IAPM and versions of the IntAPM of Adler and Dumas (1983). Hence, exchange rate risk affects expected returns in both utility-based and arbitrage-motivated international valuation concepts in a similar way. The IntAPT version introduced by Solnik (1983b) does not include an explicit adjustment for the cost of hedging. In contrast to Ikeda (1991), Solnik (1983b) starts with the conjecture that returns denominated in an arbitrarily chosen numéraire currency are generated by a factor model.

The Solnik Pricing Condition

The IntAPT pricing restriction proposed by Solnik (1983b) crucially depends on the presumption that all exchange rates follow the same k-factor model as do asset returns. To demonstrate this in the framework previously outlined, it is assumed that the unexpected exchange rate shifts in Equation 2.43 are generated by:

$$\upsilon_i^d = \gamma_{i1}^d \cdot \delta_1 + \gamma_{i2}^d \cdot \delta_2 + \cdots + \gamma_{ik}^d \cdot \delta_k + \iota_i^d \qquad (2.47)$$

for $i = 1, 2, \ldots, L$ (currencies), where γ_{ij}^d, $j = 1, 2, \ldots, k$, denotes the sensitivity of the change in the exchange rate between the domestic currency and the currency in country i to shifts in the value of the jth international risk factor. i_i^d is the error term; all the other variables have already been defined. Once again, the standard assumptions of a linear factor structure apply. Thus, Equation 2.45 of the model of Ikeda (1991) reduces to:

$$R_i^d = E\left[R_i^d\right] + \beta_{i1}^d \cdot \delta_1 + \beta_{i2}^d \cdot \delta_2 + \cdots + \beta_{ik}^d \cdot \delta_k + \varepsilon_i^d$$
$$\text{with } \beta_{ij}^d = \beta_{ij}^i + \gamma_{ij}^d, j = 1, 2, \cdots k$$
$$\text{and } \varepsilon_i^d = \varepsilon_i^i + \iota_i^d \qquad (2.48)$$

for $i = 1, 2, \ldots, L$ (assets), which is the return generating k-factor model introduced by Solnik (1983b). The model holds for any asset in any country i, stated in terms of a numéraire currency rather than the respective local currency.[23] In such a setting, the coefficients β_{ij}^d, $j = 1, 2, \ldots, k$, embody both the factor risk of local asset returns as well as the factor risk of the respective exchange rate. Because, in general, factor returns do not have to be translated into currency units, the assumed factor structure is invariant to the currency chosen to denominate asset returns. Hence, condition (3) is satisfied; while conditions (1) and (2) hold inherently in this setting.

If asset returns are generated by a k-factor model as specified in Equation 2.48, then the cross-section of expected returns in the international setting is spanned in the following way:

$$E\left[R_i^d\right] = R_{fd}^d + \lambda_1^d \cdot \beta_{i1}^d + \lambda_2^d \cdot \beta_{i2}^d + \cdots + \lambda_k^d \cdot \beta_{ik}^d \tag{2.49}$$

for $i = 1, 2, \ldots, L$ (assets), holding for any numéraire currency, that is, $d = 1, 2, \ldots, L$. R_{fd}^d denotes the risk-free interest rate in the domestic country. The coefficients λ_j^d, $j = 1, 2, \ldots, k$, are the prices of international factor risk. However, in contrast to the risk premiums in Ikeda's (1991) model, these prices include a compensation for exchange rate risk. Recall, in the setting of Solnik (1983b), asset returns are unhedged against exchange rate risk in principle. Consequently, the IntAPT pricing restriction shows up in terms of "total" factor premiums.

In fact, if a certain factor structure is assumed to hold for a set of asset returns computed in some numéraire currency, it is implicitly presumed that the evolution of international exchange rates with respect to that currency is consistent with the same factor model. Then, the resulting pricing restriction has a structure similar to the closed-economy APT. From an empirical point of view, it might be difficult, if not impossible, to specify international risk factors that commonly affect both asset returns and currency returns.[24] However, if the set of risk factors is augmented by individual exchange rate changes, this problem can be reduced in principle. The resulting specification would be similar to the multi-beta IntAPM developed by Adler and Dumas (1983): They are, however, hard to distinguish from each other empirically.

SUMMING UP THE MAIN STREAMS

International asset pricing theories differ with respect to the assumptions made on consumption and investment opportunity sets in different countries. Because the appreciation of nominal asset returns is heterogeneous across investors from different countries, the international setting is more complex than the domestic one. As a matter of fact, the dynamics of exchange rates for currencies and different local inflation rates make it more difficult to develop a consistent framework to explain the cross-section of expected returns. Nevertheless, like the pricing theories in the domestic setting, international valuation concepts end up with linear beta pricing conditions as well. The main streams in the theory of international asset pricing are summarized as follows.

The IntCAPM outlined by Stulz (1984, 1995) allows the application of standard mean-variance portfolio theory in an international environment. However, the assumtions necessary to develop the Int-CAPM include few genuine features of an international setting such as differences in consumption and investment opportunity sets and deviations from PPP. The model ends up with a standard single-beta CAPM stated in real terms, where systematic risk is measured by the covariance of an asset's return with the return on a world market portfolio.

The SS-IAPM of Solnik (1974a) and Sercu (1980) offers some basic understanding concerning portfolio selection and equilibrium pricing when investors are faced with exchange rate risk—when PPP does not hold all the time. The model yields a linear single-beta pricing relationship consistent with the idea that investors can always completely hedge their international investments against unforeseen exchange rate shifts by either going short in foreign currency bonds (Solnik, 1974a) or buying forward contracts (Sercu, 1980). This result critically relies on the assumption that inflation rates are zero, or, at least negligible, in all countries. This is, of course, a restrictive presumption.

The IntAPMs of Stulz (1981a) and Adler and Dumas (1983) do not impose a presumption on domestic inflation rates. Thus, domestic bond investments are generally not safe in real terms as with the SS-IAPM and covariances between asset returns and changes in the level of consumption good prices become relevant parameters for portfolio choice. As a result, any investor's optimal portfolio of risky assets depends on the country of residence (i.e., on the price index used to calculate real income). The standard menu of mutual funds for portfolio selection in a certain country is augmented by a country-specific portfolio of risky assets that provides the best possible hedge against inflation in that country. Thus, expected returns should also depend on asset return-inflation covariances and not on the exposure to world market movements alone. Adler and Dumas (1983) suggest a multi-beta IntAPM to price assets in accordance with their market risk as well as their potential to hedge against inflation in all countries. Stulz (1981a) develops a consumption-beta IntAPM that explains expected returns directly by the covariance between asset returns and the growth rate of real consumption in a country. However, the model of Adler and Dumas (1983) is more useful for empirical work because it provides an intuitive framework for adjusting standard beta pricing models to an international setting, where PPP deviations induce exchange rate risk.

Definitely, utility-based models yield valuable insights into the mechanisms that affect risk and return of assets in an international environment. But these concepts are often difficult to implement in practice. The IntAPT represents a reasonable alternative framework to describe the international cross-section of expected asset returns. If a certain factor structure can be assumed to hold for a set of internationally traded assets as well as currencies, the model of Solnik (1983b) provides a multi-beta pricing restriction as a benchmark for expected returns denominated in any numéraire currency. Even if the consistency of asset returns with a factor structure is given only in terms of local currency, expected returns are spanned according to the APT pricing equation, as shown by Ikeda (1991). Yet, the requirement is that returns are hedged against exchange rate risk.

Overall, multi-beta pricing models such as the IntAPT presumably provide the most flexible framework to analyze the structure of international asset returns. These models can be used for empirical work more readily than the utility-based equilibrium models.

CHAPTER 3

The Anatomy of Volatility and Stock Market Correlations

EXECUTIVE SUMMARY

- This chapter empirically investigates the asymmetry of volatility and correlation coefficients between stock markets. The findings are important for portfolio decisions and value-at-risk computations for international portfolios.
- Stock market volatility is higher when markets go down. Our statistical model shows that bad news (negative return surprises) will lead to higher volatility than good news.
- In periods of high volatility, stock markets become more correlated; and in periods of low volatility, they are less correlated.
- Higher correlations are detected when equity markets go down simultaneously, as well as when real economic activity is shrinking.
- International diversification benefits seem to vanish in exactly those market environments when they are most strongly needed.
- However, because the unconditional risk parameters are closer to the downside measures than to the upside measures, the downside risk of portfolios is not substantially biased if risk parameters are not conditioned on the direction of the market.

INTRODUCTION

The correlation structure of international stock returns plays an important role in the financial literature. In their seminal work, Levy

51

and Sarnat (1970), Grubel (1968), and Solnik (1974c), advocate international diversification based on the low correlations of national stock market returns. This argument, however, has come under attack. First, correlations between stock markets have increased considerably. Second, like the expected rate of return, correlations arc not constant over time. The implications of time-varying correlations are analyzed in this chapter.

The changing interdependence of national equity markets is also a major issue in the practice of asset management. Investment professionals offer several arguments:

- Stock market correlations are high in periods of high volatility, and lower in periods of low volatility.
- The correlations are higher when national equity markets go down.
- The correlations are higher in some periods of the business cycle (i.e., they change with the overall economic activity).

Potentially, if these arguments contained some truth, they would have important implications for asset allocation decisions and risk measurement. For example, if correlation coefficients are positively related to market volatility, the implication is that investors do not get the full benefits of international risk diversification in exactly those situations where they are most desirable. Kaplanis (1988) demonstrates that the correlation and covariance matrices of international stock returns are unstable over time. Similarly, Longin and Solnik (1995) reject the hypothesis of constant conditional correlations. More important, they find evidence for higher correlation in periods of high volatility. Erb, Harvey, and Viskanta (1994) report higher correlations during recessions than during boom periods and indicate that specific instrument variables can be used to compute reasonable forecasts of correlations. Solnik, Boucrelle, and Le Fur (1996) also find that markets become more synchronized when they are more volatile. This seems to be true for both international stock and bond returns. Longin and Solnik (2001) focus directly on the statistical properties of extreme returns. They specify the multivariate distribution of extreme returns implied by a given distribution of returns and study the structure of international equity markets during extremely volatile periods. Their results indicate that the correlation of large positive returns is not inconsistent with the assumption of multivariate normality. However, the correlation of large negative returns is much higher than normality would imply. They conclude that the benefits of international risk reduction in extremely volatile periods seem exaggerated.

The purpose of this chapter is twofold. We first show that the correlation coefficients between international stock markets not only are unstable over time but also exhibit systematic characteristics with respect to market volatility, the direction of the market, and the business cycle. The literature, however, provides little evidence about the implications of changing correlations for different areas of financial management. Therefore, we present instructive examples for the effects on international equity diversification, risk management (in particular, the computation of shortfall risks and the value-at-risk), and option pricing in the second part of this chapter.

Looking only at correlations, we cannot reach conclusions about market integration. In an asset pricing context, stock markets could be fully integrated, no matter whether their returns are correlated or not correlated. For example, the industry mixes within each country may be sufficiently different to induce low equity correlation (e.g., Roll, 1992). Therefore, this chapter solely focuses on the interdependences between markets and does not provide a strict asset pricing test of market integration.[1]

In this chapter, we first describe the stock returns used in our analysis. We then demonstrate the asymmetrical behavior of stock market volatility and present a model that captures this effect. Next, we analyze the correlation structure of international stock returns. Finally, we discuss the investment implications of our empirical observations.

DATA AND DESCRIPTIVE STATISTICS

Throughout most of this chapter, we use monthly returns on selected stock market indices, as provided by Morgan Stanley Capital

International (MSCI). All indices are constructed as performance indices, with dividends reinvested. Returns are continuously compounded and translated into Swiss francs. Our sample covers the time period from January 1970 to August 1998, which generates 343 monthly return observations for each time series. Statistical characterizations of these returns can be found in Table 3.1.

Average returns over this long sample period vary significantly across markets. While Hong Kong boosted annual returns above 12 percent, Australian investors could have earned a meager 4.3 percent. However, Hong Kong's high returns have been accompanied by extremely high risk, as measured by an annualized standard deviation of almost 41 percent. On the other extreme, the Swiss stock market's volatility was only 16.9 percent. To put these numbers into perspective, note that they imply daily average changes of 2.1 percent in Hong Kong, compared with only 0.9 percent in Switzerland. Most returns are left-skewed, as indicated by mainly negative numbers in

TABLE 3.1 Descriptive Statistics for International Stock Market Returns

	Mean (%)	SD (%)	Skewness	Kurtosis
Australia	4.3	28.9	−0.680	6.402
Austria	7.4	19.6	−1.770	14.848
Canada	5.8	22.3	0.165	7.284
France	8.9	22.8	−0.504	5.397
Germany	8.8	19.3	−0.324	4.744
Hong Kong	12.6	40.9	−0.616	5.296
Italy	8.4	22.4	−0.889	8.046
Netherlands	12.3	18.3	−0.294	3.871
Singapore	7.0	31.8	−0.527	6.079
Spain	7.2	24.0	−0.688	9.647
Switzerland	10.5	16.9	−0.659	5.564
United Kingdom	9.3	24.7	−0.638	5.820
United States	8.4	20.3	0.027	8.169
Average	8.5	24.0	−0.569	7.013

Note: The table shows descriptive statistics for monthly MSCI stock market returns over the period from 1970.01 to 1998.08. All returns are continuously compounded and denominated in Swiss francs. Means and standard deviations (SD) are reported on an annual basis.

the fourth column of Table 3.1. Finally, the kurtosis coefficient is significantly above 3 for most markets. This implies that extreme return realizations occurred more frequently than it could have been expected if returns were normally distributed. This phenomenon is often referred to as *fat tails*.

Our main interest, however, is the behavior of correlations. To start with, Table 3.2 reports the coefficients of correlation between all countries over the entire sample period. Correlations differ significantly depending on the pair of countries under analysis. The lowest values we report are around 0.3 (e.g., most correlation coefficients for Hong Kong). On the other hand, high values can go beyond 0.7. Average correlations for each country and the overall average coefficient for all countries together are reported below the correlation matrix. The total average for all numbers in the matrix is 0.477.

The important point to notice is that the usual correlation measure represents average comovements in both upmarkets and downmarkets. In contrast, separate correlation estimates in different market environments potentially can detect whether correlations increase or decrease in downmarkets. This is our main focus, and it is at the heart of international diversification: Increased correlations in downmarkets imply reduced benefits of international portfolio diversification.

The first step in this analysis is to explore whether the volatility of stock markets is different in upstates compared with downstates. Therefore, we subdivide the entire history of stock returns for each country into upmarkets and downmarkets. A month is classified as upmarket if the respective return is above average; the reverse is true for downmarkets. Given the series of m up- and n downmarkets, we compute the following up- and downvolatility measures, σ_{up} and σ_{down}:

$$\sigma_{up} = \sqrt{\frac{1}{m-1} \sum_{t=1}^{m} \left(r_{up,\,t} - mr_{full} \right)^2} \qquad (3.1)$$

$$\sigma_{down} = \sqrt{\frac{1}{n-1} \sum_{t=1}^{n} \left(r_{down,\,t} - mr_{full} \right)^2} \qquad (3.2)$$

TABLE 3.2 Matrix of Stock Market Correlations

	Australia	Austria	Canada	France	Germany	Hong Kong	Italy	Netherlands	Singapore	Spain	Switzerland	United Kingdom	United States
Australia	1.000												
Austria	0.328	1.000											
Canada	0.411	0.500	1.000										
France	0.584	0.426	0.595	1.000									
Germany	0.282	0.469	0.351	0.382	1.000								
Hong Kong	0.175	0.359	0.369	0.328	0.334	1.000							
Italy	0.407	0.670	0.618	0.687	0.505	0.417	1.000						
Netherlands	0.282	0.558	0.375	0.373	0.620	0.371	0.535	1.000					
Singapore	0.358	0.466	0.450	0.440	0.341	0.422	0.495	0.334	1.000				
Spain	0.421	0.542	0.575	0.669	0.424	0.355	0.701	0.487	0.410	1.000			
Switzerland	0.290	0.687	0.452	0.394	0.472	0.363	0.527	0.554	0.467	0.490	1.000		
United Kingdom	0.303	0.620	0.572	0.476	0.463	0.385	0.687	0.570	0.454	0.581	0.563	1.000	
United States	0.323	0.815	0.520	0.491	0.467	0.377	0.712	0.603	0.502	0.597	0.626	0.623	1.000
Average	0.347	0.537	0.482	0.487	0.426	0.355	0.580	0.472	0.428	0.521	0.491	0.525	0.555
Ø (Average)	0.477												

Note: The table shows the correlation coefficients of monthly MSCI stock market returns over the period from 1970.01 to 1998.08. All returns are continuously compounded and denominated in Swiss francs.

The mean of the full sample, denoted as mr_{full}, is subtracted from the up- and downreturns of the two subsamples, not their individual means. The reason is that we want to compare two volatility measures with respect to a common mean. This procedure also guarantees that the volatility of the full sample always falls between up- and downvolatility.

Table 3.3 displays the up- and downvolatility for our sample of international stock markets. It shows that the volatility of upreturns typically is smaller than the volatility of downreturns for all developed stock markets, except Austria. The average upvolatility is 22.4 percent, while the average downvolatility is 25.8 percent. The difference is especially pronounced in Australia (24.8% vs. 33.2%), Italy (20.2% vs. 24.9%), and the highly volatile Far East stock markets. This finding suggests that stock markets are more sensitive to bad

TABLE 3.3 Up- and Downvolatility

	Full Sample Volatility (%)	Up-volatility (%)	Down-volatility (%)	Number of Upstates	Number of Downstates
Australia	28.9	24.8	33.2	182	161
Austria	19.6	21.3	18.2	157	186
Canada	22.3	21.4	23.2	172	171
France	22.8	21.6	24.0	176	167
Germany	19.3	17.7	21.0	180	163
Hong Kong	40.9	36.9	45.1	179	164
Italy	22.4	20.2	24.9	192	151
Netherlands	18.3	17.4	19.2	172	171
Singapore	31.8	29.9	33.8	177	166
Spain	24.0	22.6	25.5	172	171
Switzerland	16.9	15.6	18.2	175	168
United Kingdom	24.7	23.6	26.6	185	158
United States	20.3	18.8	21.9	177	166
Average	24.0	22.4	25.8		

Note: The table shows three volatility numbers for each stock market: Either the volatility is computed over the full sample from 1970.01 to 1998.08, for upmarkets, or for downmarkets. Up- and downmarkets are classified on the basis of whether returns are above or below their average value in a specific month. All returns are continuously compounded and denominated in Swiss francs.

news than to good news. Next, we want to develop a statistical model of volatility that can explain this asymmetrical pattern.

AN ASYMMETRICAL MODEL OF VOLATILITY

In the previous section, we simply looked at historical volatility in different states of the world. A more sophisticated approach for analyzing stock market volatility is to adopt a GARCH model. GARCH stands for Generalized Autoregressive Conditional Heteroscedasticity; it is a rich and flexible modeling technique that has gained considerable attention in the finance literature.[2] The GARCH setup allows users to model and forecast the conditional variance, or, to be more precise, the conditional volatility of asset returns. In general, the attribute *conditional* refers to the properties of a random variable when some other random variables are known. It is assumed that the volatility of next period's return is a function of a set of information available today. This is in contrast to the unconditional volatility discussed earlier. Volatility that could be forecasted on the basis of publicly available information obviously would have important implications for the asset allocation process. Those investors seeking to avoid risk could reduce their exposure to assets whose volatility were predicted to increase. On the other hand, investors might rationally choose to take higher risk and require a higher expected rate of return. The notion that equilibrium asset prices should respond to forecasts of volatility is an essential feature of virtually all asset pricing models. They posit that equilibrium asset prices are related to forecasts of volatility, as well as to the degree of risk aversion.

The best indication for predictable changes in volatility is *volatility clustering*. This refers to the observation that large swings in prices tend to be followed by large swings of random direction, whereas small price changes are followed by small shifts. This finding holds not only for returns, but also for squared returns and absolute returns. Assuming a zero mean return over short horizons, squared returns are proxies for the instantaneous variance of returns, whereas absolute returns are proxies for the instantaneous standard deviation. Empirical evidence demonstrates that autocorrelations are highest in absolute return series, slightly lower in squared return series, and lowest in the original return series, implying persistence in volatility not present in the original return series. This observation is referred to as *heteroscedasticity,* meaning unequal volatility of a set of random variables. Figure 3.1 demonstrates the estimation results for a simple GARCH(1,1) specification applied to Swiss stock returns. The model looks as follows:

$$r_{t+1} = c + \varepsilon_{t+1} \text{ with } \sigma^2_{t+1} = \omega + \alpha\varepsilon^2_t + \beta\sigma^2_t$$

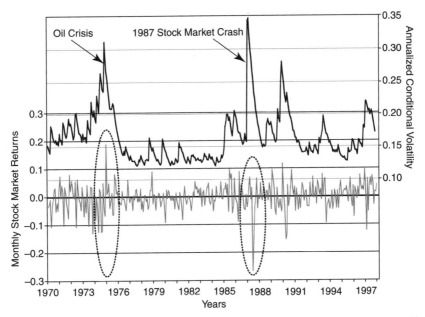

FIGURE 3.1   Returns and volatility forecasts: The Swiss case. A GARCH(1,1) specification is estimated for the Swiss stock market. The lower line plots monthly returns. The upper line displays the corresponding conditional (annualized) standard deviation, computed as the square root of the fitted values from the GARCH(1,1) setup presented in the text.

Returns over the period from t to $t + 1$ are denoted as r_{t+1}. The mean equation specifies returns simply as a constant, c, plus noise, ε_{t+1}. Therefore, the expected return is constant. σ^2_{t+1} is the conditional variance (i.e., the one-period ahead expected variance based on past information). It depends on a mean ω, last period's squared forecast error ε^2_t (the ARCH term), and last period's forecasted variance σ^2_t (the GARCH term). Both ARCH and GARCH terms are included with a one-period lag, hence a GARCH(1,1) specification for the conditional variance. The standard technique to estimate a GARCH(1,1) model is maximum likelihood estimation, assuming that the errors are conditionally normally distributed. The estimation results show strong statistical evidence for conditional heteroscedasticity in Swiss stock returns. Both estimated coefficients, α and β, are statistically significant at the 1 percent level. We report the detailed estimation results of a slightly more complicated model in Table 3.4. At this point, a graphical representation is more instructive.

The lower line in Figure 3.1 plots realized monthly stock returns. The upper line describes the time evolution of (annualized) conditional stock market volatility, computed as the square root of the fitted values from the GARCH(1,1) specification. Volatility clustering is strongly apparent in the figure: There are extreme price movements during the oil crises in the mid-1970s, the crash in 1987, and the short recession at the beginning of the 1990s. The conditional volatility increases accordingly by incorporating the most recent forecast error (news about volatility from the previous period, the ARCH term) and last period's conditional variance (the GARCH term). This specification is often compared with the way traders predict volatility. If previous returns were unexpectedly large in either the upward or downward direction, traders might increase the estimate of the variance for the next period accordingly. They would measure volatility over various time periods and use what they consider to be the most appropriate moving average.

The GARCH(1,1) specification implies a symmetrical model of conditional volatility (i.e., upstate and downstate volatility are

TABLE 3.4 Asymmetric Volatility Clustering (EGARCH)

	Coefficient Estimates			
	ω	α	γ	β
CAC 40	−0.477	0.128	−0.087	0.950
	−2.468	3.388	−3.086**	40.501
DAX	−0.543	0.216	−0.068	0.949
	−3.689	5.402	−2.954**	55.260
FTSE 100	−4.934	0.122	−0.075	0.384
	−1.826	1.544	−1.357	1.118
Hang Seng	−0.557	0.276	−0.075	0.939
	−5.817	5.860	−2.720**	73.019
MIB 30	−0.461	0.129	−0.017	0.948
	−0.878	1.504	−0.597	13.811
SPI	−0.677	0.256	−0.068	0.939
	−3.566	4.635	−2.792**	43.761
S&P 500	−0.337	0.149	−0.041	0.974
	−2.305	3.079	−1.841*	65.897

Note: The table reports the results of the EGARCH specification. Weekly returns of selected national stock market indexes are used over the period from 1988.01 to 1998.08. All returns are continuously compounded and denominated in local currency. The sign and the accompanying statistical significance of the γ coefficient reveal whether asymmetric news impacts have been observed. *t*-values are reported underneath the coefficient estimates.

*Denotes statistical significance at the 10 percent level of significance.
**Denotes statistical significance at the 1 percent level of significance.

treated as equal in the basic specification). Table 3.2, however, suggests that downward movements are followed by higher volatility than upward movements. Hence, we need a more elaborate model to account for this asymmetry in the conditional volatility. One of the most widely applied models is the EGARCH specification originally proposed by Nelson (1991):

$$r_{t+1} = c + \varepsilon_{t+1} \text{ with } \sigma^2_{t+1} = \exp\left(\omega + \beta\log(\sigma^2_t) + \alpha\left|\frac{\varepsilon_t}{\sigma_t}\right| + \gamma\frac{\varepsilon_t}{\sigma_t}\right) \quad (3.3)$$

We use the simplest possible specification for the mean equation, with only a constant, c, for expected returns.[3] The left-hand side of the conditional variance specification is exponential, implying that the conditional variance is guaranteed to be nonnegative. Most important, the coefficient γ captures possible asymmetries in the conditional variance. Intuition suggests that bad news has a stronger impact on the conditional variance ("leverage effect") than good news. Surprises on the stock market are modeled as standardized residuals, $z_t = \varepsilon_t / \sigma_t$, defined as the deviation of last period's stock return from the constant expected value, ε_t, divided by the conditional standard deviation, σ_t.

We assume that good news (when $z_t = \varepsilon_t / \sigma_t > 0$) and bad news (when $z_t = \varepsilon_t / \sigma_t < 0$) have different effects on the conditional volatility. Therefore, the news impact is asymmetrical if $\gamma \neq 0$. The presence of a leverage effect can be verified by testing whether $\gamma < 0$. Monthly sampling turns out to be inappropriate for our purpose, so we switch to weekly data to estimate the EGARCH specification. In particular, we use weekly data (in local currencies) of broad and liquid national stock market indices over the period from 1988.01 to 1998.08. Estimation results are reported in Table 3.4. Again, the α and β coefficients are highly significant, indicating strong GARCH effects (heteroscedasticity). The crucial insight, however, is that all γ coefficients are negative, most of them at the 5 percent level of significance. Therefore, the evidence for the presence of a leverage effect is overwhelming. Bad news and good news really have different effects on the conditional volatility.

The effect can be better visualized by plotting the estimated news impact curves on the basis of coefficient estimates. We plot the volatility forecast σ_{t+1} against the standardized impact $z_t = \varepsilon_t / \sigma_t$, where

$$\sigma_{t+1} = \sqrt{\exp\left[\hat{\omega} + \hat{\beta}\log(\overline{\sigma}_t^2) + \hat{\alpha}|z_t| + \hat{\gamma}z_t\right]} \qquad (3.4)$$

This expression estimates the one-period-ahead impact of news conditional on last period's variance and the standardized impact.

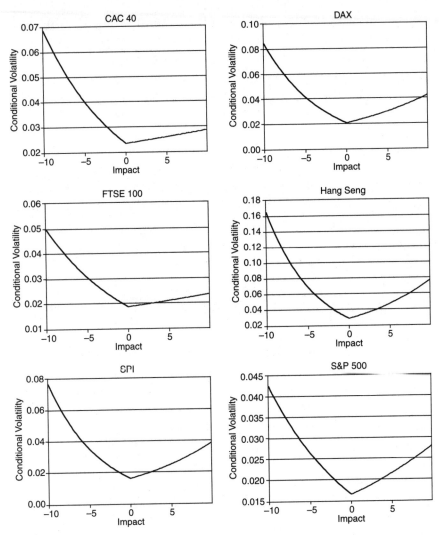

FIGURE 3.2 Estimated news impact curves. News impact curves are estimated for weekly returns of selected national stock market indices over the period from 1988.01 to 1998.08. The horizontal axis indicates the nature and size of return surprises; the vertical axis indicates the impact on conditional volatility. All returns are continuously compounded and denominated in local currency. Estimated coefficients from the EGARCH specification are used to construct the news impact curves around the mean of the estimated conditional variance series for each country.

All hat variables denote estimated parameters from the EGARCH estimation. To get a proper benchmark, we fix for each country last period's variance σ_t^2 as the mean of the estimated conditional variance series $\overline{\sigma}_t^2$. Figure 3.2 shows the resulting news impact curves. Positive and negative return surprises are drawn on the horizontal axis, the impact on conditional volatility on the vertical axis. Our notion that the EGARCH model captures the asymmetry in the effect of news on volatility is verified: The slope of the news impact curve is steeper along the negative range than the positive range. This is the leverage effect: Bad return surprises in one period have greater impact on stock market volatility in the following period than good news of similar magnitude. The importance of this finding for asset allocation and asset pricing cannot be overemphasized.

THE CORRELATION STRUCTURE OF INTERNATIONAL STOCK RETURNS

Correlation and Volatility

Although it would be convenient to have a model for stock market correlations like the one that describes stock market volatility, things become a lot more difficult. Perhaps not surprisingly, economic models for stock market correlations are scarce. The standard neoclassical setup relates national stock market correlations to the correlations of national consumption growth rates (for a review, see Lewis, 1999). Dumas, Harvey, and Ruiz (1999) use a sophisticated econometric setup to extract the driving force of equity market correlations out of national consumption growth rates. They argue that this common component is a good proxy for the movements of an unobservable world business cycle. Developing a proper pricing rule under either integrated or segmented markets, they can then infer the right degree of comovement between national stock markets. However, their approach is beyond the scope of this chapter. In what follows, we concentrate on analyzing past behavior of stock market correlations to show some patterns of major importance for the asset allocation process.

Figure 3.3 shows that the correlations of the major European stock markets and the United States with the Swiss stock market vary over time and across countries. Again, all returns have been calculated in Swiss francs. Moving windows of the previous 36 months are used to compute rolling (annualized) standard deviations and correlations. Hence, the first estimators are available on January 1, 1973. For example, the correlation between Switzerland and Germany was very high during the worldwide bull markets in the mid-1970s, decreased considerably during the 1980s, and rose to 0.8 during the crash in October 1987. Correlations decreased in the aftermath of the crash, rising again to around 0.6 only recently. Lower correlations during the first half of the 1990s do not contradict the increasing degree of stock market integration. While correlation is a purely statistical concept based on historical data, integration denotes the consistent pricing of global risk. The correlation patterns are similar across countries. Sharp increases are observed during the oil shock in 1973/1974, and all the moving averages display the well-known jump during the 1987 crash. In contrast to the other major markets, there is no drop in the correlations between Switzerland and the United States in the mid-1990s, probably because both markets experienced sharp price increases during this period.

Figure 3.3 also shows the time evolution of the volatility of the respective national indices. To make the analysis consistent, they have been computed using moving windows of 36 months. A mere look at the parallel movements of the different lines in all four graphs of the figure is sufficient to verify our initial notion that correlations tend to be higher in states of high market volatility. This is very bad news from the standpoint of asset managers. It is precisely when national markets become volatile that the benefits of international diversification are needed most.

To make sure that our graphical intuition is correct, we provide a statistical verification using the regression approach proposed by Solnik, Boucrelle, and Le Fur (1996). For each pair of countries, they regress the moving correlations on both countries' rolling volatility. Autocorrelation is an issue at this point. A 36-month moving average contains a 35-month overlap between two successive values of

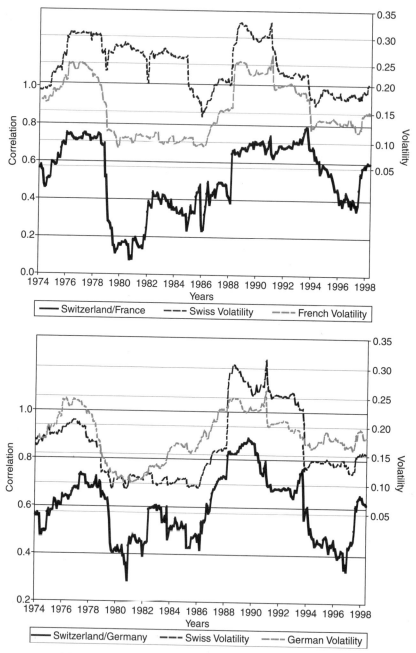

FIGURE 3.3 Stock market correlations and volatility.

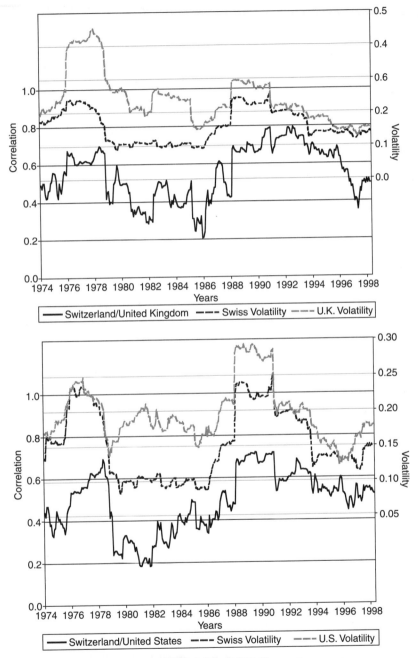

FIGURE 3.3 (continued)

correlation and standard deviation. Standard econometric proce-
dures to correct for this bias do not help in the presence of such high
and persistent autocorrelation. Therefore, for two countries i and j,
we compute monthly innovations of three-year moving correlation
coefficients, $\Delta\rho_{ij}$, and both volatility, $\Delta\sigma_i$ and $\Delta\sigma_j$. These shocks are
uncorrelated over time. Hence, it is now possible to regress the
changes of the correlation coefficients on a constant and the changes
of the associated volatility estimates:

$$\Delta\rho_{ij,t} = \alpha + \beta_1 \Delta\sigma_{j,t} + \beta_2 \Delta\sigma_{i,t} + u_{ij,t} \tag{3.5}$$

For each of the $j = 1, 2, \ldots, 13$ reference countries in our sample,
this generates a set of 12 regression equations. The results for two reference countries, Switzerland and the United States, are displayed in
Tables 3.5 and 3.6, respectively. In the Swiss case, our initial hypothesis of higher correlations during more volatile periods is confirmed.

TABLE 3.5   Correlation and Volatility: The Swiss Case

	Exogenous Variables				
	Volatility (Swiss)	t-value	Volatility (Non-Swiss)	t-value	Adjusted R^2
Australia	8.451	7.408	4.423	9.713	0.575
Austria	6.635	7.509	1.911	2.439	0.200
Canada	6.916	6.367	5.162	6.101	0.381
France	9.0126	8.542	2.460	2.844	0.349
Germany	5.864	5.482	3.425	3.008	0.276
Hong Kong	12.474	8.301	0.584	1.205	0.284
Italy	6.444	5.775	6.279	5.640	0.209
Netherlands	6.561	6.643	3.567	3.990	0.447
Singapore	11.410	7.909	2.819	4.676	0.454
Spain	8.131	7.398	2.618	3.176	0.242
United Kingdom	5.310	4.722	5.569	8.366	0.454
United States	7.627	7.175	3.636	3.859	0.354

Note: The changes of the correlation coefficients between the Swiss stock market
and other MSCI markets are regressed on a constant and the innovations in the associated national volatility. Monthly MSCI stock market returns over the period
from 1970.01 to 1998.08 are used. All are denominated is Swiss francs.

TABLE 3.6 Correlation and Volatility: The U.S. Case

	Exogenous Variables				
	Volatility (U.S.)	*t*-value	Volatility (Non-U.S.)	*t*-value	Adjusted R^2
Australia	4.758	4.481	3.713	7.767	0.513
Austria	6.803	7.598	0.322	0.360	0.165
Canada	2.937	4.375	1.365	2.305	0.287
France	6.576	7.228	2.295	2.727	0.239
Germany	5.918	6.480	5.635	5.139	0.312
Hong Kong	2.752	1.651	0.366	0.605	0.019
Italy	4.742	4.682	4.602	4.037	0.134
Netherlands	1.366	1.893	6.220	8.440	0.377
Singapore	3.667	3.260	2.779	5.239	0.274
Spain	5.550	6.223	3.368	4.464	0.238
Switzerland	3.636	3.859	7.627	7.175	0.354
United Kingdom	4.135	5.555	3.990	8.026	0.401

Note: The changes of the correlation coefficients between the United States stock market and other MSCI markets are regressed on a constant and the innovations in the associated national volatility. Monthly MSCI stock market returns over the period from 1970.01 to 1998.08 are used. All are denominated is Swiss francs.

With the exception of Hong Kong, the relationship between volatility and correlation is strong and statistically significant. The R-square values are considerably high, ranging from 0.200 to 0.575.

However, it is unclear whether the domestic or the foreign volatility is the more important factor to explain correlations. The two volatility are correlated, and it is hard to statistically separate local from foreign influences in the presence of multicollinearity. However, as in the approach of Solnik, Boucrelle, and Le Fur (1996), including only one volatility (either Swiss or local) significantly reduces the R-square. We do not report the constant term. Because the dependent variable is the innovation in correlation, the constant term represents a trend. Although always positive and thus indicating an upward trend in correlation, it is never statistically significant.

Results are similar when using the U.S. stock market as the reference market. Table 3.6 provides the results. Again, the positive relationship is statistically significant for most pairs of countries. Contrary to what one might expect, U.S. volatility is generally not particularly important in explaining the comovement with other stock markets; this even though it tends to lead all other markets.

Solnik, Boucrelle, and Le Fur (1996) argue that these findings could be explained on the basis of a simple factor model. National stock markets are affected both by world factors common to all countries and by national factors specific to one country. If national factors dominate, correlations are low. Strong shocks that occur to the world factors affect all markets and increase correlations between national stock markets. Harvey (1995b) indirectly verifies this notion in another study. He uses data for emerging stock markets, whose correlations with the developed stock markets are relatively small (but have been considerably increasing). Indeed, local factors do a decent job in predicting stock returns in these countries, whereas world factors have little impact. The globalization of the world economy and the resulting importance of world factors seem to be the driving forces for the interplay between international correlation and market volatility. This observation, however, does not necessarily carry implications for the pricing of global risks.

A final observation is that the relationship between correlation and volatility is particularly strong when volatility is high. In Figure 3.4, the simple averages of volatility in two countries are plotted against the moving correlations between the same two countries. Autocorrelation is again a problem. Despite its limited statistical accuracy, this representation is instructive and highlights that in states of high volatility, the strength of the relationship between high volatility and high correlations increases. The plots are closely scattered around an upward sloping regression line.[4] In contrast, in states of low volatility, correlations are also low and the plots are widely scattered above and below the line-of-best-fit in the lower left-hand region of all four graphs.

Upmarket and Downmarket Correlations

The usual measure of correlation represents average comovements in both up- and downmarkets. Separate correlation estimates in different return environments can detect whether correlation increases or

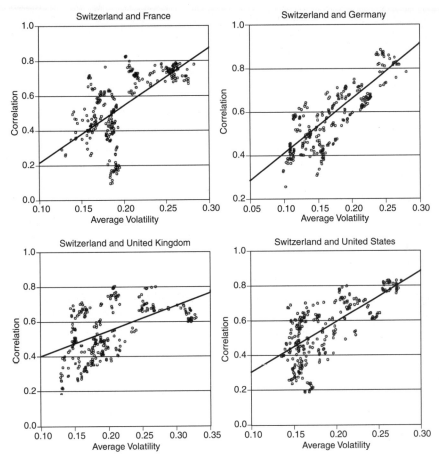

FIGURE 3.4   The strength of the link between volatility and correlation. Using the Swiss stock market as the reference, simple averages of two countries' volatility are plotted against the sliding correlations between the same pair of countries. MSCI stock market returns on a monthly basis are used over the period from 1970.01 to 1998.08. All returns are denominated in Swiss francs.

decreases in downmarkets. Increased correlations in downmarkets reduce the benefits of portfolio diversification even further. We have just shown that correlations increase when markets become more volatile. If we were to find that correlations also increase just when markets go down (i.e., in response to downside volatility), asset managers would be confronted with the worst possible combination. To explore this possibility, we extend the notion of up- and down-markets to the bivariate case, following Erb, Harvey, and Viskanta (1994). In particular, we measure correlation conditional on the realized return. For a specific pair of countries, a month is classified as an "up-up" market if both market returns are above average (positive semicorrelation), whereas a "down-down" market is defined as a month where both returns are less than average (negative semicorrelation). Unconditional correlation coefficients are computed for up-up and down-down markets; the results are displayed in Table 3.7.

In Table 3.7, the down-down correlations are substantially higher than the up-up correlations. This observation holds for all the markets analyzed in our sample. The average of the down-down correlations is 0.512, and the mean of the up-up correlations is 0.211. There is surprisingly low diversity across the individual markets. The average down-correlation of the Swiss stock market with respect to the remaining markets is 0.556, whereas the average up-correlation of the Swiss stock market with the other markets is 0.279. Interestingly, comparing the coefficients in Table 3.7 with those in Table 3.2 reveals that the overall coefficients are much closer to the downside correlations than to the upside coefficients. The overall average of correlations over the total sample in Table 3.2 was 0.477, which is similar to the down-down coefficient of 0.512, but substantially higher than the up-up coefficient of 0.211. This observation has important implications for downside risk measures. We refer to this interesting observation again later on, but there is no immediate explanation for this phenomenon. If ex post returns are rational expectation proxies for expected returns, this may indicate that risk premiums exhibit stronger common components during bad states. It may also help to explain why people do not hold stocks to the extent one would expect under constant relative risk aversion. Finally, by grouping into up-up and down-down correlations, we do not particularly focus on extreme returns. Looking only at the bottom and top percentiles of realized returns (instead of simply splitting the sample using the average returns) would probably be a more appropriate procedure. Longin and Solnik (2001) explicitly model the multivariate tail distribution. However, their analysis requires extreme

TABLE 3.7 Semi-Correlations on Global Stock Markets

	Australia	Austria	Canada	France	Germany	Hong Kong	Italy	Netherlands	Singapore	Spain	Switzerland	United Kingdom	United States	Average	Ø (Average)
Australia		0.290	0.714	0.595	0.531	0.560	0.307	0.678	0.573	0.477	0.214	0.536	0.671	0.548	0.512
Austria	0.063		0.278	0.439	0.626	0.240	0.384	0.329	0.463	0.443	0.230	0.242	0.337	0.494	
Canada	0.372	0.030		0.470	0.473	0.532	0.375	0.646	0.523	0.420	0.180	0.578	0.742	0.509	
France	0.179	0.047	0.129		0.613	0.477	0.221	0.649	0.563	0.457	0.396	0.481	0.541	0.505	
Germany	-0.015	0.265	0.057	0.349		0.495	0.341	0.657	0.598	0.535	0.448	0.495	0.555	0.507	
Hong Kong	0.243	-0.089	0.391	0.004	0.101		0.453	0.573	0.646	0.368	0.211	0.425	0.530	0.498	
Italy	0.177	0.127	0.092	0.299	0.054	0.044		0.381	0.333	0.334	0.203	0.252	0.380	0.485	
Netherlands	0.160	0.175	0.364	0.385	0.333	0.425	C.063		0.498	0.361	0.388	0.595	0.652	0.510	
Singapore	0.215	-0.020	0.319	0.299	0.053	0.505	C.175	0.236		0.477	0.376	0.496	0.656	0.498	
Spain	0.145	0.336	0.243	0.156	0.232	0.018	0.243	0.216	-0.020		0.121	0.317	0.442	0.481	
Switzerland	0.582	0.437	0.608	0.562	0.683	0.508	0.379	0.707	0.609	0.401		0.582	0.611	0.556	
United Kingdom	0.357	-0.016	0.382	0.382	0.116	0.367	0.106	0.380	0.484	0.034	0.361		0.601	0.509	
United States	0.251	0.116	0.617	0.175	0.060	0.150	-0.013	0.261	0.267	0.256	0.223	0.224		0.560	
Average	0.197	0.105	0.265	0.233	0.171	0.198	0.131	0.282	0.241	0.165	0.279	0.265	0.216		
Ø (Average)	0.211														

Note: The table reports the semi-correlations of monthly MSCI stock market returns over the period from 1970.01 to 1998.08. All returns are continuously compounded and denominated in Swiss francs. Up-up (both markets experience returns above their averages) correlations are shown above the diagonal, down-down (both markets experience returns below their averages) correlations on the right-hand side.

value theory, which we have avoided to keep the analysis accessible. Another appealing and more tractable approach to identify outliers has been suggested by Chow, Jaquier, Kritzman, and Lowry (1999). They construct multivariate confidence intervals to distinguish extreme returns from "normal" returns, allowing for unequal variances and nonzero correlations.

Business Cycles and Correlations

There is ample evidence that expected stock returns are related to the business cycle. Expected returns tend to be high during recessions and low during recoveries. The general notion is that investors want to smooth consumption patterns and, therefore, dislike recessions. Fortunately, the stock market acts like a big insurance market. By changing weights in recession-sensitive stocks, investors whose income is particularly hurt by recessions can purchase insurance against that loss from people who are not hurt by recessions. But they must pay a premium to do so, which is why the investor is willing to take on recession-related risk.[5] In fact, linking stock returns to time-varying business cycle risk seems to be the most elegant route to preserve the theory of efficient markets that has dominated the asset pricing literature since the mid-1960s.

Because correlation is a measure of the comovement of stock returns in two markets, business cycles in both countries may also influence the correlation. Instead of splitting the sample according to the ups and downs of the underlying stock markets, we now use the business cycles dates defined by the National Bureau of Economic Research (NBER) to classify stock market returns. The U.S. business cycles need not be representative for other countries, but there is no similar business cycle measurement standard for the other markets. We compute separate correlations for expansion and recession months. The results are shown in Table 3.8. Although the general pattern of the results is the same as before, the differences between the two sets of correlation coefficients are much smaller. Nevertheless, the average country-by-country expansion correlations are again lower in all cases than the corresponding recession coefficients. The average

TABLE 3.8 Stock Market Correlations through Business Cycles

	Australia	Austria	Canada	France	Germany	Hong Kong	Italy	Netherlands	Singapore	Spain	Switzerland	United Kingdom	United States	Average	Ø (Average)
Australia		0.323	0.705	0.591	0.460	0.492	0.326	0.601	0.525	0.544	0.437	0.584	0.690	0.576	0.577
Austria	0.262		0.388	0.558	0.743	0.404	0.596	0.423	0.538	0.651	0.349	0.343	0.456	0.556	
Canada	0.668	0.297		0.589	0.441	0.515	0.363	0.680	0.567	0.521	0.503	0.653	0.781	0.565	
France	0.391	0.357	0.462		0.661	0.545	0.500	0.664	0.621	0.614	0.521	0.596	0.570	0.570	
Germany	0.359	0.508	0.417	0.570		0.422	0.583	0.669	0.538	0.624	0.636	0.564	0.521	0.565	
Hong Kong	0.434	0.241	0.427	0.240	0.319		0.473	0.587	0.745	0.449	0.339	0.644	0.549	0.562	
Italy	0.374	0.066	0.371	0.320	0.255	0.279		0.476	0.507	0.705	0.311	0.429	0.415	0.567	
Netherlands	0.494	0.404	0.643	0.598	0.681	0.426	0.397		0.623	0.516	0.648	0.778	0.673	0.588	
Singapore	0.518	0.204	0.524	0.263	0.300	0.559	0.353	0.448		0.413	0.385	0.715	0.661	0.584	
Spain	0.436	0.280	0.450	0.408	0.386	0.300	0.341	0.478	0.299		0.354	0.436	0.522	0.576	
Switzerland	0.553	0.559	0.605	0.721	0.719	0.489	0.505	0.801	0.630	0.538		0.650	0.634	0.617	
United Kingdom	0.541	0.293	0.589	0.557	0.440	0.356	0.373	0.636	0.479	0.456	0.537		0.602	0.586	
United States	0.587	0.269	0.823	0.486	0.474	0.412	0.363	0.699	0.540	0.484	0.566	0.617		0.590	
Average	0.463	0.410	0.442	0.436	0.432	0.420	0.425	0.461	0.444	0.459	0.465	0.503	0.527		
Ø (Average)	0.453														

Note: The table reports the correlations of monthly MSCI stock market returns over the period from 1970.01 to 1998.08 through business cycles. All returns are continuously compounded and denominated in Swiss francs. The dating of the business cycle is taken from the National Bureau of Economic Research (NBER). Expansion correlations are shown to the left of the diagonal and recession correlations on the right-hand side.

expansion correlation is 0.453, and the average recession correlation is 0.577. The difference is fairly low for the U.S. stock market (0.527 vs. 0.590), which is surprising because the NBER business cycle definition should be most relevant for the U.S. stock market.

Although our results may be sensitive to the way the NBER classifies business cycles, the general notion is that correlations are related to the business cycle. Correlations are highest when any two countries are in a common recession, and they are lower during recoveries. This means that the same forces that drive expected returns may also affect correlations. In fact, Erb, Harvey, and Viskanta (1994) show that much of the variability in correlations can be predicted using instrument variables such as dividend yields and interest rate spreads.

INVESTMENT IMPLICATIONS

In this section, we illustrate some practical implications for these important empirical patterns of volatility and correlation. The difference of volatility and correlations between up- and downmarkets implies that the risk reduction potential of diversification strategies is limited in downmarkets. This also implies that the commonly used downside risk measures, such as shortfall risk or value-at-risk, exhibit a downward bias if equally estimated over up- and downmarket cycles. Finally, we address the possible implications for option pricing.

In a related study, Harlow (1991) shows that portfolios constructed to take asymmetry explicitly into account outperform standard mean-variance portfolios. Chow, Jaquier, Kritzman, and Lowry (1999) suggest computing two separate covariance matrices: one for normal observations to represent a quiet risk regime, and the other from the outlier observations to represent a stressful regime. Focusing on stressful periods alone would induce investors to hold unduly conservative portfolios that fail to achieve long-term performance objectives. On the other hand, optimizing portfolios on the basis of the full-sample covariance matrix would also be suboptimal because such portfolios might not even survive. Therefore, their approach is

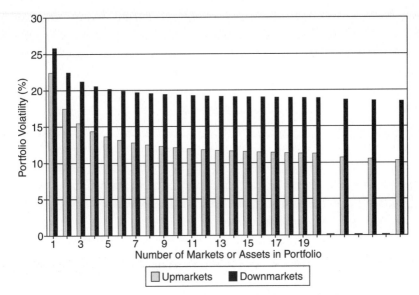

FIGURE 3.5 Diversification in up- and downmarkets: The global case. The limiting value for the up-volatility is 10.3 percent, for the down-volatility 18.5 percent.

to blend both matrices into a single one, assigning to the outlier sample a greater probability than its empirical frequency and accounting for differences in risk aversion.[6] In what follows, we explore naive diversification strategies and the error that results from failing to take into account the differences between the normal regime and the downmarket regime.

Diversification in Upmarkets and Downmarkets

The diversification curves in Figure 3.5 illustrate how the volatility of diversified portfolios (denoted as σ_p) decreases with the number of included markets in up- and downmarkets. The calculations are based on the following formula:

$$\sigma_P = \sqrt{\overline{Var} - \frac{1}{n}\overline{Cov}} \qquad (3.6)$$

where $\overline{Var}$ and $\overline{Cov}$ denote the average variance and covariance across all 13 markets in our sample. These parameters are based on the following estimates: an average upcorrelation of 0.211, an average upvolatility of 0.224, an average downcorrelation of 0.512, and an average downvolatility 0.258. It is immediately clear from Figure 3.5 that the volatility mismatch between up- and downmarkets is much more pronounced for diversified portfolios. This is caused by the anticyclical behavior of correlations. Although the upvolatility of a well-diversified portfolio reduces to 10.3 percent, the downvolatility remains at 18.5 percent, roughly 80 percent higher.

This result also holds from a purely Swiss perspective. Figure 3.6 is based on an average upcorrelation of 0.279, an average upvolatility of 0.156, an average downcorrelation of 0.556, and an average downvolatility of 0.182. The limiting volatility of a well-diversified portfolio is 8.2 percent in upmarkets, but 13.6 percent in downmarkets. Again, this is roughly 65 percent larger.

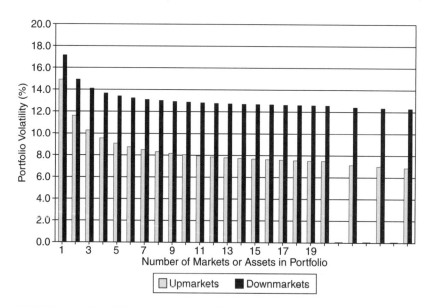

FIGURE 3.6   Diversification in up- and downmarkets: The Swiss case. The limiting value for the upvolatility is 13.6 percent, for the downvolatility 8.2 percent.

Shortfall Risk

Investment risk is often associated with the probability that the return of an investment is below a certain individual return target. As opposed to the notion of volatility, this is a downside-oriented risk measure, also known as *shortfall risk*. For example, given an expected annual return of 10 percent and a volatility of 24 percent, the probability of observing a negative annual return (i.e., assuming a threshold return of 0%) is 33.8 percent; or the probability of a return below −10 percent is 20.2 percent. These figures are based on normal return distributions.

A natural question is how different up- and down-volatility affect the magnitude of shortfall risk. To investigate this problem, we compare shortfall probabilities based on two volatility estimates (but the same mean): the overall volatility and the downmarket volatility. The average volatility across all markets is 24 percent, and the respective downside volatility is 25.8 percent (see Table 3.3). Given an average return of 10 percent and assuming a threshold return of 0 percent, overall volatility implies a shortfall probability of 33.8 percent, whereas the higher downside volatility implies a probability of 34.9 percent shortfall probability. Thus, overall volatility underestimates the true shortfall risk only marginally, by 1.1 percent. For other threshold returns, −10 percent and −20 percent, the intuition is similar: The respective bias is 1.7 percent in both cases. Table 3.9 summarizes these results. An investment horizon of 1 year is assumed in all computations.

Because correlation coefficients increase in downmarkets, the bias should increase if one analyzes the shortfall risk of diversified portfolios. We therefore compute shortfall probabilities for equally weighted portfolios including 10 markets. For simplicity, the same volatility and correlation coefficients (their average values) are assumed for all markets. The results in the lower panel of Table 3.9 show that the bias in shortfall probabilities is, at best, only marginally higher than in the undiversified case. This surprising result leads us to conclude that the increase of volatility and correlations in downmarkets does not substantially increase shortfall risk measures.

TABLE 3.9 Shortfall Risk: The Global Case

	Overall Market		Downmarkets		Shortfall Probability Overall Market Downmarket Deviation		
					Threshold Return (%)		
	Correlation	Volatility (%)	Correlation	Volatility (%)	0	−10	−20
Global Averages							
					33.8	20.2	10.6
N = 1	—	24.0	—	25.8	34.9	21.9	12.2
					1.1	1.7	1.7
					28.4	12.7	4.3
N = 10	0.477	17.5	0.512	19.3	30.2	15.0	6.0
					1.8	2.3	1.7

Note: Global data is used to compute shortfall risks. The expected return is assumed 10 percent; the time horizon underlying all calculations is one year. We both look at the undiversified case (N = 1) and a diversified portfolio consisting of 10 markets (N = 10) with equal volatility and correlation coefficients.

This conclusion is only valid as long as the normality assumption underlying the computations is supported by the data.[7]

Table 3.10 replicates the same analysis with Swiss data and shows that the results are qualitatively similar. If a threshold return of 0 percent is chosen, the bias is 1.4 percent for undiversified portfolios and 2.4 percent for a portfolio including 10 markets. Overall, the impact of the correlation effect is small because the downside correlation is close to the overall sample correlation. Recall that the average correlation was 0.477 over the entire sample. The average downmarket correlation of 0.512 is only slightly higher. On the other hand, the average upmarket correlation of 0.211 is significantly lower than the total average (see Tables 3.2 and 3.7).

Value-at-Risk

A concept closely related to shortfall risk is value-at-risk (VaR). For computing VaR, the starting point is a specific, permissible shortfall

TABLE 3.10 Shortfall Risk: The Swiss Case

| | Overall Market | | Downmarkets | | Shortfall Probability Overall Market Downmarket Deviation Threshold Return (%) | | |
	Correlation	Volatility (%)	Correlation	Volatility (%)	0	−10	−20
	Swiss Averages						
					27.7	11.8	3.8
N = 1	—	16.9	—	18.2	29.1	13.6	5.0
					1.4	1.8	1.2
					21.6	5.8	0.9
N = 10	0.521	12.7	0.556	14.1	23.9	7.8	1.7
					2.4	2.0	0.8

Note: Swiss data is used to compute shortfall risks. The expected return is assumed 10 percent; the time horizon underlying all calculations is one year. We both look at the undiversified case ($N = 1$) and a diversified portfolio consisting of 10 markets ($N = 10$) with equal volatility and correlation coefficients.

probability (e.g., 1%) during a certain time horizon (e.g., 3 months). VaR can then be understood as the amount of capital required to cover a loss with a prespecified probability within a specific period.[8] For example, given an overall volatility of 24 percent, the probability of losing more than 8.83 percent of the current capital within two weeks (10 trading days) is 1 percent, assuming a lognormal distribution for the capital and a mean of 0 percent for the continuously computed returns. Therefore, 8.83 percent is the value-at-risk. If the VaR is computed assuming a downside volatility of 25.8 percent, which is again the average value across all markets in bad states, then the VaR increases to 9.46 percent. Thus, the overall volatility underestimates the VaR by just 0.63 percentage points. Of course, the figures would change if the user were to select other confidence levels (90, 95, and 99.9%) or time horizons. The results are summarized in Table 3.11. The two-week, 99 percent VaR is the relevant figure for the capital requirements to cover market risks as suggested by the Basle Committee.

TABLE 3.11 Value-at-Risk for Undiversified Portfolios: The Global Case

Confidence (%)	Average Volatility 24.00%			Downside Volatility 25.80%			Deviation		
	10D	3M	1Y	10D	3M	1Y	10D	3M	1Y
90.0	4.96	14.25	26.48	5.33	15.24	28.15	0.36	0.98	1.68
95.0	6.33	17.91	32.62	6.78	19.12	34.58	0.46	1.21	1.97
99.0	8.83	24.36	42.78	9.46	25.93	45.13	0.63	1.57	2.35
99.9	11.55	30.98	52.37	12.36	32.88	54.94	0.81	1.89	2.58

Note: Global data for undiversified portfolios is used to compute the value-at-risk for different confidence levels and different time horizons. A lognormal distribution is assumed for capital and a mean of 0 percent for continuously computed returns. The deviation refers to the percentage difference in the value-at-risk when higher downside volatility, instead of overall volatility, is used in the computations. D, M, and Y denote days, months, and years, respectively.

The results show that the bias from neglecting asymmetrical volatility ranges from 0.36 percent (10 days, 10% shortfall probability) to 2.58 percent (1 year, 0.1% shortfall probability). These are moderate deviations. Given our results in the previous section, the picture does not change if diversified portfolios are examined. The results in Table 3.12 show that the respective bias ranges from 0.37

TABLE 3.12 Value-at-Risk for Diversified Portfolios: The Global Case

Confidence (%)	Average Volatility 17.50%			Downside Volatility 19.30%			Deviation		
	10D	3M	1Y	10D	3M	1Y	10D	3M	1Y
90.0	3.64	10.61	20.09	4.01	11.63	21.91	0.37	1.03	1.82
95.0	4.65	13.40	25.01	5.12	14.68	27.20	0.47	1.27	2.19
99.0	6.52	18.42	33.44	7.16	20.11	36.17	0.65	1.69	2.73
99.9	8.56	23.69	41.77	9.40	25.79	44.92	0.84	2.09	3.15

Note: Global data for diversified portfolios is used to compute the value-at-risk for different confidence levels and different time horizons. A lognormal distribution is assumed for capital and a mean of 0 percent for continuously computed returns. The deviation refers to the percentage difference in the value-at-risk when higher downside volatility, instead of overall volatility, is used in the computations. D, M, and Y denote days, months, and years, respectively.

TABLE 3.13 Value-at-Risk for Undiversified Portfolios: The Swiss Case

Confidence (%)	Average Volatility 16.90%			Downside Volatility 18.20%			Deviation		
	10D	3M	1Y	10D	3M	1Y	10D	3M	1Y
90.0	3.52	10.26	19.47	3.79	11.01	20.80	0.27	0.74	1.33
95.0	4.50	12.98	24.27	4.83	13.90	25.87	0.34	0.93	1.60
99.0	6.30	17.85	32.51	6.77	19.08	34.52	0.47	1.23	2.01
99.9	8.28	22.98	40.68	8.89	24.51	43.02	0.61	1.53	2.34

Note: Swiss data for undiversified portfolios is used to compute the value-at-risk for different confidence levels and different time horizons. A lognormal distribution is assumed for capital and a mean of 0 percent for continuously computed returns. The deviation refers to the percentage difference in the value-at-risk when higher downside volatility, instead of overall volatility, is used in the computations. D, M, and Y denote days, months, and years, respectively.

percent to 3.15 percent, which is only slightly higher than in the undiversified case. The impact of the correlation effect is small, because the downside correlation is close to the overall correlation (0.512 vs. 0.477, respectively).

The figures are not much different if Swiss data is used instead of global risk coefficients. The results are displayed in Tables 3.13 and 3.14, respectively. They reveal that the biases are of the same

TABLE 3.14 Value-at-Risk for Diversified Portfolios: The Swiss Case

Confidence (%)	Average Volatility 12.70%			Downside Volatility 14.10%			Deviation		
	10D	3M	1Y	10D	3M	1Y	10D	3M	1Y
90.0	2.66	7.82	15.02	2.95	8.64	16.53	0.29	0.82	1.51
95.0	3.40	9.92	18.85	3.77	10.95	20.70	0.37	1.03	1.85
99.0	4.77	13.73	25.58	5.28	15.13	27.96	0.51	1.39	2.38
99.9	6.29	17.82	32.46	6.96	19.58	35.32	0.67	1.76	2.86

Note: Swiss data for diversified portfolios is used to compute the value-at-risk for different confidence levels and different time horizons. A lognormal distribution is assumed for capital and a mean of 0 percent for continuously computed returns. The deviation refers to the percentage difference in the value-at-risk when higher downside volatility, instead of overall volatility, is used in the computations. D, M, and Y denote days, months, and years, respectively.

magnitude as those reported for global data. For the undiversified portfolio, the two-week, 99 percent VaR results in a bias of 0.47 percent (compared with 0.63%); and for the portfolio diversified across 10 markets, the bias is 0.51 percent (compared with 0.65%).

The results for the other specifications (i.e., confidence levels and time horizons) are similar. Hence, one implication of this section is that the current regulatory standards for calculating VaR figures need no fundamental adjustment. The VaR based on effective downside volatilites and correlations is only marginally (less than 1%) higher than those calculated for an overall sample. Again, this conclusion rests on the assumption that the underlying returns are normally distributed. No test is provided in this chapter that either supports or rejects this assumption. It could well be true that fat tails, skewness, and so forth have a more drastic effect on VaR figures than modifying volatility (given normality).

Option Pricing

Finally, we investigate how the disparity between up- and downvolatility affects option prices. This question is difficult to address in a Black-Scholes framework assuming normally distributed returns. To get a rough estimate of the bias, we use a simple binomial setting that is flexible enough to incorporate different implied up- and downvolatility in modeling the stock price process.

In Figure 3.7, we assume symmetrical logarithmic returns, based on a volatility of 24 percent (which is the average across all markets,

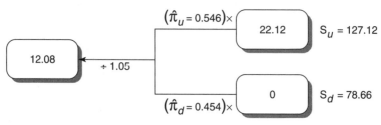

FIGURE 3.7 Option pricing with symmetric volatility.

as indicated in Table 3.2). The multiplicative binomial volatility coefficients are then

$$u = \exp(0.2) = 1.2712 \text{ and } d = -\exp(0.2) = u^{-1} = 0.7866 \qquad (3.7)$$

If we assume a current stock price of 100, the end-of-period stock price is 127.12 in the upstate, and 78.66 in the downstate. Further, a risk-free interest rate, denoted as r_f, of 5 percent is assumed. We price a 1-year, at-the-money call option with an exercise price equal to the forward price (i.e., 105). The future payoff of the option is 22.12 in the upstate, and zero in the downstate. To find the arbitrage-free value of the option, we compute the risk-neutral probabilities, which are

$$\pi_u = \frac{(1+r_f)-d}{u-d} = \frac{1.05-0.7866}{1.2712-0.7866} = 0.546 \qquad (3.8)$$

in the upstate, and $\pi_d = 0.454$ in the downstate. This implies a call option price of 12.08, which can be considered as the discrete-time analogue to the Black-Scholes price.

We now price the same option by using different volatility underlying the up- and downmovement. Based on the figures in Table 3.2, the upfactor derived from the 22.4 percent upvolatility is

$$u = \exp(0.224) = 1.2511$$

and the downfactor derived from the 25.8 percent downvolatility is

$$d = -\exp(0.258) = 0.7726$$

The end-of-period stock prices and option payoffs are displayed in Figure 3.8. The new risk-neutral probability calculation for the upstate is

$$\pi_u = \frac{(1+r_f)-d}{u-d} = \frac{1.05-0.7726}{1.2511-0.7726} = 0.582 \qquad (3.9)$$

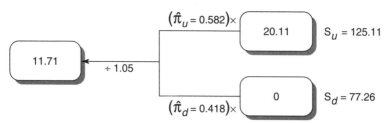

FIGURE 3.8 Option pricing with symmetric volatility.

which is slightly higher than in the symmetrical logarithmic return case. The resulting option price is 11.71, which is only 0.37 or 3 percent less than in the symmetrical logarithmic return case. Again, the asymmetrical volatility profile does not have a substantial impact on option prices. The numerical example is only indicative, and the conclusion cannot be generalized. However, volatility patterns with these characteristics can be modeled in a Black-Scholes framework (e.g., using the CEV-model developed by Cox & Ross, 1976).

CONCLUSION

The changing interdependence of national equity markets is an issue of major relevance for asset management. Indeed, we found the following empirical regularities:

- Stock market volatility is higher when markets go down. We presented a statistical model which demonstrates that bad news (return surprises) will lead to higher volatility than good news.
- In periods of high volatility, stock markets become more highly correlated, and they are less correlated in periods of low volatility.
- Higher correlations are detected when equity markets go down simultaneously as well as in periods of shrinking real economic activity.

Potentially, these findings impose dramatic challenges for asset managers. Our results strongly indicate that investors do not get the full benefits of international risk diversification in those situations when they are most desired. Surprisingly, however, the implications for traditional risk measures are not as strong as might be assumed at first sight. Both shortfall risk and value-at-risk are affected by asymmetrical volatility and correlations, but not excessively. Likewise, option prices diverge only slightly once different volatility regimes for up- and downstates are taken into account. Admittedly, our approach has been simplistic and ad hoc. In particular, we assumed multivariate normality of outliers (downstate returns) to demonstrate investment implications. If this assumption is violated, a linear correlation measure is no longer accurate to model the dependence structure of returns. Nevertheless, our results indicate that although the time-variation in volatility and correlation causes problems for asset managers, the problems are manageable. This is the good news of this chapter: Rational investors should not do without international portfolio diversification, but they must always keep the changing interdependence of national equity markets in mind and adapt their investment strategies accordingly.

CHAPTER 4

The Correlation Breakdown in International Stock Markets

EXECUTIVE SUMMARY

- This chapter addresses some major structural characteristics of correlation coefficients between stock markets over time: Does correlation significantly fluctuate over time? Is there a particular pattern, such as a positive time trend? Is correlation positively related to volatility? Is there a correlation breakdown as often claimed?
- Correlation matrices exhibit large jumps through time. There is also overwhelming empirical evidence that average correlation (and hence systematic risks) has increased almost 40 percent compared with the early 1970s.
- Correlation and volatility are strongly positively related. An examination of the tails of the return distributions demonstrates that the correlation structure of large returns is asymmetrical.
- Most of the results are bad news for risk managers and internationally diversified investors. The continuously changing correlation pattern makes it difficult to select an ex ante optimal investment strategy. In addition, the observed general increase in correlation erodes the advantage of international risk diversification.
- Variance-covariance matrices estimated from different risk regimes may provide a better representation of a portfolio's riskiness during periods of market turbulence than a variance-covariance matrix estimated from the full sample of observations.

This supports the use of downside-risk approaches to investment decisions.

MOTIVATION

Recent experience with emerging market investments and hedge funds has highlighted that risk parameters are unstable and that international equity correlations can rise quickly and dramatically. Likewise, the global stock market crash in October 1987 increased research interest into how financial disturbances transmit from one market to another and fostered a more cautious attitude toward international diversification and risk management. First, due to the progressive removal of impediments to international investment, international financial markets have become increasingly integrated. Integrated markets, however, are likely to be more correlated and thus could erode the advantages of international risk diversification in the long run. Second, recent studies suggest that the case for international risk diversification may have been overstated because the risk protection brought by diversifying assets across markets is likely to be reduced when it is needed most—during periods of high volatility or, worse, extreme negative price movements. So-called correlation breakdowns, if they occur, undermine diversification and hedging operations based on correlations estimated from historical data because they may be inaccurate precisely when they are most desired.

The crucial role of correlations in global asset allocation decisions is emphasized repeatedly in this book. On the one hand, the preceding chapter demonstrates that international equity markets are more highly correlated in periods of high volatility and that correlations are higher when stock markets go down simultaneously and in some periods of the business cycle. On the other hand, Chapter 8 reveals that the correlation structure generally does not provide sufficient information for determining whether a country or sector approach should be implemented in diversifying portfolios. Consequently, we also address whether sector- or country-based portfolios are more robust in stock market turmoils there.

This chapter investigates several questions. Does correlation really and significantly fluctuate over time? If yes, is any particular pattern emerging? Is there a positive time trend for correlations? Is correlation positively related to volatility? What actually is an extreme event on financial markets? Does correlation breakdown really occur? If yes, does it occur for all countries in the same way and what are the consequences for risk and asset management?

Some implications of changing volatility and correlations were analyzed in Chapter 3. There, it is argued that increased volatility and correlations in downmarkets do not substantially increase shortfall and value-at-risk measures. However, this conclusion is only valid as long as the data support the normality assumption of the underlying return distribution. Thus, this conclusion is incomplete because the analysis is not focused on extreme returns. To overcome this problem, this chapter provides additional information by focusing directly on the tails of the return distributions.

Finally, we introduce a procedure for blending variance-covariance matrices from different risk regimes. This enables investors to express views about the likelihood of each risk regime and to differentiate their risk aversion to them.

ANALYSIS OF THE STOCK RETURN SERIES

In financial markets theory, an important assumption is that continuously compounded stock market returns are multivariate normally distributed. This assumption is also a prerequisite for using linear correlation to measure dependence between international equity returns. However, although the assumption of (multivariate) normality is broadly applied in almost every area of finance, there is also, starting with Mandelbrot (1963) and Fama (1965), overwhelming empirical evidence that empirical distributions of stock returns are significantly different from Gaussian distributions. But if returns are nonnormal, linear correlation cannot capture the whole dependence structure between them.

Description of the Data

The sample was restricted to Switzerland (CHF) and the Group of Seven countries (United States (USD), United Kingdom (GBP), Canada (CAD), Germany (DEM), Italy (ITL), France (FRF), and Japan (JPY)). These are the eight largest markets, and their combined stock market capitalization is more than 90 percent of that of the world. For each market, monthly nominal returns are calculated in local currency. The sample period is from January 1973 to December 1999.

Summary Statistics

Summary statistics for the monthly returns appear in Table 4.1. Over the total period from January 1973 to December 1999, annualized mean returns range from 6.26 percent for Japan to 12.41 percent for Italy across the markets. Except for Italy, the medians are higher than the means, indicating that the distributions tend to be skewed to the left for these countries. Maximum and minimum values differ greatly from the mean in all countries. Here, the United Kingdom shows the most distinct extreme monthly observations (maximum: +40.05%

TABLE 4.1 Summary Statistics for Monthly Returns of the Equity Markets

	CHF	USD	GBP	CAD	DEM	ITL	FRF	JPY
Mean (annual %)	7.97	9.65	10.89	7.06	7.98	12.41	11.71	6.27
Median (annual %)	12.73	12.66	16.69	8.60	8.87	1.21	19.31	7.32
Maximum (%)	18.25	15.81	40.05	14.96	14.34	27.71	20.42	17.45
Minimum (%)	−27.46	−24.10	−31.82	−23.56	−26.82	−22.38	−24.53	−24.43
Volatility (%)	16.53	15.08	20.46	16.70	17.00	25.53	21.85	18.28
Skewness	−1.07	−0.67	0.23	−0.89	−0.73	0.27	−0.48	−0.31
Kurtosis	8.47	6.89	11.63	6.96	6.36	3.97	4.72	5.32
Jarque-Bera	465.6	228.3	1008.2	255.2	181.0	16.6	52.4	77.4
Probability	0.000*	0.000*	0.000*	0.000*	0.000*	0.000*	0.000*	0.000*

Note: The table shows descriptive statistics for monthly stock market returns over the period from 1973.01 to 1999.12 (324 observations). The stock market indices are collected from Thomson Financial Datastream.

*Denotes statistical significance at the 5 percent level of significance.

and minimum: −31.82%, compared with an annualized mean of 10.89%). Annualized standard deviation (volatility) of the returns is lowest in the United States with 15.08 percent, whereas the returns in Italy are the most volatile (25.53%).

The coefficients of skewness and kurtosis permit evaluation of the distributional characteristics of the returns. If returns are exactly normally distributed, the skewness is equal to zero and the kurtosis is equal to three. As indicated, Table 4.1 shows that except for Italy and the United Kingdom, all stock market returns are negatively skewed. Here, Switzerland seems to have the most negatively skewed and therefore asymmetrical market. The high values of the kurtosis support that financial time series tend to be heavy-tailed. This means that there are too many observations around the mean and, in contrast, too many outliers (extreme events). To examine the combined effect of skewness and kurtosis, the Jarque-Bera test of normality is conducted. Not surprisingly, the null hypothesis of normally distributed returns is rejected on the 5 percent level of significance for all markets.

International Equity Market Correlations

So far, each time series has been analyzed separately. The following section turns to the empirical dependence structure of international stock markets. Table 4.2 reports linear correlations calculated over the whole sample period, mirroring the long-term interdependence of the international equity markets. The highest correlation coefficient is 72.99 percent, documented for Canada and the United States, and the lowest is 28.66 percent, reflecting the relationship between returns in Italy and Japan. Switzerland exhibits the highest equally weighted average correlation with the other seven stock markets: The average coefficient is as high as 56.73 percent. High average values are also measured for the United States (52.56%), France (50.82%), and United Kingdom (50.31%). The lowest mean correlation with other markets is measured for Japan (32.93%), followed by Italy (39.44%).

Moreover, the correlation matrix reveals certain "regional correlation clusters." Typically, high correlation coefficients are documented

TABLE 4.2   Correlation Matrix over the Period 1973.01 to 1999.12

	CHF	USD	GBP	CAD	DEM	ITL	FRF	JPY	Average
CHF	1	64.44	61.13	58.14	69.50	45.91	58.70	39.26	56.73
USD		1	64.06	72.99	47.59	32.73	53.04	33.05	52.56
GBP			1	56.59	45.45	39.43	52.23	33.29	50.31
CAD				1	42.47	36.45	51.81	31.28	49.96
DEM					1	42.94	56.73	31.69	48.05
ITL						1	42.94	28.66	39.44
FRF							1	33.26	50.82
JPY								1	32.93
Total average									47.60

Note: The table shows linear correlation coefficients for monthly stock market returns over the period from 1973.01 to 1999.12 (324 observations). All values are multiplied by 100 (percentage).

for countries that are located in the same region. Examples are the United States and Canada (72.99%), Switzerland and Germany (69.50%), and Switzerland and France (58.70%). The U.K. market, on the other hand, seems to be more correlated with the U.S. and Canadian markets than with other European stock markets (except Switzerland).

It is often claimed that international equity market correlations are unstable over time. Studies such as Erb, Harvey, and Viskanta (1994), Longin and Solnik (1995), Solnik, Boucrelle, and Le Fur (1996), and Oertmann (1997), to name just a few, document that correlation matrices are unstable over time. Conversely, other studies such as Kaplanis (1988) or Forbes and Rigobon (1999) conclude that the relationship between international equity markets is less unstable as often claimed. To explore this issue, the preceding sample period is divided into three subperiods (January 1973 to December 1986, 1987, and January 1988 to December 1999). Table 4.3 reports equally weighted average correlations and volatility for these three subperiods.

In comparing these values, it becomes evident that average correlation has increased notably from 40.55 percent in the period from January 1973 to December 1986 to 55.16 percent in the period from

TABLE 4.3   Correlations and Volatility over Different Time Periods

	CHF	USD	GBP	CAD	DEM	ITL	FRF	JPY	Average
Equally Weighted Average Correlations									
1973.01–1999.12	56.73	52.56	50.31	49.96	48.05	39.44	50.82	32.93	47.60
1973.01–1986.12	49.14	45.81	44.04	42.37	35.57	32.63	41.79	33.02	40.55
1988.01–1999.12	62.90	58.20	58.48	55.38	61.06	49.65	60.20	35.42	55.16
1987.01–1987.12	76.56	74.65	73.99	76.96	63.90	55.91	78.64	48.52	68.64
Volatility									
1973.01–1999.12	16.51	15.06	20.43	16.67	16.97	25.49	21.82	18.25	18.90
1973.01–1986.12	13.98	15.26	22.78	17.33	14.97	27.19	23.18	14.04	18.59
1988.01–1999.12	16.94	12.42	14.61	14.40	16.89	23.23	19.26	21.67	17.43
1987.01–1987.12	31.46	30.64	37.89	28.43	31.39	21.81	26.86	23.27	28.97

Note: The table shows equally weighted average correlations and volatility for the following subperiods: January 1973 to December 1986, 1987; and January 1988 to December 1999. All values are multiplied by 100 (percentage).

January 1988 to December 1999. Even more, in 1987 (including the October 1987 stock market crash), average correlation between the international stock market returns was as high as 68.44 percent. Thus, stock market interdependence seems largely to have grown in times of the market crash. Compared with the average correlation computed over the whole sample period (47.60%), it is evident that correlations fluctuate considerably over time.

TIME-MEASURED OBSERVATIONS

The previous section provides preliminary evidence that correlations fluctuate widely over time. Additionally, it is often stated that correlations increase in periods of high market turbulence. Another question is whether the growth in international capital flows and market integration raised the general level of correlation in the past 30 years. This section investigates the comovement structure of international equity markets in depth. It is shown that, like the expected rates of returns, correlations and volatility vary widely according to the particular time period considered, that there is a positive relationship between correlation and volatility, and that average correlation has increased considerably since the early 1970s.

It is not easy to define an appropriate historical analysis. Hence, in the first part of this section, volatility, covariances, and correlations are estimated on the basis of a moving estimation window. As this has several disadvantages, the argument in the second part is based on re-alized volatility and correlation constructed from daily data.

Moving Estimation Windows

It has long been recognized that the sizes and signs of correlations often depend on the sample period and the investment horizon cho-sen. So, initially (like the analysis in the preceding chapter), the com-putation of volatility, covariances, and correlations is based on moving estimation windows that include T preceding monthly re-turns data. Figure 4.1 shows correlations, covariances, and volatility for Switzerland and the United States calculated for estimation win-dows with a length of 36 months.

Any first inspection of Figure 4.1 suggests that volatility, covari-ance, and correlation change markedly through time. In addition, the correlation structure is sensitive to extreme events such as the Octo-ber 1987 stock market crash. As soon as October 1987 falls into the calculation period, correlation increases dramatically and persists at these high levels for the whole sampling period.

Figure 4.1 also shows that correlation tends to be higher in peri-ods of high market volatility. It seems that U.S. and Swiss volatility, and the correlation between them, follow a similar pattern over time. Indeed, not only is there a significant positive relationship be-tween volatility and correlation, but this relationship is even more pronounced if volatility is high. In the literature, there is also over-whelming evidence that correlation and volatility are positively re-lated. Longin and Solnik (1995) find that their forecasts of correlations increase in periods of high (conditional) volatility. Fur-ther, Solnik, Boucrelle, and Le Fur (1996) statistically verify that markets tend to move more in parallel in high volatility states using

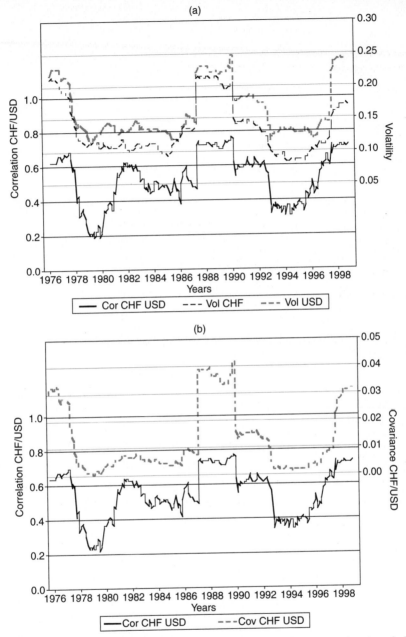

FIGURE 4.1 Correlations, volatility, and covariances for Switzerland and the United States. The figure shows linear correlations and volatility (a) and covariances (b) for Switzerland and the United States over the period from 1976.01 to 1999.12. Length of moving window is 36 months. All calculations are based on monthly returns.

a regression approach and confirm the hypothesis. To sum up, covariances seem to increase faster than variances.

Figure 4.2 shows the effect of omitting outliers on correlations and covariances between Switzerland and the United States. Inspection of the graphs indicates that correlations and covariances are generally lower in absence of these extreme events. Although this is especially distinct for the period containing the October 1987 stock market crash, the recent increase in correlation is—surprisingly—hardly affected by the large market movements in August, September, and October 1998. The effect of omitting extreme negative and positive returns is more distinct for the covariances than for the correlations. In contrast to correlations, covariances are significantly lower in the periods containing the oil shocks in the early 1970s, the October 1987 crash, and the crises in Asia and Russia.

Realized Correlation Constructed from Daily Data

So far, the computation of volatility, covariances, and correlations has been based on moving estimation windows that included T previous monthly returns data. However, a major disadvantage of moving averages is that the resulting time series are heavily autocorrelated and thus difficult to handle in further econometric analysis. To overcome this difficulty associated with the use of overlapping samples, Schwert (1989) and French, Schwert, and Stambaugh (1987) estimate the monthly standard deviation of stock returns using daily returns. They argue that using nonoverlapping samples of daily returns creates an estimation error that is uncorrelated through time. Also, because volatility are not constant over time, a more precise estimate of the standard deviation for a particular month is obtained by using only returns within that month. Their argument, however, is based solely on volatility and not on covariances or correlations. Yet, investigating international dependence structures founded on daily data causes a major problem: National stock markets operate in diverse time zones with different opening and closing times, thereby making return observations nonsynchronous. Thus, daily returns reflect information revealed over different time intervals.

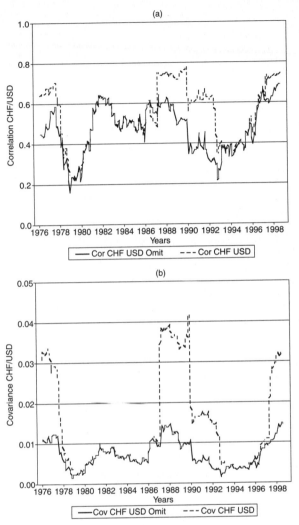

FIGURE 4.2 Correlations and covariances for Switzerland and the United States: Extreme negative and positive monthly returns omitted. The figure shows linear correlations (a) and covariances (b) for Switzerland and the United States over the period from 1976.01 to 1999.12. Length of moving window is 36 months. All calculations are based on monthly returns. The negative and positive monthly returns omitted correspond to the following months: Switzerland: 10.87 (−27.5%), 8.98 (−20.3%), 9.98 (−16.6%), 8.90 (−14.9%), 9.74 (−12.7%), 10.98 (18.3%), 1.75 (15.8%), 5.90 (12.3%), 2.91 (9.7%), 1.97 (9.2%); United States: 10.87 (−24.1%), 11.73 (−13.9%), 9.74 (−13.8%), 8.98 (−11.8%), 7.74 (−9.9%), 10.74 (15.8%), 1.87 (13.3%), 1.75 (12.6%), 10.98 (12.3%), 1.76 (10.7%).

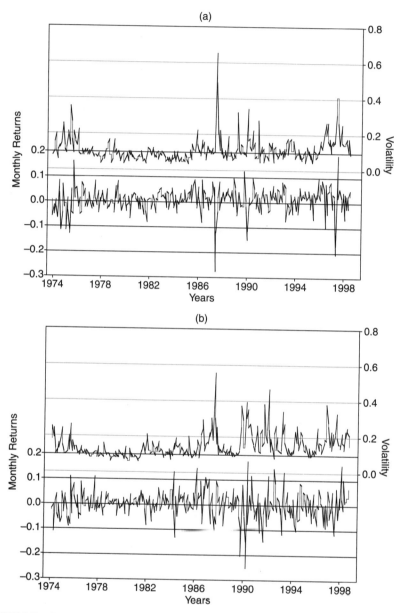

FIGURE 4.3 Returns and volatility for Switzerland and Japan. The figure shows monthly returns and the corresponding realized monthly volatility for Switzerland (a) and Japan (b). Realized volatility are constructed from moving-average, two-day returns (monthly sampled).

To control for markets in different countries not being open during the same time, Forbes and Rigobon (1999) propose to use moving-average, two-day returns. Thus, the rest of this section is based on moving-average, two-day return series that are chopped into monthly blocks within homoskedasticity is assumed.

Figure 4.3 shows the monthly return series and the corresponding time series of realized volatility for Switzerland and Japan, constructed from daily data and sampled for monthly periods. In Switzerland, especially the large price movements during the early 1970s, the October 1987 stock market crash, and the Asian and Russian crises in 1998 caused volatility to rocket. For the most part, the 1990s in Japan were very volatile. In general, the volatility clustering patterns are only apparent.

Similarly, Figure 4.4 shows the return series for the Swiss market and the realized covariances between Switzerland and the United States and Germany, respectively. Here the peak in October 1987 is distinct indicating that the October 1987 stock market crash was indeed an exceptional occurrence, at least within the sample period starting in 1973. Figure 4.4 also seems to give some preliminary evidence that the covariances increased over the final decade.

Figure 4.5 plots the (equally weighted) average realized correlation for Switzerland and (still constructed from daily return data, but sampled for yearly periods) average realized correlation for Switzerland, the United States, the United Kingdom, Germany, and Japan. It is evident that the estimates of average realized correlations are volatile, reaching levels as high as 0.8 and as low as −0.1. Moreover, the smoothed series shows that there is a distinct upward shift in average correlation and that average correlation is strongly synchronized across the countries.

Is There a Time Trend?

It is often stated that the progressive removal of impediments to international investment, as well as the growing political, economic, and financial integration positively affected international market linkages.[1] To investigate whether correlation (and volatility) exhibited such a positive time trend, simple least-squares lines were fitted

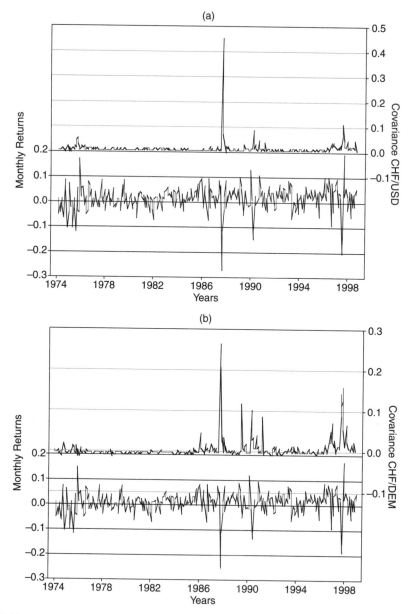

FIGURE 4.4 Covariances between Switzerland and the United States, and Germany. The figure shows monthly returns and the corresponding realized monthly covariances between Switzerland and the United States (a) and Switzerland and Germany (b). Realized covariances are constructed from moving-average, two-day returns (monthly sampled).

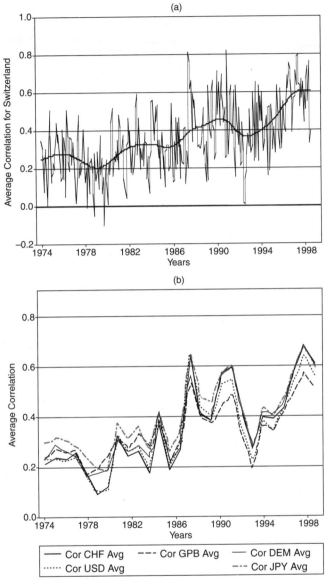

FIGURE 4.5 Average correlation for Switzerland (monthly sampled) and for Switzerland, United States, United Kingdom, Germany, and Japan (yearly sampled). The figure plots equally weighted average realized correlation for Switzerland (a) and equally weighted average realized correlation based on moving-average, two-day returns, but sampled for yearly periods for Switzerland, the United States, the United Kingdom, Germany, and Japan (b). The smoothed series (a) corresponds to the Hodrick and Prescott (1997) filter.

over the total sample period (January 1973 to December 1999) for the monthly sampled realized volatility and correlations. The results are reported in Table 4.4.

Table 4.4 indicates that, in general, there is no time trend in volatility. In contrast, however, average realized correlations have significantly increased for all countries. Here, the highest increase is measured for Japan (40.9%) and the lowest for Germany (26.1%). Average correlation for Switzerland has increased 35.4 percent since January 1973. On the whole, average correlation increased almost 40 percent over the past three decades. These results are fully in line with the findings presented in Solnik and Roulet (2000), and especially in Longin and Solnik (1995). Longin and Solnik (1995) do not find a secular increase in expected market volatility, but they find an average increase in conditional correlation of 36 percent over the period from 1960 to 1990. On the other hand, they also claim that such a constant linear trend is not consistent with the definition of a correlation coefficient. Although this is certainly true, no theory exists for other forms of time trends. Solnik, Boucrelle, and Le Fur (1996) also fit simple least-squares lines over their total sample period. They conclude no trend is easy to identify in their samples. However, as they work with moving estimation windows and thus with heavily autocorrelated time series, their results should be interpreted with caution.

TABLE 4.4 Time Trends: Correlation and Volatility

	CHF	USD	GBP	CAD	DEM	ITL	FRF	JPY	Average
Correlation									
β	1.09*	1.18*	1.11*	1.02*	0.81*	0.87*	1.00*	1.26*	1.23*
Total	35.4%	38.3%	36.0%	33.2%	26.1%	28.1%	32.3%	40.9%	39.8%
Volatility									
β	0.15*	0.07	−0.28*	−0.04	0.19*	−0.07	−0.09	0.31*	0.01
Total	4.80%	2.14%	−8.97%	−1.13%	6.16%	−2.37%	−2.98%	9.91%	0.39%

Note: The table shows the coefficients for a time trend for equally weighted average realized correlations and volatility over the period from 1973.01 to 1999.12. The coefficients are multiplied with 1000. Heteroskedasticity and autocorrelation consistent standard errors and covariances (according to Newey & West, 1987).

*Denotes statistical significance at the 5 percent level of significance.

EVENT-MEASURED OBSERVATIONS

The previous section demonstrated that international correlation increases in periods of high market turbulence, irrespective of the direction of the markets. In addition, however, it is often claimed that the correlation structure of large returns is asymmetrical: International correlation of large negative stock returns differs from that of usual or positive returns. Correlation is said to be highest in periods of extremely volatile downmarkets or bear markets. The following section investigates whether the correlation between international stock markets really exhibits systematic characteristics in the direction of their movements.[2] Because return distributions are not multivariate normal, the usual standard deviation and correlation of returns do not provide sufficient information. Thus, focusing directly on the properties of extreme returns (the tails of the return distributions) provides additional information. In practical application, however, this raises the question of how to define an (extreme) event on financial markets. In any case, the literature provides no clear answer.

Correlation Breakdown

It is widely argued that when one equity market dives, so, generally, do others. Correlations tend to 100 percent as volatility rockets and the markets crash. According to Boyer, Gibson, and Loretan (1999), this pattern of extreme synchronized rises and falls in financial markets is then termed *correlation breakdown*. If returns are drawn from a symmetrical distribution such as the multivariate normal distribution, however, correlations in up- and downmarkets should be indistinguishable. For this reason, the usual measure of linear correlation represents average comovement in both up- and downmarkets. As already shown, however, returns are not symmetrical but skewed to the left. Thus, only separate correlation estimates in different return environments detect whether correlation increases or decreases in downmarkets.

Based on Erb, Harvey, and Viskanta (1994), the preceding chapter applied a semicorrelation analysis to demonstrate that correlations are higher in downmarkets when the data are segmented by ex post returns. In doing so, correlations for months with below-average returns (negative semicorrelation) and for months with above-average returns (positive semicorrelation) were calculated. A month was classified as up/up if, for a specific pair of countries, both market returns are above average; whereas a down/down market was defined as a month where both returns are less than average. Under the assumption of symmetrical return distributions, there is no statistical reason why returns above the mean should have a different correlation from the returns below the mean. However, the empirical findings indicated that down correlations are generally higher than up correlations. Longin and Solnik (2001), on the other hand, use the results of extreme value theory to model the multivariate distribution of large returns for monthly data from 1959 to 1996 for the five largest stock markets (United States, United Kingdom, France, Germany, and Japan). They find in a bivariate framework that the correlation of large negative returns (more precisely, returns of both countries that are below a given threshold) is much higher than normality would suggest. In contrast, they find correlation between the United States and the other four markets is not inconsistent with the assumption of multivariate normality for large positive returns. They conclude that the benefits of international risk reduction in extremely volatile periods have been overstated. In a third example, given in Chow, Jacquier, Kritzman, and Lowry (1999), the vector distance from multivariate average is a measure for identifying multivariate outliers. Hence, a multivariate outlier represents a set of contemporaneous returns that is collectively unusual in the sense that either the performance of an individual asset or the interaction of a combination of assets is unusual.

What Actually Is an (Extreme) Event on Financial Markets?

Both Erb, Harvey, and Viskanta (1994) and thus the analysis in the preceding chapter, and Longin and Solnik (2001) implicitly assume that an extreme event is associated with returns being below a predetermined threshold for both countries at the same time. Yet, is this actually a relevant extreme event for international investors? One might argue that if the returns in both countries are below a certain level, the aim of diversification has already been missed. It is exactly the imperfect correlation that should help to avoid those uncomfortable situations with both markets diving. But if such a situation is already present, investors are no longer interested in any correlation. Using their definition of an extreme event, a second difficulty arises, too. How can those events be interpreted where one market is up and the other market is down and, consequently, correlation is negative? The approach of estimating multivariate outliers suggested by Chow, Jacquier, Kritzman, and Lowry (1999) is also difficult to justify. Their definition of stress as periods that are unusual (possibly containing extreme negative and positive returns) raises the question: Are investors equally risk-averse to negative and positive (multivariate) outliers? The answer is most definitely no. Altogether, it seems important to define what and why certain situations on financial markets are classified as stress events. Thus, the following analysis is based on the following two definitions of an (extreme) event:

1. An (extreme) event for an investor in country j is given when the monthly return of stock market j exceeds a (exogenously) given threshold.
2. An (extreme) event for an investor in country j is given when the monthly return of a world market portfolio exceeds a (exogenously) given threshold.

Whereas the first definition avoids the difficulties associated with the approaches suggested by Erb, Harvey, and Viskanta (1994), Longin and Solnik (2001), and Chow, Jacquier, Kritzman, and Lowry (1999), respectively, the second definition seems to be particularly suitable for investors already internationally diversified.

Empirical Evidence: Based on Realized Correlations

A first opportunity is to consider realized monthly volatility, covariances, and correlations constructed from daily data as described earlier. Figure 4.6 plots Swiss volatility and average covariance versus

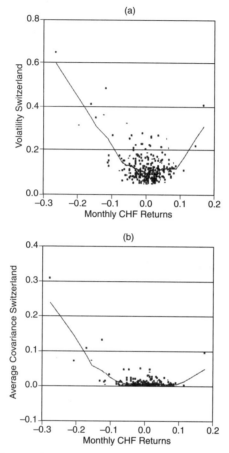

FIGURE 4.6 Volatility and average covariances for Switzerland versus monthly Swiss market returns. The figure plots fitted locally weighted polynomial regressions through volatility (a) and equally weighted average covariances (b) for Switzerland versus monthly Swiss market returns.

Swiss returns. The asymmetry of the volatility and the covariances because of extreme negative returns is only apparent. The most negative return belongs to the October 1987 stock market crash. This was the month when both volatility and covariance peaked.

Figure 4.7 extends the analysis to average realized correlation for Switzerland and the United States. To a less degree, a similar asymmetry of correlation is also apparent.

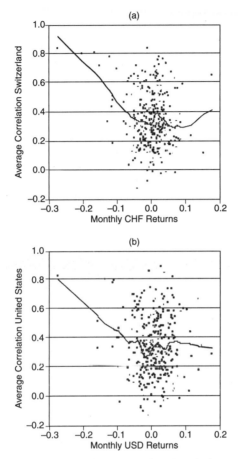

FIGURE 4.7 Average correlations for Switzerland and the United States versus the respective monthly returns. The figure plots fitted locally weighted polynomial regressions through equally weighted average correlations for Switzerland (a) and the United States (b) versus the respective monthly returns.

The preceding analysis is sensitive to some individual (extreme) observation pairs. These are inherent to financial markets and therefore should not be dismissed as special cases. Accordingly, the following analysis focuses directly on the tails of the monthly return distributions.

Empirical Evidence: Based on Monthly Return Data

The first part of this section is based on the first definition, that an (extreme) event for an investor in country j is given when the monthly return of stock market j exceeds a (exogenously) given threshold. More formally, for country j the conditional correlation is calculated as follows:

$$\rho_{i,j}\big|\underline{\theta}<r_j<\bar{\theta}=\frac{E\left[\left(r_j-\mu_j\big|\underline{\theta}<r_j<\bar{\theta}\right)\left(r_i-\mu_i\right)\right]}{\sqrt{E\left[\left(r_j-\mu_j\right)^2\big|\underline{\theta}<r_j<\bar{\theta}\right]}\sqrt{E\left[\left(r_i-\mu_i\right)^2\right]}}$$

(4.1)

with $\underline{\theta}=-\infty$ for $\bar{\theta}=-8\%(1),-6\%(2),-4\%(3),-2\%(4),0\%(5)$
and $\bar{\theta}=+\infty$ for $\underline{\theta}=0\%(6),+2\%(7),+4\%(8),+6\%(9),+8\%(10)$

where the numbers given in the brackets relate to a particular risk regime.

Figure 4.8 shows the correlation between Switzerland, the United States, and Japan with each of these three markets once being the home market.

When Switzerland is the home market (a), the correlation between Switzerland and Germany increases with negative returns and decreases with positive returns. The correlation between Switzerland and the United States, however, is higher when returns are either very low or very high. In contrast, the correlation between Switzerland and Japan is quite unlike the one just described for the U.S. market. Here, the correlation coefficient peaks approximately in the middle of the return distribution and is lowest at both ends of the distribution.

The picture for American investors with the U.S. market as home market (b) is worse. Here, lower returns are associated with much higher correlations. In distinct contrast, Japanese investors are in a safe position. For the Japanese market as home market (c), correlations are lowest the more extreme the returns become, irrespective of their direction.

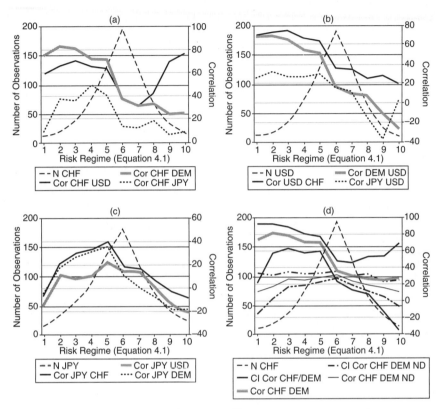

FIGURE 4.8 Conditional correlation coefficients: Swiss, U.S., and Japanese markets as home markets. The figure plots conditional correlation coefficients: Swiss (a), U.S. (b), and Japanese markets (c) as home markets. Graph (d) shows confidence intervals for correlation coefficients between Switzerland (home market) and Germany both for empirical and simulated multivariate normally distributed returns.

Turning to statistical significance, Figure 4.8 also plots confidence intervals for the correlation coefficients between Switzerland and Germany based on the empirical and simulated multivariate normal distributions (in each case the Swiss market as home market). Inspection of Graph (d) indicates that correlations for negative returns are significantly different from the respective correlations calculated for simulated multivariate normally distributed returns. Because of the small number of observations, however, the statistical significance disappears for correlations calculated if the Swiss market is below the −8 percent threshold.

Figure 4.9 shows (equally weighted) average empirical correlations for Switzerland and the United States but also graphs the respective average correlations for simulated multivariate normally distributed returns. As indicated in Longin and Solnik (2001), if all correlation coefficients between any two components of a multivariate normal process are strictly lower than one (in absolute value), then the components of the maximum tend toward independence. In particular, the asymptotic correlation of extreme returns is then equal to zero. Figure 4.9 confirms this issue. In contrast to the normal distribution, the average correlation for the Swiss market as home market is again higher for extreme returns, irrespective of direction. This is again completely different for the U.S. market. Here, average correlation tends to decrease with the absolute size of the threshold for positive returns, as expected with multivariate normality, but tends to increase for negative returns. Hence, the probability of simultaneous large losses is much larger than under the assumption of multivariate normality.

The final part of this section is based on the second definition of an extreme event: An extreme event for an investor in country j is given when the monthly return of a world market portfolio (here approximated by the MSCI-World Index in local currencies) exceeds an exogenously given threshold. For country j, the conditional correlation is calculated as follows:

$$\rho_{i,j}\big|\underline{\theta} < r_{World} < \bar{\theta} = \frac{E\left[\left(r_j - \mu_j\big|\underline{\theta} < r_{World} < \bar{\theta}\right)\left(r_i - \mu_i\right)\right]}{\sqrt{E\left[\left(r_j - \mu_j\right)^2\big|\underline{\theta} < r_{World} < \bar{\theta}\right]}\sqrt{E\left[\left(r_i - \mu_i\right)^2\right]}} \quad (4.2)$$

The results for the Swiss, the U.S., and the Japanese markets are depicted in Figure 4.10.

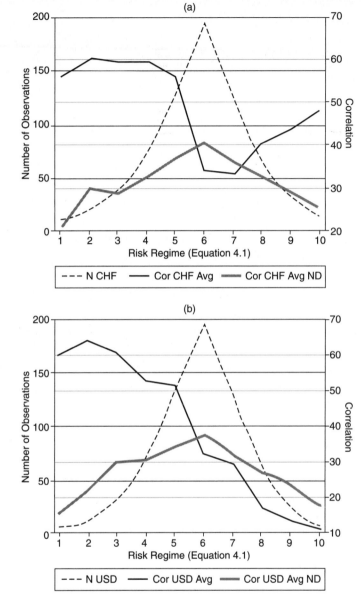

FIGURE 4.9 Conditional average correlation coefficients for the Swiss and
U.S. market as home market: Empirical and simulated multivariate
normally distributed returns. The figure shows conditional equally
weighted average correlation coefficients for the Swiss (a) and U.S. market
(b) as home market both for empirical and simulated multivariate
normally distributed monthly return data. ND = Multivariate normal
distribution.

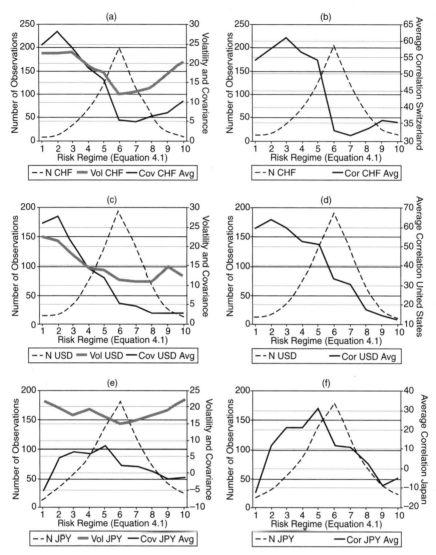

FIGURE 4.10 Conditional volatility, average covariances, and correlations for Switzerland, the United States, and Japan: World market return as threshold return. The figure shows conditional volatility and equally weighted average covariances for Switzerland (a), the United States (c), and Japan (e). Equally weighted average correlations for the same markets are depicted on the right hand side in graphs b, d, and f, respectively. In all cases, the world market return approximated by the MSCI-World Index serves as threshold return.

Both volatility and average covariances are given on the left-hand side (a,c,e) and average correlations are shown on the right-hand side (b,d,f) of Figure 4.10. The U.S. and the Japanese markets show little difference from the previous analysis. In the Swiss market, however, the picture slightly worsens. Using the second definition, average correlation now decreases when returns increase, much like the U.S. market.

Implications for Asset Management

The main purpose of the preceding section was to investigate the asymmetrical correlation structure of large returns. Using two definitions of an extreme event, the empirical results indicate that the correlation structure of large returns is asymmetrical. Generally, the most asymmetrical market is the U.S. market. Here, correlation is highest for large negative returns and lowest for large positive returns. So the probability of simultaneous large losses is much larger than under the assumption of multivariate normality. Although the Swiss market shows significant higher correlation for large negative returns, correlation is also high for large positive returns. However, a completely different picture evolves for the Japanese market. For both extreme negative and positive market movements, average correlation tends to be zero or even negative.

The argument that correlation is positively related to the direction of the market is potentially important for at least three reasons. First, it has strong implications for both asset allocation decisions and risk management. If correlations are higher during bear markets than during bull markets, and bear market moves are greater than bull market moves, the benefits of international diversification may be less impressive than conventional wisdom predicts. It is in periods of extreme negative returns that the benefits of international risk diversification are most desired and that the question of international correlation is most relevant to risk-averse agents. Second, what appears in normal circumstances to be a good hedge might become a very good hedge with an increase in correlation, or, might lead to a doubling up of the respective position. Finally, it may help to explain the equity home bias puzzle, arguably one of the most important puzzles in international finance.[3]

OPTIMAL PORTFOLIOS FROM EVENT-VARYING VARIANCE-COVARIANCE MATRICES

According to Markowitz (1952), one of the inputs required by investors seeking to hold efficient (internationally diversified) portfolios is an ex ante estimate of the variance-covariance matrix of the stock market returns. However, the use of ex post covariance measures as proxies of the ex ante measures is only justified if the international dependence structure is stable and if returns are multivariate normal. Yet, the previous sections show that both assumptions fail in reality. Even worse, the instability is particularly distinct in periods of extremely volatile bear markets. Consequently, the common use of constant variances and covariances in global asset allocation within a mean-variance optimization framework might lead to suboptimal portfolios. In the same way, if the portfolios cannot withstand exceptional periods of market turbulence, they may not even survive and thus cannot generate long-term performance. Therefore, portfolios need to be constructed on the basis of carefully estimated variance-covariance matrices. Although a number of estimation methods have been developed in the literature, this section is restricted to a method recently proposed by Chow, Jacquier, Kritzman, and Lowry (1999). They propose computing two separate variance-covariance matrices, one for normal observations to represent a quiet risk regime, and the other from outlier observations to represent a stressful regime. Their approach is then to blend both variance-covariance matrices into a single one, thereby accounting for different risk aversions and possibly assigning the outlier sample a greater probability than its empirical frequency. Based on the second definition of extreme events (i.e., risk regimes), this section extends their procedure to more than two risk regimes.

To identify optimal portfolios based on investors' attitude toward k different risk regimes, the full-sample variance-covariance matrix can be replaced by

$$\sum_{i=1}^{k} p_i \Sigma_i \qquad (4.3)$$

where p_i is the probability of falling within risk regime i and sums to unity. Substituting these variance-covariance matrices into the standard equation for expected utility $E[U]$ of a portfolio with a weight vector w yields

$$E[U] = \bar{w}'\bar{\mu} - \lambda\left[p_1\bar{w}'\Sigma_1\bar{w} + \cdots + p_k\bar{w}'\Sigma_k\bar{w}\right] \qquad (4.4)$$

where λ equals risk aversion to full-sample risk. Equation 4.4 expresses views about the respective probabilities of the different risk regimes, but it assumes that investors are equally risk-averse to all risk regimes. To differentiate the risk aversion to various risk regimes, the latter are assigned values that reflect the respective relative risk aversion. These values are then rescaled so that they sum to 2 according to

$$\lambda_i^* = \frac{2\lambda_i}{\sum_{i=1}^{k}\lambda_i} \qquad (4.5)$$

Finally, the probability-weighted variance-covariance matrices are multiplied by their respective rescaled risk aversion parameters, resulting in

$$E[U] = \bar{w}'\bar{\mu} - \lambda\left[\lambda_1^* p_1\bar{w}'\Sigma_1\bar{w} + \cdots + \lambda_k^* p_k\bar{w}'\Sigma_k\bar{w}\right] = \bar{w}'\bar{\mu} - \lambda\left[\bar{w}'\Sigma^*\bar{w}\right] \qquad (4.6)$$

with

$$\Sigma^* = \sum_{i=1}^{k}\lambda_i^* p_i \Sigma_i \qquad (4.7)$$

Table 4.5 shows the characteristics of two standard mean-variance optimal portfolios based on full-sample risk parameters and

TABLE 4.5 Optimal Portfolios from Blended and Full-Sample Variance-Covariance Matrices

Risk Regimes i	1	2	3	4	5	6	7	8	9	10
Risk aversion λ_i^*	0.57	0.62	0.67	0.15	0	0	0	0	0	0
Probability p_i	1.4	1.7	4.9	10.1	19.0	31.4	18.2	8.7	2.9	1.4

	Mean (%)	Maximum (%)	Minimum (%)	Volatility (%)	Skewness	Kurtosis	Jarque-Bera	Probability
Full-sample Σ	6.00	10.05	−19.05	13.24	−1.07	6.86	262.07	0.00*
Blended Σ^*	6.00	15.65	−14.22	15.48	−0.21	3.99	15.54	0.00*

Portfolio Weights	CHF (%)	USD (%)	GBP (%)	CAD (%)	DEM (%)	ITL (%)	FRF (%)	JPY (%)
Full-sample Σ	12.3	15.0	−12.5	38.8	33.4	−4.6	−18.4	36.0
Blended Σ^*	−3.9	47.1	−18.3	36.7	−2.9	−17.0	−2.6	61.0

Note: The table depicts optimal portfolios from blended and full-sample variance-covariance matrices. The numbers defining the different risk regimes are defined in Equation 4.1.

*Denotes statistical significance at the 5 percent level of significance.

blended risk parameters under the following assumptions. First, the portfolios' expected return is 6 percent per annum, and the mean returns for the markets correspond to the ones given in Table 4.1 (in both cases). Second, the probabilities of falling within risk regime i correspond to the empirical ones. Finally, the risk aversion parameters are not chosen arbitrarily, but optimized such that the minimum monthly return observation is maximized (the least negative) and all λ_i are positive (to ensure risk aversion).

The results indicate that the resulting portfolio, based on the full-sample variance-covariance matrix, is skewed to the left and heavy-tailed. Also, the minimum monthly portfolio return, at −19 percent, is quite low. In contrast, the second portfolio, based on the blended risk parameters, is only slightly skewed to the left and hardly heavy-tailed. The minimum monthly portfolio return, at −14 percent, is still low, but definitely higher than in the first portfolio. The respective rescaled risk aversion parameters λ_i^* show that only the first four risk regimes are relevant for the calculation of the portfolio. These correspond to the left tail of the return distribution. Not surprisingly, the composition of the optimal portfolio shifts such that the second portfolio is (more) heavily exposed to the Japanese stock market.

Thus, constructing a portfolio that is almost normally distributed (and hence without negative outliers) corresponds to assuming high risk aversion toward stress periods such as defined in the risk regimes 1 to 4. A variance-covariance matrix estimated or blended from stress events characterizes a portfolio's riskiness during market turbulence better than a full-sample variance-covariance matrix. Mean-variance optimization based on a blended variance-covariance matrix produces portfolio strategies with realized returns that have less downside risk exposure than those determined using a full-sample variance-covariance matrix. It accomplishes this goal without sacrificing expected return. Overall, the results support the use of downside risk approaches for investment decisions that focus on return dispersions below a specified target or benchmark return, as proposed by Harlow (1991). These measures are attractive because they are likely to be consistent with investors' perception of risk. Optimization based on downside measures produces portfolio strategies with realized returns that have less downside risk exposure than those determined using variance.

CONCLUSION

International equity market returns are not multivariate normally distributed because there are too many extreme (negative) observations. Although this is a well-known phenomenon, it can cause correlation to be unstable over time. Indeed, it is important to remember that correlation matrices exhibit large jumps through time. There is also overwhelming empirical evidence that average correlation (and hence systematic risk) has increased almost 40 percent since the early 1970s. In addition, correlation and volatility are positively related. Turning directly to the tails of the return distributions shows that the correlation structure of large returns is asymmetrical. Using two different definitions of extreme events, the empirical findings suggest that the most asymmetrical market is the U.S. market.

Correlation for the U.S. equity market is highest for large negative returns and lowest for large positive returns. Although the Swiss market likewise exhibits higher correlation for large negative returns, correlation also seems to be high for large positive returns. A completely different picture evolves for the Japanese stock market. For both extreme negative and positive market movements, average correlation tends to be zero or even negative, which is in fact in line with the behavior of simulated multivariate normally distributed returns.

Most of the results are bad news for internationally diversified investors. The continuously changing correlation pattern makes it difficult to select an ex ante optimal investment strategy. In addition, the observed general increase in correlation has steadily eroded the advantage of international risk diversification. The positive link between correlation and market volatility means that investors and risk managers do not get the full benefits of international risk diversification in those situations where it is most desirable—during high volatility regimes associated with negative returns.

Finally, variance-covariance matrices estimated from different risk regimes provide a better representation of a portfolio's riskiness during market turbulence than a variance-covariance matrix estimated from the full sample of observations. This supports the use of downside-risk approaches to investment decisions.

CHAPTER 5

Global Economic Risk Profiles

Analyzing Value and Volatility Drivers in Global Markets

EXECUTIVE SUMMARY

- This chapter explores the common characteristics of returns as well as expected returns across international stock and bond markets.
- First, factor model regressions show how, and to what extent, multiple global economic forces drive the variation of returns on international stock and bond markets. We introduce the concept of the global economic risk profile (GERP) of global investments.
- Second, beta pricing models are implemented to examine the cross-section of unconditionally expected returns.
- Our empirical results reveal three (out of seven) major sources that explain the differences in expected returns across international stock and bond markets: (1) the worldwide variation of stock markets, (2) shifts in global long-term interest rates, and (3) the variation of exchange rates between major currencies.

INTRODUCTION

Since the economies around the world have become more and more integrated, capital markets are increasingly affected by global rather than country-specific risk factors. From an asset-pricing perspective, relevant questions in this type of setting include:

■ What global forces affect the variation of asset returns on international markets?
■ What are the performance attributes of international investments?
■ Do international markets offer long-term rewards for exposing a portfolio to global sources of risk?
■ What global forces cause common variation of expected returns across international asset classes?

Several empirical studies have contributed valuable insights about the global tradeoff between risk and return on international stock markets (see, Brown & Otsuki, 1993; Cho, Eun, & Senbet, 1986; Dumas & Solnik, 1995; Ferson & Harvey, 1993, 1994; Gultekin, Gultekin, & Penati, 1989; Harvey, 1991, 1995a, 1995b; Korajczyk & Viallet, 1990). This research on international asset pricing has significantly improved our understanding of global financial markets. However, empirical evidence on the pervasive risks of investing on international capital markets is still deficient. Despite the importance of international bonds in managed global portfolios, very little attention has been paid to the global forces driving the returns on international bond markets. The main purpose of this chapter is to study empirically the common characteristics of returns and expected returns across global stock and bond markets. Global investors need a detailed analysis of the sources of shared return variation for these asset classes to optimally diversify their portfolios and to control the associated risks. Our empirical methodology follows Ferson and Harvey (1994), who investigated global economic risks for international stock market returns.

This chapter starts with a review of the methodological framework used in analzing the structure of international stock and bond returns. There is a description of the data sample and a brief discussion of the specification of global risk factors (volatility drivers). The following section introduces the global economic risk profiles (GERP) of stock and bond markets. Finally, the cross-sectional structure of these risk profiles (factor sensitivities) is used to test the pricing potential of the underlying risk factors. We find that only three out of the seven global risk factors qualify as value drivers.

EMPIRICAL METHODOLOGY

An unconditional beta pricing model is used to examine the structure of returns and expected returns across international stock and bond markets. Analyzing the pricing of global risks in an unconditional framework is particularly useful from the viewpoint of investors usually thinking in terms of time-stable long-run compensations. Our valuation framework is consistent with the Arbitrage Pricing Theory (APT) developed by Ross (1976), Huberman (1982), Chamberlain (1983), Chamberlain and Rothschild (1983), Ingersoll (1984), and others. A theoretical foundation for using the APT in an international context is given by Solnik (1983). To set up the model, we assume that:

- Multiple risk factors have an impact on variances as well as on long-term expected returns of international assets.
- Only global factors are sources of systematic risk.
- A set of observable economic factors is a valid representation of the true factor structure driving returns.

We distinguish between *volatility drivers* and *value drivers* in the following ways: Volatility drivers are global factors that explain a certain amount of volatility in stock and bond returns but do not necessarily affect their long-term expected returns. Volatility drivers are estimated within the context of factor models. A subset of volatility drivers also qualifies as value drivers, or so-called priced risk factors. The exposure of stocks and bonds to value drivers is associated with a nonzero expected return, hence a risk premium. Value drivers are estimated in the context of a specific asset-pricing model, such as the Capital Asset Pricing Model (CAPM) or the Arbitrage Pricing Theory (APT), using cross-sectional data (see Figure 5.1). Although

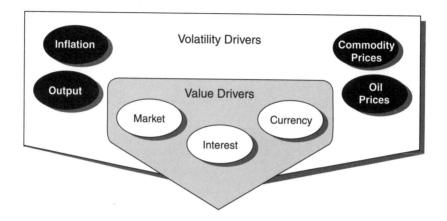

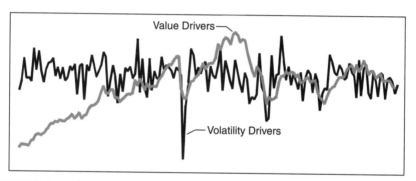

FIGURE 5.1   Value and volatility drivers. Volatility drivers cause (short term) stock and bond return volatility. Value drivers determine expected returns of stocks and bonds; they represent priced factors. Value drivers are typically subsets of volatility drivers.

economically different, volatility and value drivers can be analyzed within the same analytical framework, as described in the following subsections.

The Return-Generating Process

The following linear k-factor model describes the relation between returns, expected returns, and the factors inherently affecting the returns on international stock and bond markets:

$$r_{it} = E[r_{it}] + \beta_{i1} \cdot \delta_{1t} + \beta_{i2} \cdot \delta_{2t} + \cdots + \beta_{ik} \cdot \delta_{kt} + \varepsilon_{it} \qquad (5.1)$$
$$\text{for } i = 1, 2, \ldots, n$$

where r_{it} represents the return on the ith stock or bond market in excess of the risk-free interest rate observed for period t, beginning at time $t - 1$ and ending at time t. The excess return on any market i, $i = 1, 2, \ldots, n$, is calculated as $r_{it} = R_{it} - R_{ft}$, where R_{it} stands for the continuously compounded period t return on the ith market, and R_{ft} is the corresponding interest rate on a risk-free investment over the same period. $E[r_{it}]$ stands for the unconditionally expected excess return on market i, respectively. The variables $\delta_{1t}, \ldots, \delta_{kt}$, denote the unexpected changes in the values of common global risk factors, measured over the same time interval. The coefficients $\beta_{i1}, \ldots, \beta_{ik}$, are the global factor betas of the ith market, also referred to as the market's factor risk profile, determined on the basis of excess returns. Finally, ε_{it} is an idiosyncratic residual with bounded variance. The error terms ε_{it}, $i = 1, 2, \ldots, n$, are allowed to be cross-sectionally correlated such that, formally, Equation 5.1 constitutes an approximate factor model.

It is assumed that the k-factor model adequately explains international excess returns denominated in a single numéraire currency. Only the unexpected components of the changes in the risk factors enter the analysis. Such innovations are determined using a simple vector autoregressive model (VAR). The residuals of the VAR system make up the time series of unexpected changes in the global risk factors.

The Pricing Restriction

Assuming that the model in Equation 5.1 adequately characterizes the return-generating process on international stock and bond markets, it is postulated that the cross-section of long-term expected returns is described by the subsequent beta pricing relationship:

$$E[r_i] = \lambda_1 \cdot \beta_{i1} + \lambda_2 \cdot \beta_{i2} + \cdots + \lambda_k \cdot \beta_{ik}$$
$$\text{for } i = 1, 2, \ldots, n \qquad (5.2)$$

where the λ coefficients, $\lambda_1, \ldots, \lambda_k$, represent unconditional (time-constant) global rewards for a market's unconditional exposure to unexpected changes of the k global risk factors, $\delta_{1t}, \ldots, \delta_{kt}$. Combining Equations 5.1 and 5.2 yields the following empirically testable nonlinear relationship between excess returns, factors changes, and factor rewards:

$$rr_{it} = \sum_{j=1}^{k} \lambda_j \cdot \beta_{ij} + \sum_{j=1}^{k} \beta_{ij} \cdot \delta_{jt} + \varepsilon_{it}$$
$$\text{for } i = 1, 2, \ldots, n \tag{5.3}$$

Accordingly, the period-by-period excess return on any market i, $i = 1, 2, \ldots, n$, is decomposed into (1) an expected component corresponding to the market's factor risk profile and the global risk premiums, (2) an unexpected component captured by the market's exposure to unexpected changes in the common factors, and (3) an idiosyncratic residual. Hence, the model in Equation 5.3 includes the specifications of both the return-generating process and the pricing restriction. When the model implements a cross-section of time series of asset returns, factor betas and factor prices (risk premiums) can be estimated simultaneously. Ferson and Harvey (1994) use the same model to examine the pricing of global risks on international stock markets.

DATA DESCRIPTION

Stock and Bond Market Returns

The cross-section of international asset returns covered in our analysis includes 17 stock markets and 8 bond markets. These markets are represented by total return indices as provided by Morgan Stanley Capital International (MSCI) and Salomon Brothers. The MSCI stock indices included in our sample represent about 60 percent of the world stock market capitalization. Inevitably, the number of bond markets is smaller than the number of equity markets, since free and active bond markets have not been developed in all 17 countries. Even for the bond markets included in the sample, some differences in the degree of liberalization must be taken into account. Nevertheless, the 8 Salomon Brothers government bond indices represent a substantial part of the world bond market capitalization.

Throughout, we apply continuously compounded excess returns measured in Swiss francs. The local currency returns are translated into Swiss franc returns using the effective exchange rate on the last trading day of each month. The one-month Eurocurrency interest rate for Swiss francs quoted in London, at the beginning of each month, is applied as the risk-free interest rate to compute excess returns. Table 5.1 shows summary statistics for the world stock and bond market excess returns from 1982.02 to 1995.02. Detailed results for the individual markets can be found in Oertmann (1997).

Specification of Global Risk Factors

Seven global factors are predetermined to represent possible pervasive sources of risk for international investments, denoted δ_{jt}, $j = 1, 2, \ldots,$ 7, in the valuation framework. We consistently apply aggregate information on potential global sources of systematic risk. Five of the seven global factors are constructed by aggregating economic data from the G7 countries. These major industrialized countries are Canada, France, Germany, Italy, Japan, the United Kingdom, and the United

TABLE 5.1   Summary Statistics for Excess Returns on International Assets

	Swiss Francs		Local Currency	
	Mean (% Annual)	SD (% Annual)	Mean (% Annual)	SD (% Annual)
World stock markets	5.807	17.546	5.036	13.960
World bond markets	4.157	9.878	3.715	6.157

Note: Means and standard deviations are annualized values, calculated on the basis of continuously compounded monthly excess returns over the period from 1982.02 to 1995.02. For the excess returns denominated in Swiss francs, the one-month Eurocurrency interest rate for Swiss francs is applied as the risk-free rate. Excess returns calculated in local currency are based on local risk-free interest rates.

States. The remaining two (non-G7) risk factors are derived from economic and financial time-series representing information on global aggregates. The predetermined global risk factors are displayed in Table 5.2.

These global factors can be described as follows:

- The G7 inflation rate change is constructed from monthly log changes in the consumer price indices (CPI) in the G7 countries. The price index data is originally collected by the International Monetary Fund (IMF).
- The change in G7 industrial production is the weighted average of the contemporaneous monthly industrial production growth rates in the respective countries. The production indices are taken from the national government databases.
- The change in the level of G7 long-term interest rates is constructed on the basis of the yields on long-term government bonds in the G7 currencies. The monthly yield data is provided by IMF.
- The change in G7 short-term interest rates is based on the 3-month Eurocurrency rates for the G7 currencies. Contrary to other authors, we include both an aggregate long-term rate and an aggregate short-term rate in the analysis to capture the information about changing slopes of the term structure.
- The price of the G7 currencies is calculated as the trade-weighted average of the respective exchange rates to the Swiss franc. The weights correspond to the relative shares of the total export of Swiss firms to these countries.

TABLE 5.2 Global Risk Factors

ING7C	Change in the global (G7) inflation rate
IPG7C	Change in global (G7) industrial production
ILG7C	Change in global (G7) long-term interest rates
ISG7C	Change in global (G7) short-term (3 months) interest rates
CHG7C	Change in the value of a basket of major (G7) currencies measured in CHF
DJCIC	Change in the Dow Jones commodity price index
WDSTR	Excess return on the world market portfolio

- The exchange rate data are provided by the IMF. The monthly price changes of this currency basket mirror changes in the external value of the Swiss franc.
- The monthly log changes in the Dow Jones commodity index mirror changes in commodity prices worldwide.
- Finally, the world market portfolio is proxied by the MSCI world index. This is a value-weighted combination of the total returns of 1,585 stocks listed on the stock exchanges in the United States, Europe, Canada, Australia, New Zealand, and the Far East (as of March 21, 1995). The 22 countries included represent more than 90 percent of the total world market capitalization. The monthly index changes are denominated in Swiss francs, in excess of the one-month Eurocurrency interest rate.

The standard models of international asset pricing theory motivate some of these factors (e.g., the models developed by Adler & Dumas, 1983; Sercu, 1980; Solnik, 1974a; Stulz, 1981a). Earlier empirical studies on multi-beta asset pricing in the international environment provide further guidelines for our model (e.g., the work of Brown & Otsuki, 1993; Dumas & Solnik, 1995; Ferson & Harvey, 1993, 1994; Harvey, 1995b; Harvey, Solnik, & Zhou, 1994). Finally, empirical research on the pricing of risks on national stock and bond markets influences our strategy of factor selection; pathbreaking papers in this field are Chen, Roll, and Ross (1986), Fama and French (1993), Elton, Gruber, and Blake (1995), and Ferson and Korajczyk (1995). Descriptive statistics for the time series of the global risk factors appear in Table 5.3.

GERP—A FIRST INSPECTION OF THE MARKETS' RISK PROFILES

In this section, the relationship between market returns and global factor changes is analyzed in the framework of simple multifactor model regressions, following the approach of Ferson and Harvey (1994). Such regressions provide valuable insights on the factor risk

TABLE 5.3   Statistics for the Predetermined Global Risk Factors

	Change			Correlations between Total Factor Changes						
	Mean (% Annual)	SD (% Annual)	AC(1)	WDSTR	ING7C	IPG7C	ISG7C	ILG7C	CHG7C	DJCIC
WDSTR	5.807	17.546	−0.146	1.000	−0.078	−0.154	−0.118	−0.211	0.507	0.000
ING7C	3.587	0.757	0.319		1.000	−0.029	0.107	0.249	0.176	−0.032
IPG7C	2.423	2.120	−0.118			1.000	0.207	0.139	−0.016	0.090
ISG7C	−6.848	14.135	0.143				1.000	0.552	0.094	0.110
ILG7C	−4.733	10.200	0.403					1.000	0.095	0.074
CHG7C	−1.601	5.584	0.090						1.000	−0.091
DJCIC	1.021	9.530	−0.097							1.000

Notes: WDSTR = World stock market excess return denominated in Swiss francs; ING7C = G7 inflation rate change; IPG7C = Change in industrial production in the G7 countries; ISG7C = Change in the level of G7 short-term interest rates; ILG7C = Change in the level of G7 long-term interest rates; CHG7C = Change in the price of a trade-weighted basket of the G7 currencies measured in Swiss francs; DJCIC = Change in the Dow Jones commodity price index. SD = Standard deviation; and AC(1) = First-order autocorrelation. The sample period runs from 1982.02 to 1995.02.

profile of the stock and bond markets in the sample. Identifying factor risk profiles has many applications in portfolio management:

■ *Fundamental analysis.* Factor exposures and the explanatory power of factor models provide valuable information on the economic determinants of volatility. This enables an efficient allocation of resources in the data gathering and transformation process of financial analysis.

■ *Diversification.* The cross-sectional patterns of factor risk profiles provide valuable information on the diversification effects across the markets. A well-diversified portfolio takes into consideration not only the idiosyncratic risk of individual stocks, but also the various risk factors—and the factor exposures provide the necessary information.

■ *Pricing potential.* Cross-sectional differences in expected returns can be related to risk factors if their respective factor exposures differ across stocks (and are different from zero).

■ *Hedging.* Factor exposures are the basis for minimum-variance hedging strategies.

The multifactor regression applied in this section is an empirical version of the general factor model in Equation 5.1. For any international stock or bond market, the specification of the regression can be written as:

$$r_{it} = a_i + \beta_{i1} \cdot \delta_{1t} + \beta_{i2} \cdot \delta_{2t} + \cdots + \beta_{i7} \cdot \delta_{7t} + \varepsilon_{it} \tag{5.4}$$

$$i = 1, \ldots, 17 \text{ (stock markets)}; \; i = 1, \ldots, 8 \text{ (bond markets)}$$

The variables and coefficients were described earlier. The regression analysis is conducted within a system of seemingly unrelated equations of the preceding type for either asset class. The factor betas are determined simultaneously for the cross-section of 17 stock markets and for the cross-section of 8 bond markets. Estimation of the system is performed using Zellner's (1962) seemingly unrelated regression (SUR) method.[1] The results of the regression procedure are displayed in Appendix Table 5A.1 on page 143.

Factor Profiles for Stock Markets

A rough inspection of the global economic risk profiles (GERP) demonstrates surprising similarity across markets, at least with respect to their signs. The only mixed results can be observed for IPG7C (industrial production) and ISG7C (short-term interest rates). Of course, the coefficients substantially differ. To facilitate comparison, Figure 5.2 depicts the *t*-values of the sensitivity coefficients for representative stock and bond markets. In terms of statistical significance (*t*-statistics exceeding 2), the world stock market returns, global long-term interest rates, global exchange rates, and to a certain extent, global inflation are the most important factors.

To better understand the interpretation of the *t*-values, compare the values of the exposures of the British and the Swiss stock markets. In their dependence on the world stock market (WDSTR), the Swiss and British stock markets are virtually identical; hence there are no diversification benefits for this risk factor. However, the

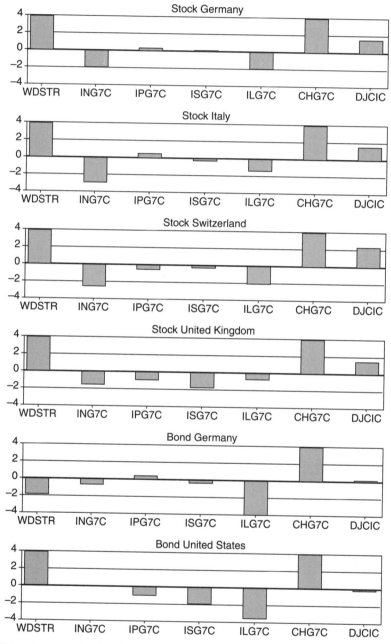

FIGURE 5.2 Magnitude of *t*-values of factor betas for selected stock and bond markets.

dependence of a portfolio of Swiss stocks on long-term global interest rate risk (ILG7C) can be substantially reduced by also holding British stocks. The contrary is true for short-term global interest rate risk (ISG7C), against which the British stock market is more sensitive than the Swiss stock market. However, the bars in Figure 5.2 do not represent the exposures themselves, but their respective *t*-values.

Factor Profiles for Bond Markets

The general picture of the bond market factor profiles (see again Table 5A.1 on page 143) is similar to the previous results. Not surprisingly, the signs of the interest rates exposures are more consistent across the bond markets. In terms of statistical significance, the global long-term interest rate (ILG7C) and the global exchange rate (CHG7C) have the strongest effect on bond returns. For example, take the *t*-values of the Swiss and U.S. bond market exposures. There is no benefit in the diversification of short- and long-term interest rate risk because the sensitivities are similar. However, in terms of global exchange rate risk (CHD7C) and global market risk (WDSTR), U.S. stockholders gain a substantial diversification benefit by holding Swiss stocks. Nothing is said about the expected return consequences—this requires information on the market price of risk associated with the risk factors. This issue is addressed in the final section of this chapter.

Explanatory Power of the Factor Models

The seven global risk factors explain between 16.4 percent (Austria) and 77.5 percent (United States) of the excess return variance on the stock markets with an average of 48.4 percent across all 17 countries. The R-square values achieved for the cross-section of bond markets range from 21.2 percent (Switzerland) to 61.5 percent (United States), with an average of 39.7 percent. Altogether, the fraction of return variance captured by the predetermined factors is larger for the stock markets. Estimation of a simple one-factor model including only the world market proxy (such a model can be regarded as an empirical version of the international CAPM) yields an average adjusted

R-square of 0.434 across the stock markets; the seven-factor model produces an average value of 0.460 using this measure. Evidently, the world market factor alone accounts for a large portion of the return variance on stock markets. The improvement in explanatory power obtained by considering the economic risk factors in addition to the world market index is by far more pronounced for the bond markets. The average adjusted R-square increases from 0.161 to 0.369 when switching from the one-factor model to the seven-factor model.

DISCRIMINATING BETWEEN VOLATILITY AND VALUE DRIVERS

The analysis in the preceding section has not been able to discriminate between value and volatility drivers. This distinction is of utmost importance. As the name suggests, volatility drivers cause variation in bond and stock returns, but they tell us nothing about the expected returns on stocks and bonds. We need further tests to identify the economic factors affecting the long-term, or expected, returns on our asset classes, the so-called value drivers. The volatility drivers previously analyzed are natural candidates to qualify as value drivers. Of course, other variables could be used as well.

In our unconditional setting, whether factors are priced can only be tested from cross-sectional data on stock and bond market exposures (factor sensitivities, or simply betas). The general notion is that assets with different risk exposures must be associated with different expected returns. This section addresses tests of the pricing potential of a given set of volatility drivers based on the cross-sectional structure of factor sensitivities. This gives us candidates of potential value drivers. However, whether these factors are actually priced (associated with a risk premium) will be tested in the subsequent section.

Testing the Pricing Potential of the Risk Factors: Wald Tests

Two different types of hypotheses are examined with respect to the cross-section of beta coefficients associated with each of the seven predetermined global risk factors. Our first null hypothesis investigates whether the betas belonging to a risk factor are statistically significant across markets. For each global factor, this hypothesis asserts that the factor betas are equal to zero for all the markets. A factor whose betas are all zero is generally not applicable for explaining the variance of returns.

The rejection of this (first) hypothesis is not sufficient to determine the pricing potential of factors. Even if the returns in all markets are significantly driven by a certain global factor, the factor exposures may not be associated with a long-term reward. Another requirement is that the beta coefficients corresponding to a factor must be significantly different in their numerical values across markets. Therefore, a second null hypothesis to be tested is that the factor betas are jointly equal across markets. Pricing tests should exclude global factors for which this null hypothesis cannot be rejected.

The Wald test statistics are asymptotically chi-square distributed with degrees of freedom equal to the number of restrictions implemented. Tests are run separately for the cross-section of stock markets and for the cross-section of bond markets. The chi-square test statistics together with the corresponding p-values are reported in Table 5.4.

Potential Value Drivers for Stock Markets

The results of the Wald tests as applied to stock markets indicate that the null hypothesis of jointly zero factor betas is rejected for the world stock market excess return, the G7 inflation rate change, the change in G7 industrial production, the measure of G7 long-term interest rates, the change in the price of the G7 currency basket, and the commodity price index. The rejection is most pronounced for the world stock market and the exchange rate factor (these exhibit the largest chi-square statistics). With the exception of the short-term interest rate variable, therefore, all predetermined global factors seem to significantly move international stock markets. However, not all the factors that have passed this first inspection show up with a broad enough range of betas to potentially account for cross-sectional differences in long-term average returns. The hypothesis of equal factor betas across

TABLE 5.4 Testing the Global Factors' Cross-Sectional Influence

	Chi-Square Test Statistics and p-Values						
	Global Risk Factors						
	WDSTR	ING7C	IPG7C	ISG7C	ILG7C	CHG7C	DJCIC
	Stock Markets						
Hyp 1 (17 df)	997.151	33.493	51.180	11.711	47.202	514.536	33.103
	0.000	0.009	0.000	0.817	0.000	0.000	0.011
Hyp 2 (16 df)	77.919	15.271	26.227	11.710	29.516	57.928	15.087
	0.000	0.505	0.051	0.764	0.021	0.000	0.518
	Bond Markets						
Hyp 1 (8 df)	51.305	8.961	2.384	18.189	46.249	311.617	6.223
	0.000	0.346	0.966	0.019	0.000	0.000	0.622
Hyp 2 (7 df)	47.833	7.521	2.384	13.166	20.042	243.340	3.354
	0.000	0.377	0.956	0.068	0.005	0.000	0.850

Notes: The table shows the output of Wald tests. WDSTR = World stock market excess return; ING7C = G7 inflation rate; IPG7C = Change in industrial production in the G7 countries; ISG7C and ILG7C = Variables for the change in G7 short-term (3 months) and G7 long-term interest rates; CHG7C = Change in the price of a trade weighted basket of the G7 currencies measured in Swiss Francs; DJCIC = Change in the Dow Jones commodity price index. The Wald test restrictions are implemented over the period from 1982.02 to 1995.02 in the following SUR system of equations:

$$r_{it} + a_i = \beta_{i1} \cdot \delta_{1t} + \beta_{i2} \cdot \delta_{2t} + \dots + \beta_{i7} \cdot \delta_{7t} + \varepsilon_{it}$$
$$i = 1, \dots, 17 \text{ (stock markets); } i = 1, \dots, 8 \text{ (bond markets); } t = 1, 2, \dots, T$$

The Wald test hypotheses on regression coefficients are:
Hypothesis 1: The factor betas are equal to zero for all the markets

$$H_0: \beta_{ij} = 0, i = 1, \dots, 17 \text{ (stock markets); } i = 1, \dots, 8 \text{ (bond markets)}$$

Hypothesis 2: The factor betas are jointly equal across the markets

$$H_0: \beta_{ij} = \beta_j, i = 1, \dots, 17 \text{ (stock markets); } i = 1, \dots, 8 \text{ (bond markets)}$$

df = Degrees of freedom. p-values are given below the test statistics.

the stock markets is rejected only for the world market factor, the change in G7 industrial production, the shift in G7 long-term interest rates, and the exchange rate factor. The global inflation factor and the change in the prices of commodities seem to have a significant, but similar impact on international stock returns. In summary, four risk factors are left as potential candidates for priced sources of risk across international stock markets: the world stock market factor (WDSTR), the change in G7 industrial production (IPG7C), the shift in G7 long-term interest rates (ILG7C), and the exchange rate factor (CHG7C).

Potential Value Drivers for Bond Markets

The Wald test rejects the null hypothesis of jointly zero factor sensitivities in the cross-section of bond markets at the 10 percent level of significance for the excess return on the world stock market, the measures of both G7 short-term and long-term interest rate shifts, and the change in the price of the G7 currencies measured in Swiss francs. These four risk factors pass the second test regarding the cross-sectional variance of factor betas as well. As with the stock markets, the rejection of the first hypothesis is most apparent for the world market proxy and the exchange rate factor. The shift in global inflation rates, the change in the level of global output, and the movement of global commodity prices do not have a considerable influence on international bond returns.

Choosing the Common Factors

This section has identified global risk factors that not only affect the variance of international market returns, but also might explain differences between expected returns across countries and asset classes. Table 5.5 provides a summary that shows the candidate factors are not exactly the same for the stocks and bond markets.

Three common factors for stocks and bonds can be found:

1. The world stock market excess return, WDSTR.
2. The change in the level of G7 long-term interest rates, ILG7C.
3. The change in the price of the G7 currency basket, CHG7C.

In the next section, we examine the association between the international stock and bond markets' exposures to changes of these global factors and the long-term average (expected) returns observed across markets.

TABLE 5.5   Discriminating Volatility and Value Drivers: Wald Tests

	Pricing Impact on		
Volatility Drivers	17 Stock Markets	8 Bond Markets	Joint
Inflation	No	No	No
Output	Yes	No	No
Commodity prices	No	No	No
Stock market	Yes	Yes	**Yes**
Short interest	No	Yes	No
Long interest	Yes	Yes	**Yes**
Currency	Yes	Yes	**Yes**

Note: Data includes monthly returns from 1982.02 to 1995.02 for 17 stock and 8 bond markets.

ASSESSING THE POWER OF VALUE DRIVERS: TESTING THE PRICING EQUATION

In the previous section, we analyzed which of the seven risk factors (volatility drivers) have the potential to explain cross-sectional differences in average stock and bond returns (which of the factors are potential value drivers). Three common factors were identified. In this section, we test whether these factors are indeed priced (associated with nonzero risk premiums in the cross-section of stock and bond returns). The model in Equation 5.3 serves as the starting point for our unconditional beta pricing test. The model is estimated by the following system of restricted seemingly unrelated regression equations:

$$
\begin{pmatrix} r_{1t} \\ \vdots \\ r_{nt} \end{pmatrix} = \lambda_1 \cdot \begin{pmatrix} \beta_{11} \\ \vdots \\ \beta_{n1} \end{pmatrix} + \ldots + \lambda_k \cdot \begin{pmatrix} \beta_{1k} \\ \vdots \\ \beta_{nk} \end{pmatrix} + \begin{pmatrix} \beta_{11} \cdots \beta_{1k} \\ \vdots \\ \beta_{n1} \cdots \beta_{nk} \end{pmatrix} \cdot \begin{pmatrix} \delta_{1t} \\ \vdots \\ \delta_{kt} \end{pmatrix} + \begin{pmatrix} \varepsilon_{1t} \\ \vdots \\ \varepsilon_{nt} \end{pmatrix} \quad (5.5)
$$

where r_{it}, $i = 1, \ldots, n$, stands for the continuously compounded monthly excess return on the ith market. The variables $\delta_{1t}, \ldots, \delta_{kt}$ represent the contemporaneous unexpected monthly changes of the global risk factors in the test. The regression coefficients $\beta_{i1}, \ldots, \beta_{ik}$,

$i = 1, \ldots, n$ are the factor sensitivities (factor betas) of the ith market's return, and $\lambda_1, \ldots, \lambda_k$ denote the corresponding factor risk premiums (factor prices). Finally, ε_{it}, $i = 1, \ldots, n$, captures the idiosyncratic component of the monthly return on the ith market.

The preceding system of equations includes restrictions: (1) Each of the factor prices is constrained to be equal across the markets, and (2) the regression intercept is assumed to be equal to zero. Both of these restrictions are enforced by APT-motivated beta pricing theory. The parameters to be estimated by processing time-series and cross-sectional return data simultaneously are the factor sensitivities, $\beta_{i1}, \ldots, \beta_{ik}$, $i = 1, \ldots, n$, and the factor risk premiums, $\lambda_1, \ldots, \lambda_k$. Hence, the number of coefficients in the system is $[(n \cdot k) + k]$. Simultaneous estimation of factor betas and factor prices in the framework of a restricted relative pricing model has been popularized by several authors, and, in particular, goes back to the work of Burmeister and McElroy (1988). Following the empirical approach of Ferson and Harvey (1994), we estimate the system of equations using Hansen's (1982) Generalized Method of Moments (GMM).

The system of equations is implemented for a cross-section of asset returns including the 17 stock markets and 8 bond markets. Hence, we assume a priori that international stock and bond markets are integrated with respect to the pricing of global risks.

Table 5.6 reports the empirical results for two alternative specifications of system in Equation 5.5:

1. A single-factor model specified in accordance with an international CAPM, including only the world stock market excess return.
2. A three-factor model along with the world stock market excess return, the change in the level of G7 long-term interest rates, and the change in the price of the G7 currency basket as global sources of risk.

The table shows the factor risk premiums that are estimated simultaneously together with the factor betas over the period from 1982.02 to 1995.02. More detailed results including the t-statistics

TABLE 5.6   Estimation Results of Beta Pricing Test

		Global Risk Premia			
International CAPM		3-Factor Model			
λ_j (Monthly %)	GMM χ^2 Statistic	λ_j (Monthly %)			GMM χ^2 Statistic
WDSTR	(p-Value)	WDSTR	ILG7C	CHG7C	(p-Value)
0.526	24.893	0.259	−0.352	0.084	21.956
8.205	(0.411)	2.144	−1.406	0.904	(0.462)

Note: The reported coefficients, the monthly risk premia (factor prices), are estimated simultaneously with factor betas (not reported here) using GMM. The GMM
test statistic for the model's goodness-of-fit is chi-square distributed with 24 (22) degrees of freedom for the international CAPM (3-factor model). The sample period is
from 1982.02 to 1995.02.

based on heteroskedasticity-consistent standard errors and the mean
pricing error (MPE) for each of the national stock and bond markets
can be found in Oertmann (1997).

   Looking at the international version of the CAPM, investors re-
ceived a long-term reward for their exposure to world market risk
over the time period examined. The model identifies a world market
risk premium of 0.526 percent in excess return on a monthly basis
(6.312% per year) across stock and bond investments. The respective λ coefficient is estimated on a high significance level. Thus, the
world market beta seems to be a reasonable determinant of expected
returns on both international stock and bond markets. The GMM
test statistic for the model's goodness-of-fit does not reject the restrictions imposed by the single-factor on the cross-section of expected stock and bond returns.

   In the three-factor setting, the estimated price of world market
risk is 0.259 percent in monthly excess return, which is notably lower
than the corresponding premium in the single-factor model. The reward for global interest rate risk is minus 0.352 percent on a monthly
basis. Thus, markets that are negatively exposed to the shifts in the
global interest rate factor tend to offer investors a positive long-term
compensation for bearing this source of risk. A negative exposure to

global interest rate changes exists for most of the stock markets and all bond markets. However, the factor price for interest rate risk is only at the margin of being statistically significant. Finally, the premium for exchange rate risk shows up with a small positive value. The λ coefficient is 0.084 percent per month, indicating that a higher exposure to the exchange rate factor is associated with a slightly higher average return over the period examined. However, our evidence on such a relationship is weak; the estimated factor price for global exchange rate risk does not satisfy any conventional levels of significance.

CONCLUSION

This chapter presents empirical evidence on the value and volatility drivers for international stock and bond markets. The global economic risk profile (GERP) of stock and bond markets is investigated in the setting of factor model regressions. Our major results can be summarized as follows:

■ International stock market returns seem to be influenced by a broader variety of global risk factors than international bond market returns. Stock markets may have four to five persistent driving forces, whereas interest rate factors and shifts in global exchange rates predominantly affect the returns in bond markets.
■ Three of the seven predetermined global risk factors systematically affect the returns of both stock and bond investments: the excess return on the world market portfolio, the change in global long-term interest rates, and the change in the price of the G7 exchange rate basket. Hence, these variables seem to represent the inherent forces that cause the frequently observable comovement between international stock and bond market returns.

Next, our analysis examines whether some of the global factors that have been identified as being related to the variance of international asset returns also affect the long-term evolution of asset values.

Our investigation concentrates on those three factors that influence both stock and bond markets in the preliminary regression analysis. Both an empirical version of the international CAPM and a three-factor pricing model are estimated. The major findings of our pricing tests are:

■ The single-factor CAPM identifies a significantly positive premium for the exposure to world market risk in the long-term returns of both stock and bond markets. For some markets, however, such a model leaves relatively large pricing errors.
■ The three-factor model seems to provide a more distinctive picture of the value drivers in both stock and bond market returns. The estimation results indicate that average returns of both asset classes include rewards for interest rate risk in addition to the market premium. There also is weak evidence that exchange rate risk is priced across international assets.

Our empirical results show that multiple sources of global economic risk affect both the variability of returns and the values on international stock and bond markets. Hence, to control the variance and measure the performance of an internationally diversified portfolio including both stock and bond positions, a framework with multiple global risk factors must be preferred to the single-factor model specified in the CAPM. When return benchmarks are required for such a balanced portfolio strategy, it appears essential to include a premium for the risk of global interest changes.

APPENDIX

Table 5A.1 shows the global risk factor betas, as estimated from the specification of the regression in Equation 5.4. The factor betas are determined simultaneously for the cross-section of 17 stock markets and for the cross-section of 8 bond markets. The system of equations is estimated using Zellner's (1962) seemingly unrelated regression (SUR) method.

TABLE 5A.1 Regression of Stock and Bond Market Excess Returns on the Predetermined Global Risk Factors

| | Global Risk Factor Betas | | | | | | | | | | Adjusted |
	Intercept	WDSTR	ING7C	IPG7C	ISG7C	ILG7C	CHG7C	DJCIC	DW	R^2	R^2
	Stock Markets										
Australia	0.003	1.084	−1.864	−0.717	0.025	0.350[a]	2.655	0.672	2.221	0.490	0.465
	0.624	7.908	−0.637	−0.730	0.151	1.391	7.449	3.292			
Austria	0.005	0.410	−3.201	1.294[a]	0.127	−0.236	1.456	0.310	1.625	0.164	0.124
	1.040	2.963	−1.084	1.305	0.760	−0.928	4.046	1.505			
Belgium	0.009	0.786	−4.403	0.802[b]	−0.131[b]	−0.166	1.362	0.314	1.748	0.529	0.506
	2.931	9.060	−2.379	1.291	−1.242	−1.044	6.035	2.431			
Canada	0.000	0.873	−5.409	−0.664	−0.056	−0.088	2.303	0.386	1.964	0.662	0.646
	0.032	10.672	−3.103	−1.135	−0.565	−0.588	10.383	3.176			
Denmark	0.004	0.510	−1.039	−0.392	−0.087	−0.457	1.601	0.239	1.864	0.342	0.311
	1.075	5.165	−0.493	−0.554	−0.730	−2.518	6.232	1.630			
France	0.006	0.829	−2.504	0.445[b]	−0.015	−0.637	1.553	0.407	1.863	0.511	0.488
	1.664	8.701	−1.233	0.652	−0.135	−3.643	6.273	2.871			
Germany	0.005[b]	0.635	−4.026	0.453	0.002	−0.391	1.583	0.258[a]	1.857	0.341	0.310
	1.411	5.853	−1.739	0.582	0.015	−1.962	5.608	1.597			
Hong Kong	0.006[b]	1.168	−4.908	−1.362	0.007	0.387	2.792	0.161	1.831	0.364	0.334
	0.974	6.477	−1.276	−1.055	0.036	1.171	5.956	0.598			
Italy	0.002	0.782	−8.590	0.632	−0.037	−0.340	1.606	0.323	1.934	0.325	0.293
	0.420	5.819	−2.998	0.657	−0.228	−1.379	4.598	1.615			
Spain	0.005[a]	1.221	−1.880[b]	−1.261	0.124	−0.361[a]	0.953	0.162	1.652	0.577	0.557
	1.289	11.661	−0.842	−1.681	0.981	−1.882	3.506	0.298			
Netherlands	0.010	0.761	−3.697	−0.192	−0.010	−0.234	1.630	0.189	1.824	0.622	0.604
	3.642	10.668	−2.429	−0.376	−0.117	−1.788	8.787	1.784			
Norway	0.004[b]	1.142	0.944	−0.037	−0.045	0.263	2.004	0.416	1.808	0.473	0.448
	0.846	9.020	0.349	−0.041	−0.294	1.133	6.089	2.207			
Spain	0.004	0.910	−1.794	−0.769	0.196	−0.555	2.058	0.351	1.834	0.445	0.419
	0.996	7.857	−0.726	−0.927	1.397	−2.611	6.837	2.037			
Sweden	0.007	0.994	−3.838[a]	−0.718[b]	0.125	−0.073	2.003	0.158	1.937	0.463	0.438
	1.758	8.569	−1.552	−0.864	0.893	−0.344	6.646	0.919			
Switzerland	0.006	0.769	−3.757	−0.959	−0.017	−0.280	1.117	0.267	1.832	0.530	0.508
	2.311	10.452	−1.819		−0.193	−2.073	5.838	2.445			
United Kingdom	0.005	0.881	−2.433	−0.569	−0.157	−0.106[b]	2.016	0.161	1.958	0.617	0.599
	1.612	10.816	−1.402	−0.977	−1.593	−0.713	9.527	1.332			
United States	0.004	0.959	−3.173	−1.553	−0.049	−0.129[b]	2.281	0.190[a]	1.745	0.775	0.765
	1.911	14.599	−2.266	−3.299	−0.618	−1.076	13.362	1.947			

Notes: WDSTR = World stock market excess return denominated in Swiss francs; ING7C = G7 inflation rate change; IPG7C = Change in industrial production in the G7 countries; ISG7C = Change in the level of G7 short-term interest rates; ILG7C = Change in the level of G7 long-term interest rates; CHG7C = Change in the price of a trade-weighted basket of the G7 currencies measured in Swiss francs; DJCIC = Change in the Dow Jones commodity price index. The SUR system of equations is estimated over the period from 1982.02 to 1995.02:

$$r_{it} = a_i + \beta_{i1} \cdot \delta_{1t} + \beta_{i2} \cdot \delta_{2t} + \ldots + \beta_{i7} \cdot \delta_{7t} + \varepsilon_{it}$$
$$i = 1, \ldots, 17 \text{ (stock markets)}; \, i = 1, \ldots, 8 \text{ (bond markets)}$$

t-Statistics are reported below the coefficients (factor betas). DW = Durbin-Watson test statistic; R^2 = Coefficient of determination; Adjusted R^2 = Adjusted for degrees of freedom. All explanatory variables represent innovations.
[a] Indicates a coefficient that looses significance when the regressions are run with an outlier adjustment; the procedure to adjust for outliers drops any observation for which the residual is larger than 2 standard errors in a preliminary regression.
[b] Indicates a coefficient that attains significance when the regressions are run with an outlier adjustment; the procedure to adjust for outliers drops any observation for which the residual is larger than 2 standard errors in a preliminary regression.

(continued)

TABLE 5A.1 (*Continued*)

| | Global Risk Factor Betas | | | | | | | | | | Adjusted |
	Intercept	WDSTR	ING7C	IPG7C	ISG7C	ILG7C	CHG7C	DJCIC	DW	R²	R²
					Bond Markets						
Canada	0.003	0.318	−2.342	−0.139	−0.151[a]	−0.289	1.814	0.013	1.953	0.492	0.468
	1.186	4.327	−1.489	−0.263	−1.687	−2.135	9.448	0.127			
France	0.004	0.045	0.692	0.139	−0.033	−0.331	0.715	0.024[b]	2.195	0.381	0.352
	2.588	1.116	0.802	0.481	−0.671	−4.451	6.798	0.413			
Germany	0.002	−0.061	−0.478[b]	0.135	−0.021	−0.307	0.653	0.012	1.876	0.415	0.388
	2.234	−1.833	−0.667	0.562	−0.523	−4.990	7.475	0.251			
Japan	0.005	0.218	−0.394	0.236	−0.025	−0.301	0.681	0.048	1.774	0.246	0.210
	2.219	3.611	−0.305	0.543	−0.344	−2.699	4.311	0.533			
Netherlands	0.002	−0.034	−0.327	0.041	−0.058	−0.251	0.629	0.035	1.774	0.414	0.386
	2.317	−1.071	−0.477	0.182	−1.503	−4.245	7.520	0.740			
Switzerland	−0.000	0.007	−0.768	0.008	−0.030	−0.128	0.089	0.067	1.464	0.212	0.175
	−0.197	0.341	−1.653	0.053	−1.147	−3.192	1.578	2.092			
United Kingdom	0.002	0.098[a]	−0.045	0.188	−0.215	−0.273	1.465	0.011	1.612	0.403	0.375
	0.936	1.494	−0.032	0.396	−2.676	−2.248	8.492	0.115			
United States	0.002	0.277	−0.015	−0.427	−0.139	−0.361	1.733	−0.014	1.676	0.615	0.597
	1.261	4.746	−0.012	−1.019	−1.969	−3.358	11.364	−0.169			

Testing Market Integration

The Case of Switzerland and Germany

EXECUTIVE SUMMARY

- One of the most relevant questions in international asset pricing and international corporate finance is whether capital markets are integrated or segmented. For example, this issue is of utmost importance for the cost of capital of corporations.

- Typically, the integration of capital markets is discussed in the context of capital transfer restrictions or barriers to international investments, the emergence of global trading systems, and high or increasing correlations between the returns on different national capital markets.

- From a theoretical finance perspective, however, a capital market is integrated if assets with the same risk characteristics have the same expected returns, irrespective of the market to which they belong. Integration is conceptually related to the valuation of risky assets.

- In this chapter, we provide an empirical analysis of whether the Swiss and German stock markets are integrated with the world stock market. We use two methodologies to test the null hypothesis of integration: The first is a test of the consumption-based asset-pricing model; the second is a latent variable approach.

- The results from both tests indicate that it is not possible to reject the null hypothesis that the German and Swiss stock markets are integrated with the global stock market. This implies that the level of capital costs of publicly traded German and

Swiss companies do not differ from those of other countries belonging to the same risk class.

INTRODUCTION

Economic journalists usually see a link between the increasing globalization and the ongoing integration of the global capital markets. From an asset-pricing perspective, however, market integration means that assets in different currencies or countries display the same risk-adjusted expected returns. In integrated markets, the premium for systematic risk does not depend on the national base of an investment. Whether national equity markets are integrated or segmented is not merely an academic question, but has a decisive impact on important issues. First, segmentation directly affects the desirability of international diversification. International portfolios should display superior risk-adjusted performance because part of the domestic systematic risk can be diversified away by investing internationally without paying a price in terms of lower returns (e.g., Jorion & Khoury, 1996). Second, in a segmented capital market, some irrelevance theorems in corporate finance lose their validity. If the pricing of risk is different in a stock market and in the foreign exchange market, hedging currency risk may add value to the firm. In this case, firms face optimal hedging decisions as well as an optimal breakdown of debt into domestic and nondomestic. Finally, the company cost of capital depends on whether capital markets are integrated or segmented. The general practice is to determine firm betas with respect to a national stock price index. If capital markets are integrated, however, the market portfolio must be identified as a global aggregate (e.g., Stulz, 1995).

Integration is often linked to market access barriers for foreign investors or the extent to which they have already been dismantled. A further distinction can be made between indirect and direct access barriers. Indirect barriers might encompass the greater difficulty in gaining access to information regarding foreign shares, differences in the quality of information about companies because of dissimilar publication requirements, and all the other forms of expenditure associated with investing abroad. Direct barriers include different legal provisions and fiscal regulations as well as limitations on the percentage of a business that foreign investors may hold. Finally, legal restrictions imposed by the country of origin have to be considered. Swiss pension funds, for example, are not allowed to invest more than 30 percent of their portfolio assets into non-Swiss securities.

Financial market theory, however, requires that segmentation or integration must be strictly viewed from an asset-pricing or valuation perspective. In fact, merely analyzing the actual instances of market access restrictions does not provide adequate evidence for either segmentation or integration. Marginal investors determine the prices of financial assets, and sophisticated traders often find ways to get around these barriers with innovative financial products. In equity swaps, for example, two parties agree to exchange all the cash flows of two equity positions. Such transactions can be conducted across national borders. In fact, they are a common occurrence, especially for investments in emerging stock markets.

In this chapter, therefore, the integration of capital markets is tackled from the perspective of asset-pricing theory. Generally speaking, asset pricing is concerned with determining expected returns on risky assets. Therefore, following the definition by Campbell and Hamao (1992) and Bekaert and Harvey (1995), a capital market is integrated if investments with the same risk characteristics have identical expected returns, irrespective of the market to which they belong. Risk is measured as the sensitivity coefficient with respect to a global (world market) portfolio. Or, if investments from various countries with perfectly correlated returns have identical expected returns, capital markets are fully integrated (see Stulz, 1981a). Of course, returns must be measured in the same reference currency. Therefore, the simplest test for integration would be to compare the prices of two portfolios with perfectly correlated cash-flows from different countries. If the markets concerned were integrated, then the market prices for such investments ought to be identical at any point in time. However, the influences of risk factors specific to individual countries make it virtually impossible to construct perfectly correlated portfolios across national borders. For this reason, all empirical tests of integration are based on a specific valuation model. An asset-pricing model indicates the part of return variability that is compensated with a risk premium on international capital markets. In the world of the Capital Asset-Pricing Model (CAPM), this means that a test for integration examines whether the returns on foreign investments lie on the domestic security market line (see Wheatley, 1988). In contrast, segmentation implies that foreign assets will lie significantly away from the domestic security market line. Assuming a world with only one currency, integration describes a situation where all assets are priced according to their beta relative to a world index. On the other hand, the domestic betas should be priced in segmented markets.

However, any valuation approach implies a joint test of two hypotheses: (1) the hypothesis of integrated markets and (2) the hypothesis that the underlying asset-pricing model can capture the dynamic risk-return relationship. Thus, there are two possible reasons for rejecting the null hypothesis of integration. Either the markets under consideration are indeed segmented and/or the underlying global asset-pricing model provides only an inadequate description of the true risk-return relationship. For the CAPM, this latter observation is tantamount to stating that the world market portfolio is inefficient.

Empirical tests for integration can be either unconditional or conditional. In the former case, expected returns and variances are assumed to be constant over time. In contrast, the moments of expected returns in the latter case are modeled as time varying. Previous studies are limited mainly to a U.S. perspective. Solnik (1974b), Stehle (1977), Jorion and Schwartz (1986), Cho, Eun, and Senbet (1986), and Gultekin, Gultekin, and Penati (1989) test models with constant expected returns. Harvey (1991) develops a conditional CAPM with both the amount of risk and the risk premium variable over time. He uses Hansen's (1982) Generalized Method of Moments (GMM). As an alternative, Chan, Karolyi, and Stulz (1992) as well as De Santis and Gerard (1997) estimate a conditional CAPM using the GARCH-in-the-mean approach. This technique permits explicit modeling of the time-variation of variances and covariances. Whereas the majority of studies use national stock indices, Heston, Rouwenhorst, and Wessels (1995) use individual securities' data to investigate the null hypothesis of integration on the basis of an international factor model. Errunza and Losq (1985) choose a totally different approach. Instead of testing the null hypothesis of integration, they investigate a model that explicitly restricts access to individual markets for a particular group of investors. Finally, Bekaert and Harvey (1995) formulate a model that emulates the variation in the degree of integration over time. Such regime-switching models may be widely used in the asset allocation process in the future. Overall, the empirical results are mixed: Different estimation techniques come up with empirical evidence for both integration and segmentation, depending on the sample of markets and the time period examined.

The aim of this chapter is to test the null hypothesis of integration of the Swiss and German stock markets with the world market. This question is pertinent from two viewpoints. First, the results by Heston, Rouwenhorst, and Wessels (1995) present grounds for doubting whether the German and Swiss stock markets are integrated with the world market. Given that the two markets are among the most highly capitalized in the world, it is appropriate to take another look at these results using a different test methodology. Second, the question is particularly interesting from the perspective of the cost of capital faced by German and Swiss companies. If those markets were segmented, the expected returns for German and Swiss securities would have to be higher.[1] Only then would investors hold these securities in efficiently diversified portfolios. The requirement for a higher stock return has a direct implication in higher capital costs for German and Swiss companies.

In our empirical study, we use two different test methodologies. First, to examine the null hypothesis of stock market integration, we test a stochastic discount factor (SDF) model on a country-by-country basis. This approach is based on the seminal work by Hansen and Singleton (1982). Second, following Campbell and Hamao (1992), we specify a conditional beta pricing model in a way that can explain the variability of expected returns over time. The model contains a time-varying risk premium on a single (unobservable) risk factor in combination with a constant beta coefficient. In both cases, we cannot reject the null hypothesis of integration.

In the remainder of this chapter, we discuss the widespread misconception that the correlation between national equity markets and integration of those markets are identical concepts. We then present a consumption-based test for the integration of the German and Swiss equity markets with the world market. We continue to formulate a test methodology based on a beta pricing model with a single unobservable risk factor. Such models are known as *latent variable models* in the literature. After describing the data needed for our analysis, we discuss the empirical results.

INTEGRATION AND CORRELATION

Practitioners often argue that low correlations between international stock market returns imply market segmentation. In fact, average correlations between stock markets have been low for long periods. But since the stock market crash in October 1987, these correlations have increased markedly. Whereas the average correlations between developed stock markets were around 0.3 in the early 1980s, they climbed to around 0.6 in the 1990s. Longin and Solnik (1995) show that the null hypothesis of a constant correlation matrix over this period of time can be rejected. Figure 6.1 shows the time evolution of average correlations between the monthly excess returns of the MSCI indices for Germany and Switzerland, with the excess returns of the MSCI indices for Japan, the United Kingdom, and the United States. The latter three markets are taken as being representative for the world market. Monthly excess returns are measured in German marks or Swiss francs over the period from 1976.01 to 1997.09, using the respective interest rates for one-month deposits on the Eurocurrency market as the risk-free asset. Average correlations are computed on the basis of moving three-year time windows; hence, the first correlation estimators are available in January 1979. The

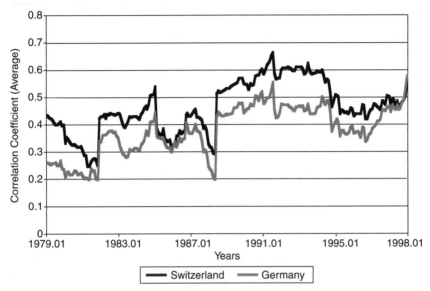

FIGURE 6.1 Moving correlations of excess returns. The figure shows the development over time of the average correlation coefficients between the excess returns on the MSCI indices for Germany and Switzerland respectively, on the one hand, and the United States, the United Kingdom, and Japan, on the other hand. Returns are measured in both German marks and Swiss francs in excess of the corresponding one-month interest rates on the Eurocurrency market over the time period from 1976.01 to 1997.09. The average correlations are presented on the basis of a moving three-years time window. The first correlation coefficient becomes available in January 1979.

abrupt increase of correlations in October 1987 indicates that the stock market crash was a global happening. From that date onward, average correlations between the two groups of countries have remained high, which is often interpreted as a sign for an increased degree of integration.

Financial market theory, however, requires a more sophisticated view. In portfolio theory, higher correlations imply a reduced potential for global diversification, or, higher global systematic risk. That information, by itself, cannot say anything about the way global risks are priced on the individual national equity markets. As stated, integration is related to valuation, which explains why even a low correlation between national equity markets can be consistent with a high degree of integration among these same markets. Adler and Dumas (1983) stress that purely national (fortuitous) influences, affecting the output of only that national economy, ought to have an effect solely on the stock prices of domestic businesses. This is not a sign of segmentation, but instead indicates efficient capital markets. Roll (1992) notes that national economies also display different forms of specialization, depending on their competitive advantages. Therefore, if the production structures are significantly different from one country to another, worldwide (fortuitous) shocks affect different countries with different intensities. Accordingly, low correlations between national equity markets are, again, not a reliable indicator for market segmentation.

TWO MODELS FOR TESTING INTEGRATION

A Consumption-Based Test for Market Integration

The classical work by Breeden (1979) and Grossman and Shiller (1981) shows that capital market equilibrium can be characterized along the optimality condition of an investor's intertemporal choice problem between consumption and investment. The authors look at the intertemporal choice problem of an investor who can trade freely in an asset i with price P_{it} at time t and can obtain a gross simple expected rate of return of $E_t(1 + R_{i, t+1})$ over the period from time t to $t + 1$. Returns are in real terms. Assume the investor consumes C_t at time t and has additive (separable) preferences over time. Let $U(C_t)$ denote the investor's period utility, which is defined over the current period's consumption. Finally, δ is a time discount factor, indicating that consumption today is worth more than consumption tomorrow. This parameter determines the relative weights the investor places on the near-term future versus the distant future, hence $\delta < 1$. With these assumptions, a standard result in modern asset-pricing theory is that the first-order condition for the optimal consumption-investment choice looks as follows:

$$U'(C_t)\, P_{it} = \delta\, E_t\big[P_{i,\,t+1} U'(C_{t+1})\big] \Rightarrow U'(C_t) = \delta\, E_t\big[(1+R_{i,\,t+1})\, U'(C_{t+1})\big] \quad (6.1)$$

This is the famous Euler equation. Although this expression may look complicated, the intuition behind it is easy to grasp. Portfolio optimality implies that even a marginal change in the fraction of asset i negatively affects the investor's utility. Along the optimal consumption path, the investor must be indifferent between the following two alternatives: (1) Use an additional dollar for consumption at time t; or (2) invest an additional dollar into asset i, sell this asset at time $t+1$, and use the proceeds for consumption in this later period. At the optimum, the marginal cost of saving an extra dollar for one period must be equal to the marginal benefit. The marginal cost is the marginal utility of a dollar of consumption at time t, $U'(C_t)$. The marginal benefit is the expected payoff of one dollar invested in asset i for one period $(1+R_{i,\,t+1})$, times the marginal utility of an extra dollar of consumption next period, $U'(C_{t+1})$, discounted back at rate δ. Expected returns must adjust to ensure that the investor is indifferent between both alternatives. Hence, capital market equilibrium can be characterized on the basis of the first-order optimality condition for intertemporal portfolio choice. Dividing the Euler equation by $U'(C_t)$, we have the following expression:

$$1 = E_t\left[(1+R_{i,\,t+1})\,\delta\,\frac{U'(C_{t+1})}{U'(C_t)}\right] = E_t\big[(1+R_{i,\,t+1})\, M_{t+1}\big] \quad (6.2)$$

where M, the coefficient of marginal utilities, represents the intertemporal marginal rate of substitution. It is also referred to as the *stochastic discount factor* (SDF), or *pricing kernel,* in the literature. This model represents the discrete version of the Consumption Capital Asset Pricing Model (CCAPM). It first appeared in the path-breaking papers by Lucas (1978) and Grossman and Shiller (1981,

1982). The continuous time version of the model goes back to Breeden (1979). Noting that a gross return is simply an asset with a price of one, the discount factor transforms future cash flows into current prices, incorporating both time and risk. A high level of future consumption implies low marginal utility in the future and thus a low discount factor. Accordingly, a low (high) value of M_{t+1} stands for good (bad) future conditions, whereby the adjectives "good" and "bad" refer to the representative investor's willingness to pay for cash flows during different states of the economy. Intuitively, for an asset with high rates of return in good states of the world (when M_{t+1} is low), today's price must be relatively low. In contrast, the price of an asset with high rates of returns in bad states of the world (when M_{t+1} is high) will be relatively high. Because the marginal utility of an additional dollar is higher in bad states than in good states, investors are willing to pay a higher price, or, the other way round, demand lower rates of return (e.g., Zimmermann, 1998). This notion can be formalized by writing the expectation of a product as the product of expectations plus a covariance term to arrive at the following CCAPM pricing restriction:[2]

$$E_t[1+R_{i,\,t+1}] = \frac{1}{E_t[M_{t+1}]}\left(1 - Cov_t[R_{i,\,t+1}, M_{t+1}]\right) \qquad (6.3)$$

This expression posits that an asset with a high expected return has a low covariance with the stochastic discount factor. The asset tends to have low returns when investors have high marginal utility. It is thus risky because it fails to deliver wealth in states when wealth is most valuable to investors. Hence, they demand a large premium to hold it (see Campbell, Lo, & MacKinlay, 1997).

To make the consumption-based model empirically testable, it is necessary to specify the utility function. It is standard in the literature to assume that investors have power utility with constant relative risk aversion, denoted as γ:

$$U(C_t) = \frac{C_t^{1-\gamma} - 1}{1-\gamma} \qquad (6.4)$$

where C_t stands for the investor's consumption in real terms. The coefficient of relative risk aversion, γ, determines the fraction of wealth that an investor is willing to pay to avoid a gamble of a given size relative to wealth. A plausible benchmark model makes relative risk aversion independent of wealth. In this case, investors at all levels of wealth make the same decisions when the risks they face and the costs of avoiding them are both expressed as fractions of wealth. Therefore, power utility's property of a constant relative risk aversion is convenient for explaining the stability of financial variables (e.g., interest rates and risk premiums) in the face of economic growth (see Campbell, Lo, & MacKinlay, 1997). With this specification, it is possible to rewrite the CCAPM as follows:

$$E_t\left[\delta\left(\frac{C_{t+1}}{C_t}\right)^{-\gamma}\left(1+R_{i,\,t+1}\right)-1\ \Big|\,Z_t\right] = E_t\big[u_{t+1}\big|Z_t\big]=0 \qquad (6.5)$$

where the expectation is now conditioned on a vector of instrumental variables available at time t, collected in Z_t. The vector u_{t+1} contains the pricing errors (the deviations of realized returns from expected returns). The vector of instrumental variables must be chosen carefully. The two requirements are that instruments must be observable at the beginning of each period and possess prediction power for stock returns over the next period. The exact specification of these variables for our tests appears in the following data description. If the model describes the risk-return relationship appropriately, expected returns should compound all information contained in the information variables. The remaining pricing errors should be unexpected and, hence, uncorrelated with the information variables. Otherwise, return expectations are not rational in the sense that they do not incorporate all relevant information.

In the standard model with power utility, the discount factor is represented by the growth rate of consumption raised to the power of the negative coefficient of relative risk aversion. Therefore, an important prediction of this specification is that expected real consumption growth and expected real asset returns are perfectly correlated. In an international context, the argument can be reversed, so that the model also provides the rationale for an integration test. If the German stock market is integrated with the world market, the German per capita consumption rates must constitute a valid discount factor that can be applied to the entire cross-section of country returns. The same rationale applies for the Swiss stock market. Given the null hypothesis of integration and assuming power utility, the model posits that the consumption rates of investors in all countries must be perfectly correlated. Intuitively, investors from different countries can share their risks by equalizing consumption rates. In this case, only global systematic risk matters for the pricing of risky assets. Buying and selling claims on consumption goods abroad can insure a country's idiosyncratic risk.[3]

Our first empirical test for stock market integration is thus based on the CCAPM in combination with power utility, where the growth rates of German and Swiss (real) consumption are used as the stochastic discount factor, respectively. As discussed, if the model describes the risk-return relationship appropriately, expected returns should compound all information contained in the information variables. The remaining pricing errors should thus be orthogonal to the available set of information (to the vector of lagged instrumental variables Z_t). The resulting orthogonality conditions can be tested simultaneously for all countries using the Generalized Method of Moments (GMM), originally proposed by Hansen (1982). This technique permits a simultaneous estimation of the time preference rate, δ, and the (constant) coefficient of relative risk aversion, γ. In a compact notation, the system of orthogonality conditions can be written as:

$$E[u \otimes Z] = 0 \qquad (6.6)$$

where $\otimes$ denotes the Kronecker product of vectors. The GMM methodology allows computing a simple test statistic to assess whether the orthogonality conditions are empirically fulfilled. Hansen (1982) shows that this test statistic follows a chi-square (χ^2) distribution.[4] If the model residuals do not fulfill the orthogonality conditions, the GMM test statistic takes on a significant value, rejecting the null hypothesis of integration. This is then an indicator that (1) the equity markets under consideration are at least partially segmented, and/or (2) the Euler equation is not capable of capturing the dynamic risk-return relationship across international stock markets. In fact, the results should be interpreted carefully. It is well known that the standard CCAPM suffers from many problems. Most importantly, it cannot explain the high historical excess returns of stocks over the risk-free rate. This is the famous "equity premium puzzle" (see Mehra & Prescott, 1985). The problem is that consumption has been very smooth in the past, requiring excessively high coefficients of relative risk aversion to duplicate the historical equity premium.[5] This problem also affects our consumption-based test for stock market integration.

A Beta Pricing Model with an Unobservable Benchmark Portfolio

In portfolio theory, mean-variance efficiency of the benchmark portfolio implies a linear relationship between the beta of an asset and its expected return if the beta is computed with respect to this efficient benchmark portfolio. The problem with empirical tests of the celebrated Capital Asset Pricing Model (CAPM) is that the true benchmark portfolio, the market portfolio, is unobservable for the econometrician. This is the essence of Roll's (1977) critique: The CAPM pricing restriction is in fact a tautology. The linear relationship between beta and expected return is merely a result of the mean-variance efficiency of an a-priori chosen benchmark portfolio. Therefore, the null hypothesis of integration may be rejected in empirical tests because of a wrongly specified benchmark portfolio. To circumvent this problem, following Gibbons and Ferson (1985), Campbell and Hamao (1992), and Bekaert and Hodrick (1992), we specify a *latent variable model*. Such models are in the tradition of beta pricing models. They allow for time variation in risk premiums, but maintain the assumption that the conditional betas are fixed parameters. In an international context, the time variation of expected stock returns is assumed to be a linear function of time-varying risk premiums on a small number of global factors, with constant conditional beta factors as coefficients of proportionality. The major restriction of the model is that expected (and not merely historical) returns are perfectly correlated across countries. This property makes the model suitable for tests of market integration. Latent variable models remain agnostic about the underlying risk factors; they are treated as being unobservable.

The stochastic discount factor pricing restriction derived in the previous section implies that the expected return on an asset depends on its conditional covariance with marginal utility. The specification as a multifactor beta pricing model follows directly if marginal utility is modeled as linearly dependent on state variables (see Cochrane, 2001). The expected return, to be realized at time $t + 1$, conditional on the information set available at time t, again denoted as Z_t, can then be written as a linear combination of risk premiums multiplied by the factor sensitivities:

$$E\left(R_{i,\,t+1}\,|\,Z_t\right) = \lambda_0\left(Z_t\right) + \sum_{j=1}^{K} b_{ij}\lambda_j\left(Z_t\right) \quad i = 0, \cdots, N \qquad (6.7)$$

This standard multifactor beta pricing framework has been heavily applied in the empirical literature.[6] The coefficient b_{ij} denotes the conditional sensitivity of the return on asset i with respect to (unexpected) changes of risk factor j, where $j = 1, \ldots, K$. Most importantly, the model posits the existence of K marketwide conditional risk premiums, denoted as $\lambda_j(Z_t)$, for $j = 1, \ldots, K$. Specifically, λ_j is the risk premium paid as compensation for a unit exposure with respect to systematic risk factor j. Risk premiums are modeled as time-varying, conditional on the time evolution of the instrumental variables in Z_t. If there is a portfolio with betas equal to zero on all K factors, then $\lambda_0(Z_t)$ is the expected return on this "zero-beta" portfolio (see Black, 1972). Conditional on publicly available information, $E\left(R_{i,\,t+1}\,|\,Z_t\right)$ describes the time variation in the expected returns on asset i. This variation in expected returns is driven by the time variation in economic risk premiums, which themselves depend on the time evolution of the instrumental variables in Z_t. In general, the betas will also be time-varying functions of the instrumental variables. However, we restrict conditional betas as fixed parameters. This is justified in light of the findings by Ferson and Harvey (1993), who show that time-varying risk premiums are the main drivers of expected returns, whereas time-varying betas are less important. The pricing restriction imposed by this model is that each country has its distinctive risk profile (i.e., its betas, or sensitivity coefficients), but the risk premiums apply equally for the entire cross-section of countries. They measure the price of a unit factor risk, which must be equal in integrated stock markets.

Cho, Eun, and Senbet (1986) point out that the number of relevant risk factors does not indicate the strength of integration within a sample of markets. Therefore, we only look at the simplest model with a single unobservable factor portfolio. For $K = 1$, the model is usually referred to as a *single latent variable model*. For the actual specification of the underlying risk, we do not take a definitive view. A plausible approach is to assume the existence of a factor related to business cycle risk, as postulated by Fama and French (1989) and Oertmann (1997).

The appendix to this chapter shows how a single-factor latent variable model can be derived out of the beta pricing restriction. We test the following system of equations using GMM again:

$$
\begin{aligned}
r_{1,\,t+1} &= \delta_0 + Z_{1,\,t}\delta_1 + Z_{2,\,t}\delta_2 + \cdots + Z_{L,\,t}\delta_L + u_{1,\,t} \\
r_{2,\,t+1} &= \left[\delta_0 + Z_{1,\,t}\delta_1 + Z_{2,\,t}\delta_2 + \cdots + Z_{L,\,t}\delta_L\right]\cdot c_2 + u_{2,\,t} \\
&\ \ \vdots \\
r_{N,\,t+1} &= \left[\delta_0 + Z_{1,\,t}\delta_1 + Z_{2,\,t}\delta_2 + \cdots + Z_{L,\,t}\delta_L\right]\cdot c_N + u_{N,\,t}
\end{aligned}
\tag{6.8}
$$

where N is the number of countries in the cross-section of the sample. r_1 denotes the excess returns on the reference asset, which are the MSCI stock market indices for Germany or Switzerland, respectively, in our setup. r_2 through to r_N stand for the excess returns of the test assets, that is, the excess returns for the United States, the United Kingdom, and Japan. They are assumed to proxy for the world stock market. δ_0 is a regression constant. Following Gibbons and Ferson (1985), the conditional expected return is modeled as a linear combination of lagged instrumental variables, $Z_t \cdot \delta_v$, with $v = 1, \ldots, L$, denotes the sensitivity coefficient of the expected return on the vth instrumental variable. The beta coefficient of the reference asset is normalized to one, without limiting the general case. The coefficients c_i, with $i = 2, \ldots, N$, are proportionality coefficients, or "relative" betas. Finally, u_i, $i = 1, \ldots, N$, denotes the pricing error associated with asset i.

The model implies that expected excess returns vary over time in accordance with the time evolution of the premium on a single risk factor. To keep the model tractable, the risk premium itself is modeled as a linear combination of lagged instrument variables, Z_t, in the first equation of the model. Note again that the model does not require that we specify the underlying risk factor. In contrast, we simply let the data speak. The expected excess returns on all other countries are proportional to the conditional expected returns on the reference asset. Constant conditional betas serve as the coefficients of proportionality. Therefore, the pricing restriction is again that the expected returns on all assets in the sample are perfectly correlated. This explains why latent variable models form the basis for empirical tests of market integration. Proposing that conditional expected returns are perfectly correlated across countries is the same as saying that the markets under consideration are integrated. Or, put the other way round, if equity markets are integrated and the predictability of excess returns is determined by the time variability of a single risk factor, then a statistically significant degree of joint variability must be detectable for expected returns on international stock markets.

The model is tested for both individual countries and simultaneously for all countries. Assuming rational expectations, integration posits that the pricing errors are all equal to zero in expectation. Provided that the empirical relationship tallies with the specification of a single latent variable model, all residuals, denoted as u_{it}, must be orthogonal to each of the lagged instrumental variables in the information set, Z_t. The resulting orthogonality restrictions can be tested using GMM, which allows a simultaneous estimation of the relative beta factors, c_i, with $i = 2, \ldots, N$, for all countries as well as the sensitivity coefficients, δ_v, with $v = 1, \ldots, L$, on the selected instrumental variables. The following orthogonality conditions are estimated:

$$E[u \otimes Z] = 0 \qquad (6.9)$$

where $\otimes$ again denotes a Kronecker product of vectors. The chi-square (χ^2) test statistic for the model's goodness-of-fit allows us to determine whether the null hypothesis of the integration of the German and/or Swiss stock market with the world market can be rejected. If the model's residuals do not satisfy these orthogonality restrictions, the GMM test statistic takes on a significant value. This is then an indicator that (1) the equity markets considered are not integrated, and/or (2) that the single latent variable model cannot capture the dynamic risk-return characteristics of the underlying national stock indices. Again, given that we always test a joint hypothesis, it is not possible to distinguish between these two interpretations.

DATA

Description of the Data for the Consumption-Based Integration Test

The data for the consumption-based integration test is sampled on a quarterly basis from January 1976 to September 1997. We use the MSCI country indices for Germany and Switzerland, as well as the indices for the United States, the United Kingdom, and Japan. The latter three markets proxy for the world stock market. Real returns are computed by deducting the change in the consumer price index for Germany and Switzerland from the total return in German marks or Swiss francs, respectively. The consumer price indices are taken from the Main Indicator Database of the Organization for Economic Cooperation and Development (OECD). The upper panel of Table 6.1 contains a description of real returns. All values are reported as annualized percentages.

Consumption data is taken from the Datastream National Government Series. As a general practice, empirical studies use consumer goods and services as data for consumption. Durable goods are usually not included in the analysis because investors derive utility over multiple periods. This is inconsistent with power utility, which assumes separability over time. However, only the aggregate figures for total consumption are available for Germany and Switzerland. Therefore, we work with total consumption data for all other countries as well. We use seasonally adjusted consumption series in real terms. Population figures from the OECD's Main Indicator Database are applied to compute per-capita consumption. The growth rates for real per-capita consumption of Germany and Switzerland are used as the discount factors in our consumption-based test for integration. The

TABLE 6.1   Descriptive Statistics of Data for the Consumption-Based Test

| | Numéraire Currency | | | | |
| | German Mark | | Swiss Franc | | |
Equity Market	Average Real Return	SD	Average Real Return	SD
Germany	7.86	19.19	7.11	20.57
Japan	8.22	23.99	7.46	24.21
Switzerland	9.97	18.50	9.22	18.22
United Kingdom	11.22	20.72	10.46	21.90
United States	9.69	19.73	8.93	20.97

Discount Factor: Real per-Capita Consumption Growth	Average Growth Rate	SD
Germany	2.53	3.97
Switzerland	0.86	1.03

Note: The means and standard deviations of real stock returns and real per-capita consumption rates are reported in percentages on an annual basis over the time period from 1976.01 to 1997.09.

lower panel of Table 6.1 shows that the annual growth of German consumption was extraordinarily high during the sample period. This might be related to the rapid growth in the wake of German unity in the early 1990s. For both Germany and Switzerland, however, the standard deviation of consumption growth is very low. This phenomenon, which can be observed in virtually all developed countries, plays a central role in the debate surrounding the equity premium puzzle. Finally, we use lagged excess returns and lagged consumption rates as instrumental variables to specify the orthogonality conditions to be tested using GMM.

Description of the Data for the Latent Variable Model

In the test for market integration using the single latent variable model, we use monthly data over the period from January 1976 to September 1997. Excess stock returns are computed by subtracting the interest rate for 1-month deposits on the Eurocurrency market for German marks and Swiss francs from the total stock returns denominated in German marks and Swiss francs. Descriptive statistics of monthly excess returns are reported in the upper part of Table 6.2. Again, all values are given as annualized percentages. For the instrumental variables, we closely follow previous literature. Instrumental variables must be publicly available at the beginning of each period and, in addition, must have some predictive power for stock market returns over the following period. Given our null hypothesis of global stock market integration, we mainly use lagged values of global aggregates as instrument variables. We use a G7 term spread (i.e., the difference between longer- and shorter-term government bonds), the G7 dividend yield, the G7 rate of inflation, and the TED-spread (i.e., the difference between the 3-month Eurocurrency interest rate for U.S. dollars and the return on the 3-month U.S. Treasury bill). These variables are standard in the literature (for a more detailed description see Ferson & Harvey, 1993). The weighting scheme applied to construct global aggregates of the instrumental variables is in accordance with the relative gross domestic products of the G7 countries. All the data

TABLE 6.2 Descriptive Statistics of Data for the Latent Variable Test

	Numéraire Currency			
	German Mark		Swiss Franc	
Equity Market	Average Excess Return	SD	Average Excess Return	SD
Germany	4.72	18.11	5.68	19.45
Japan	5.08	22.45	5.90	22.80
Switzerland	6.85	15.98	7.66	15.66
United Kingdom	8.08	21.42	8.90	22.31
United States	6.55	19.16	7.37	20.40
Global Instrumental Variables			Mean	SD
G7 dividend yield			3.211	0.799
G7 inflation rate			4.784	0.795
G7 term spread			1.071	0.730
TED spread			0.940	0.783

Note: The means and the standard deviations of excess stock returns are reported in percentages on an annual basis over the time period from 1976.01 to 1997.09. The construction of the global instrumental variables is described in the text.

for constructing these variables are taken from the OECD's Quarterly National Account Database.

EMPIRICAL RESULTS OF THE TESTS FOR INTEGRATION

Results of the Consumption-Based Test for Integration

To estimate the consumption-based integration test, we set the time discount factor to $\delta = 0.99$. This corresponds to the values reported by Hansen and Singleton (1982) and enhances the power of the chi-square (χ^2) test of the overidentifyng restrictions. The only parameter left to be estimated is thus the coefficient of relative risk aversion, γ. If one assumes that investors are risk averse, a condition for the plausibility of the estimated results is that $\gamma > 0$ applies. The orthogonality restrictions are estimated simultaneously for all countries using GMM. We use a constant, lagged stock returns, and the two periods' lagged consumption rate as instrumental variables.[7] For the four stock markets incorporated in each test, this results in 24 orthogonality conditions, one parameter to be estimated, and thus 23 degrees of freedom for the χ^2 test of the overidentifying restrictions. The empirical results are reported in Table 6.3.

For both Germany and Switzerland, the p-value of the χ^2 test statistic is not significant in any subperiod from January 1976 to September 1997. We interpret this in favor of the null hypothesis that the German and Swiss stock markets are integrated with the world stock market. The estimated coefficients of relative risk aversion have the

TABLE 6.3 Consumption-Based Test for Integration

All Markets Simultaneously	Germany			Switzerland		
	γ	t-Value	χ^2_{23} (p-Value)	γ	t-Value	χ^2_{23} (p-Value)
Total sample period (1976.01–1997.09)	2.446	1.434	0.527	3.323	0.833	0.624
Subperiod 1 (1976.01–1986.12)	2.213	1.353	0.447	3.900	1.473	0.356
Subperiod 2 (1987.01–1997.09)	0.469	0.518	0.998	0.731	0.109	0.789

Note: The following system of orthogonality conditions is tested using GMM:

$$E_t\left[\delta\left(\frac{C_{t+1}}{C_t}\right)^{-\delta}\left(1 + R_{i,t+1}\right) - 1 \mid Z_t\right] = E_t\left[u_{t+1} \mid Z_t\right] = 0$$

All variables are explained in the text. The model is tested using MSCI stock market indices for Germany and Switzerland, respectively, and the indices for the United States, the United Kingdom, and Japan. To test the null hypothesis of integration, the growth rates of (real) German and Swiss consumption are applied to capture the cross-sectional risk-return relationship. All estimates are based on a time discount factor of $\delta = 0.99$. The t-values measure the statistical significance of the estimated coefficients of risk aversion, γ. The two columns with the chi-square (χ^2) test statistics indicate the individual p-values for the null hypothesis of integration.

correct sign, but they are generally insignificant. Although the values are higher than those reported in Hansen and Singleton (1982), they are smaller than those in Wheately (1988) and Harvey (1991). In their classical study for the United States, Friend and Blume (1975) argue that the maximally plausible value is around 10 for relative risk aversion.

To check for the possibility of time variation in risk aversion, we test the model for two subperiods. The first subperiod runs from 1976.01 to 1986.12; the second is from 1987.01 to 1997.09. Risk aversion is considerably lower in the second subperiod than in the first one, but the precision of the estimated values is very low for both Germany and Switzerland. Further, the p-values of the χ^2 test statistic take on high absolute values for both markets in the later subperiod, much higher than in the earlier subperiod. A possible interpretation is that the degree of integration has increased over time. However, the testing of a joint hypothesis of market equilibrium and integration complicates all interpretations. It may well be that the consumption-based asset-pricing model is wrongly specified, but our empirical test is just not powerful enough to reject it. Alternatively, the results could also be interpreted as indicating that the historically low correlations between consumption rates in various countries are not an indication of segmentation. Instead, they might point to incomplete markets (see Solnik, 1994).

Results of the Latent Variable Test for Integration

Overall, the results of the single latent variable model underscore the findings of the consumption-based test. However, the χ^2 test statistic has the tendency to lose power as the system of orthogonality conditions increases (it is unable to reject the null hypothesis when it is false). For this reason, we test the model both for individual pairs of markets as well as for all markets together. This allows us to determine which restriction (which country) is responsible for any possible rejection of the null hypothesis in the multivariate system with all countries. A test of individual pairs of

TABLE 6.4 Latent Variable Test for Integration

Pairs of Countries	Germany $\hat{c}_1$	t	χ_4^2	Switzerland $\hat{c}_1$	t	χ_4^2
United States	0.724	1.869*	0.664	0.721	2.274**	0.838
Japan	1.204	1.949*	0.601	1.104	2.460**	0.519
United Kingdom	0.805	1.908*	0.775	0.795	2.258**	0.784

All Other Countries Simultaneously	Germany χ_{12}^2	Switzerland χ_{12}^2
Total sample period (1976.01–1997.09)	0.957	0.976
Subperiod 1 (1976.01–1986.12)	0.408	0.443
Subperiod 2 (1987.01–1997.09)	0.576	0.421

Note: The following system of orthogonality conditions is tested using GMM:

$$r_{1,t+1} = \delta_0 + Z_{1,t}\delta_1 + Z_{2,t}\delta_2 + \dots + Z_{L,t}\delta_L + u_{1,t}$$

$$r_{2,t+1} = \left[\delta_0 + Z_{1,t}\delta_1 + Z_{2,t}\delta_2 + \dots + Z_{L,t}\delta_L\right]\cdot c_2 + u_{2,t}$$

$$\vdots$$

$$r_{N,t+1} = \left[\delta_0 + Z_{1,t}\delta_1 + Z_{2,t}\delta_2 + \dots + Z_{L,t}\delta_L\right]\cdot c_N + u_{N,t}$$

All variables are explained in the text. The model is tested using MSCI stock market indices for Germany and Switzerland as the reference asset, respectively, and the indices for the United States, the United Kingdom, and Japan as the test assets. The time-varying risk premium on the single latent factor is modeled as a linear combination of lagged instrumental variables, Z_t. The null hypothesis of integration posits that the expected excess returns are perfectly correlated, with the relative beta factors, c_i, $i = 2, \dots, N$, as the proportionality coefficients. The system of equations is tested both for individual pairs of markets and for all markets together. The columns with the chi-square (χ^2) test statistic indicate the corresponding p-value for the null hypothesis of stock market integration.

*Relative beta factors are significant at the 10 percent level.

**Relative beta factors are significant at the 5 percent level.

countries produces 10 orthogonality restrictions (because we use 5 instruments) and contains 6 parameters to be estimated. Thus four degrees of freedom are left in the χ^2 test of the overidentifying restrictions. In the multivariate model for all four stock markets, the χ^2 test statistic has 12 degrees of freedom; there are 20 orthogonality conditions and 8 parameters to be estimated. The empirical results of the latent variable model are shown in Table 6.4.

Again, we cannot reject the null hypothesis that the German and Swiss equity markets are integrated with the world market. The lower panel of Table 6.4 shows that for both Germany and Switzerland, the p-value for the whole sample period is greater than 0.95 in the multivariate system with all four countries. These results are confirmed by the tests for individual pairs of countries in the upper panel of Table 6.4. It is not possible to reject the null hypothesis of integration for any of the country pairs. Finally, the values for the relative beta factors, c_i, $i = 2, \ldots, N$, are plausible and statistically significant.

The empirical results are, however, crucially tied to the assumption of constant factor sensitivities. If this assumption is not justified, then the single latent variable model is not capable of describing the risk-return structure, even if the markets are in fact integrated. Also remember that, again, we test a joint hypothesis. If the single factor beta pricing model is empirically inadmissible (if the latent benchmark portfolio is not the priced factor), then the expected excess returns fluctuate independently of one another, even if the valuation of systematic risk is in fact global. It is equally possible that the markets considered in our investigation are actually segmented. Even in this case, it would be conceivable that the markets are subject to similar shocks, which may cause synchronous variability in expected returns. Empirical tests on the basis of latent variable models are not powerful enough to distinguish between these alternative hypotheses.

CONCLUSION

The aim of the empirical work in this chapter has been to test the null hypothesis of the integration of the German and Swiss stock markets with the world stock market. Integration implies that investments with the same risk characteristics have identical expected returns, independent of their national base. A distinction is made between integration and the mere correlation of stock market returns. We apply two tests of integration: a consumption-based test and a latent variable test. Neither model leads to a rejection of the null hypothesis of the German and Swiss stock markets' integration with the world stock market. This is in striking contrast to the results by Heston, Rouwenhorst, and Wessels (1995). Our results imply that the level of capital costs of publicly traded German and Swiss companies do not differ from those of other countries belonging to the same risk class.

However, some words of caution are necessary. Market integration is conceptually related to the valuation of risky assets. Therefore, in all integration tests a joint hypothesis of market equilibrium and integration must be tested. Accordingly, there may be two reasons for rejecting the null hypothesis of integration: (1) The equity markets being considered are at least partially segmented, and/or (2) the underlying asset-pricing model cannot capture the dynamic risk-return relationship. Our econometric tests are not powerful enough to distinguish between these two hypotheses. Therefore, the empirical results must be interpreted carefully. They provide evidence for the validity of the null hypothesis of integration, but our asset-pricing models still could be misspecified. The literature related to the equity premium puzzle provides strong reasons to believe that the Consumption Capital Asset Pricing Model (CCAPM) is an inadequate description of the true risk-return relationship.

APPENDIX

In this appendix, we show the derivation of a single latent variable model from the familiar beta pricing restriction. For a more detailed discussion, see Ferson, Foerster, and Keim (1993). For notational convenience, we omit time subscripts and do not explicitly indicate the dependency of the risk premium on the instrument variables.

Formally, let b denote the $K \cdot (N + 1)$ matrix of sensitivity coefficients, with elements b_{ij}, and write the beta pricing restriction as follows:

$$E(R \mid Z) = \lambda_0 \underline{1} + \lambda b \qquad (6A.1)$$

where R is a vector of returns with dimension $(N + 1)$, l is a vector of ones with dimension $(N + 1)$, and λ is the K-dimensional vector of risk premiums. Define an N-dimensional vector of excess returns, r, where excess returns are computed relative to some arbitrarily chosen asset. This allows writing the beta pricing restriction in terms of excess returns:

$$E(r \mid Z) = \lambda \beta \qquad (6A.2)$$

where β denotes the $(K \cdot N)$ matrix of constant factor sensitivities of the excess returns with respect to unexpected changes in the K risk factors. Next, we partition the vector of N excess returns into $r = (r_1, r_2)$, where r_1 is a K vector with reference assets and r_2 the $(N - K)$ vector with test assets. The number of unobservable (latent) risk factors, K, determines the number of reference assets. Similarly, split up the matrix of the factor betas into $\beta = (\beta_1, \beta_2)$. With this specification, solve for the risk premium as a function of the reference assets to get:

$$\lambda = E(r_1 \mid Z) \beta_1^{-1} \qquad (6A.3)$$

It is then straightforward to derive the following cross-sectional pricing restriction for the $N - K$ reference assets:

$$E(r_2 \mid Z) = E(r_1 \mid Z) \beta_1^{-1} \beta_2 = E(r_1 \mid Z) C \qquad (6A.4)$$

where C is a $K \cdot (N - K)$ matrix of relative beta coefficients.

Finally, it is necessary to specify the functional form of risk premiums to make the model empirically testable. According to Gibbons and Ferson (1985), a linear relationship is assumed between risk premiums and instrumental variables, collected in the L-dimensional vector Z. The relative beta coefficients of the reference assets are normalized to one without limiting the general case. This results in the following system of equations:

$$r_1 = Z\delta_1 + u_1$$
$$r_2 = Z\delta_1 C + u_2$$

(6A.5)

where δ denotes an $(L \cdot K)$ matrix of regression coefficients. Our single latent variable model, which is the simplest type of this model, falls out immediately.

CHAPTER 7

Emerging Market Investments

Myth or Reality?

EXECUTIVE SUMMARY

- In the late 1980s, investors began pouring money into the emerging markets in Latin America and Asia. High historical average returns coupled with low correlations between emerging stock markets and developed stock markets were the driving forces for investments in these regions.
- The distributional characteristics of emerging stock market returns and simple spanning tests indicate that emerging stock markets constitute a stand-alone asset class. However, traditional portfolio theory fails to realize these global diversification benefits. Emerging markets are very attractive on an ex ante basis, but highly responsible for any poor ex post portfolio performance.
- The Stein-estimator is a useful remedy that Jorion (1985, 1986) introduced in the finance literature. Shrinkage of mean returns with high estimation errors toward the return of the minimum-variance portfolio leads to significantly improved ex post performance and more stable portfolio allocations for emerging stock market investments. However, unlike Jorion's results for an earlier time period, shrinkage seems no longer beneficial when applied to a recent sample of developed stock markets.

MOTIVATION

In the late 1980s, investors began pouring money into the emerging markets of Latin America, Asia, the Mideast, and Africa. Although several of these countries have not yet liberalized their capital markets, emerging markets in general have become more accessible for global investors over the past decade. Two main instruments are available for foreigners who want to become active in emerging stock markets: country funds and American Depositary Receipts (ADR). A closed-end country fund is an investment company that invests in a portfolio of assets in a foreign country and issues a fixed number of shares domestically. There are two distinct market-determined prices: the country fund's share price quoted on the market where it trades and its net asset value determined by the prices of the underlying shares traded on the foreign markets. American Depositary Receipts are rights to foreign shares that trade in dollars on a U.S. exchange or over the counter.[1] They can be exchanged for the underlying security in the local market at any time. The underlying shares are held in custody by the depository bank, which converts dividends and other payments into dollars for distribution to the holders of the ADR. Many countries have started or are about to reduce the barriers for foreign investors. Direct access to emerging stock markets at a reasonable cost will become much easier for investors in the near future.

The attraction of emerging markets seems intuitive. Tiny emerging markets did not ride the waves of bourses in developed markets, thereby providing a hedge against losses in more established markets. Returns can be impressive in these markets, but high returns are usually accompanied by extremely high volatility. The high historical average returns combined with low correlations between emerging markets and the developed stock markets are the driving forces for investments in these regions. Modern portfolio theory provides a comfortable theoretical argument for incorporating emerging markets into the asset allocation process. Observing increasing correlations across developed stock markets, investment managers are searching for stand-alone asset classes with distinctive risk-return characteristics. The "emerging market solution" is appealing, and most fund managers try hard to convince their sponsors that a "diversification free lunch" is available in emerging markets.[2] In addition, lack of integration can present new opportunities for global investors. In a pricing context, integration implies that risk is consistently rewarded across capital markets, and the empirical evidence indicates that emerging markets exhibit time-varying degrees of integration (see Bekaert & Harvey, 1995). This implies that assets with a high expected return could potentially be purchased at cheaper prices than comparable assets in developed countries.

This chapter thoroughly examines familiar arguments in favor of emerging market investments, using stock market data for seven developed countries (Canada, France, Germany, Japan, Switzerland, United Kingdom, and the United States) and seven emerging economies (Argentina, Brazil, Chile, India, Korea, Mexico, and Thailand) over the past two decades. The following questions are considered:

■ Is the behavior of stock market returns in emerging markets different from that of developed stock markets? Do emerging stock markets constitute a stand-alone asset class?

■ Are investments in emerging markets attractive for a globally oriented investor? Is it possible to improve the risk-return spectrum of an investor who is already diversified across the major developed stock markets?

■ Given the distributional characteristics of emerging stock returns, does the traditional mean-variance analysis provide useful answers for global asset allocation? If not, is there a simple remedy to reduce estimation error?

The results can be summarized as follows. First, emerging markets boost higher historical returns, combined with high volatility. Emerging stock market returns depart from normality more frequently and are much less correlated with the world market index than developed stock market returns. Second, the gains from diversification are real. A simple spanning test shows that, once emerging markets are added to the analysis, the shift in the efficient frontier is genuine rather than an artifact of sampling variation. The third part of this chapter shows that the standard mean-variance approach provides little help in realizing these diversification benefits. Simulating a rolling strategy of investing into the optimal portfolio of global stock markets shows how important it is to account for estimation error in expected returns. Emerging markets seem very attractive on an ex ante basis, but turn out to be highly responsible for poor ex post performance. Shrinkage toward the minimum-variance portfolio is an easy-to-implement tool that allows asset managers to improve the ex post performance.

DATA

Our data sample contains stock indices for major developed and emerging stock markets. We use total return indices from the Morgan Stanley Capital Investment (MSCI) database (with dividend reinvestment) and compute monthly returns for Canada, France, Germany, Japan, Switzerland, the United Kingdom, and the United States from 1976.01 to 1998.07. The International Finance Corporation (IFC) has provided similar indices for emerging stock markets. The emerging capital markets in Latin America and Southeast Asia have attracted particular interest. Total return indices for more than a two-decade sample period are available only for Argentina, Brazil, Chile, India, Korea, Mexico, and Thailand. All other country indices in the IFC database start in January 1985, or even later. All returns are calculated using the Swiss franc as the denomination currency. The 1-month Eurocurrency interest rate for Swiss francs is used as the risk-free asset. All summary statistics are presented in Table 7.1.[3]

To provide a more comprehensive illustration, Table 7.1 includes return characteristics for the entire set of Latin American and Southeast Asian countries in the IFC database. The mean stock returns in emerging markets range from 54 percent (Argentina) to –9 percent (Indonesia, whose sample only begins in 1990.01). This is in sharp contrast to the range of average returns in the developed markets. In the reduced MSCI sample used here, no arithmetic average for the return of any country comes close to exceeding 15 percent. In the IFC

TABLE 7.1 Summary Statistics for Emerging and Developed Stock Market Returns

	Starting Year and Month	Swiss Francs			Autocorrelations					Correlation with the World Index
		Arithmetic Mean (% Annual)	Geometric Mean (% Annual)	SD (% Annual)	ρ_1	ρ_2	ρ_3	ρ_6	ρ_{12}	
MSCI Markets										
Canada	1976.01	10.554	7.974	22.675	0.056	0.006	−0.016	0.048	0.005	0.807
France	1976.01	14.512	11.925	22.492	0.088	−0.064	0.020	−0.008	−0.020	0.682
Germany	1976.01	13.103	11.170	19.469	0.056	−0.033	0.048	−0.029	−0.004	0.631
Japan	1976.01	11.433	8.816	22.743	0.036	−0.016	0.075	0.000	−0.024	0.744
Switzerland	1976.01	14.803	13.193	15.637	0.110	0.025	−0.029	−0.039	0.006	0.712
United Kingdom	1976.01	15.938	13.436	22.114	0.072	−0.081	−0.049	−0.041	−0.098	0.814
United States	1976.01	14.350	12.259	20.250	0.045	0.039	−0.041	−0.071	0.024	0.860
IFC Markets										
Argentina	1976.01	54.241	18.766	82.049	−0.010	0.021	0.016	0.102	−0.086	0.458
Brazil	1976.01	24.080	7.411	57.888	0.015	0.006	−0.061	0.001	−0.011	0.467
Chile	1976.01	28.639	21.237	37.466	0.160	0.142	−0.051	−0.052	0.057	0.480
Colombia	1985.01	24.469	10.822	29.436	0.294	0.127	0.000	0.054	−0.024	0.185
India	1976.01	13.113	8.780	29.158	0.152	0.011	−0.120	0.022	−0.039	0.213
Indonesia	1990.01	−9.342	−20.271	46.194	0.254	−0.067	−0.010	−0.095	−0.010	0.415
Korea	1976.01	11.892	4.936	36.803	0.031	0.062	−0.092	0.068	0.069	0.403
Malaysia	1985.01	1.646	−5.066	37.026	0.174	0.160	−0.050	−0.128	0.024	0.551
Mexico	1976.01	23.448	11.417	50.681	0.225	−0.057	−0.099	−0.122	−0.029	0.635
Pakistan	1985.01	5.605	0.643	31.693	0.229	−0.049	−0.102	0.054	−0.053	0.327
Philippines	1985.01	23.717	16.127	38.528	0.329	0.058	−0.062	−0.081	0.090	0.563
Taiwan	1985.01	24.350	11.702	50.171	0.081	0.074	−0.097	−0.143	0.099	0.525
Thailand	1976.01	10.694	4.399	35.822	0.113	0.138	−0.090	−0.048	0.087	0.525
Venezuela	1985.01	17.608	5.797	49.617	0.007	0.156	0.006	0.021	−0.046	0.053

Note: All returns are in Swiss francs. The sample period runs through 1998.07. SD = Standard deviation.

emerging sample, eight countries (Argentina, Brazil, Chile, Colombia, Mexico, Philippines, Taiwan, and Venezuela) have returns that average above 15 percent. It is important to present both arithmetic and geometric returns. The geometric average reflects the average return of a buy-and-hold strategy, whereas the arithmetic average assumes rebalancing at the beginning of each period while holding the total amount invested constant over time. With high volatility, there are supposedly large differences in the arithmetic and geometric mean returns. Indeed, the problem is severe for the emerging market sample. The most dramatic example is Argentina. The arithmetic average return is 54 percent, but the geometric average return is "only" 19 percent.

A final observation is that high returns in emerging stock markets are accompanied by high volatility. Annualized volatility range from 29 percent (Colombia) to 82 percent (Argentina). In contrast, the

MSCI countries have volatility in the well-known region between 15 percent and 25 percent per year. All countries in the IFC sample exhibit volatility above the maximum volatility of 25 percent (United Kingdom) in the MSCI sample. Intuitively, excessive volatility of stock returns in emerging markets is of major importance for the asset allocation process. As discussed later in this chapter, naïve portfolio strategies fare miserably, mostly because of this high return volatility and, hence, substantial estimation errors.

Autocorrelations are also presented in Table 7.1. In the MSCI sample, only the United Kingdom has first-order autocorrelations exceeding 0.1. In the emerging market sample, seven countries have autocorrelations greater than 0.1, some of them even above 0.2. This suggests that in these countries stock returns are predictable on the basis of past information.[4] The last column in Table 7.1 shows the correlations of emerging stock markets with the MSCI (all countries) world index. The correlations are well above 0.6 for all the countries in the MSCI sample; for Canada, the United Kingdom, and the United States they are even higher than 0.8. Sample correlations are considerably smaller across the emerging market sample; for Argentina and India they become as low as 0.2.

Table 7.2 shows the correlation structure between MSCI and IFC markets. Correlations lie at the heart of the "diversification free lunch." Despite high return volatilitiy on emerging stock markets, low correlations should offer substantial diversification opportunities in a portfolio context. To save space, Table 7.2 only contains the correlations between the 14 stock markets that are analyzed in the rest of this chapter. The overall message is clear: On average, the correlations between MSCI and IFC markets (in the upper-right part of the table) are smaller than the correlations between the MSCI markets (upper-left in the table).[5] In a portfolio context, this means that the opportunity set becomes larger: Higher expected returns can be achieved at a lower level of volatility. We test this central proposition statistically in the next section of this chapter.

Finally, one might suspect that emerging market returns depart from normality. To investigate this notion, Table 7.3 reports the coefficients of skewness and kurtosis for the sample return series. If

TABLE 7.2 Correlations between International Stock Returns

	MSCI Markets						IFC markets						
	France	Germany	Japan	Switzerland	United Kingdom	United States	Argentina	Brazil	Chile	India	Korea	Mexico	Thailand
Canada	0.51	0.42	0.35	0.54	0.62	0.81	0.50	0.35	0.54	0.28	0.33	0.61	0.48
France		0.60	0.38	0.58	0.58	0.54	0.49	0.29	0.34	0.26	0.19	0.51	0.39
Germany			0.32	0.68	0.48	0.49	0.22	0.21	0.29	0.15	0.15	0.42	0.42
Japan				0.35	0.38	0.37	0.20	0.31	0.14	0.01	0.41	0.36	0.33
Switzerland					0.58	0.60	0.30	0.36	0.33	0.23	0.25	0.46	0.46
United Kingdom						0.62	0.41	0.34	0.40	0.15	0.34	0.54	0.40
United States							0.54	0.40	0.54	0.26	0.30	0.59	0.47
Argentina								0.27	0.41	0.31	0.14	0.51	0.29
Brazil									0.38	0.28	0.09	0.40	0.23
Chile										0.46	0.29	0.52	0.42
India											0.14	0.33	0.31
Korea												0.27	0.52
Mexico													0.39

Note: All returns are measured in Swiss francs. The sample is from 1976.01 to 1998.07.

TABLE 7.3 Analysis of the Distribution of Stock Market Returns

	Higher Moments of the Distribution		GMM Test of Normality	
	Skewness	Kurtosis	Chi-Square Test Statistic (χ^2)	p-Value
MSCI Markets				
Canada	−0.583	5.826	2.632	0.268
France	−0.401	4.840	3.133	0.209
Germany	−0.780	5.973	3.851	0.146
Japan	−0.268	4.049	9.092*	0.011
Switzerland	−1.008	8.164	1.657	0.437
United Kingdom	0.803	6.086	2.614**	0.271
United States	−0.741	6.130	3.091	0.213
IFC Markets				
Argentina	0.043	7.245	26.420**	0.000
Brazil	−0.377	5.541	5.210	0.074
Chile	0.270	3.782	4.814	0.090
Colombia	0.736	4.830	7.697*	0.021
India	0.328	3.558	5.285	0.071
Indonesia	−1.231	5.690	33.960**	0.000
Korea	0.538	8.119	7.543*	0.023
Malaysia	−0.153	5.424	8.094*	0.017
Mexico	−0.904	5.103	4.254	0.119
Pakistan	−0.362	6.897	11.902**	0.003
Philippines	−0.097	4.127	6.112*	0.047
Taiwan	0.229	4.605	7.659*	0.022
Thailand	−0.747	5.623	14.556**	0.001
Venezuela	−1.096	7.664	4.047	0.132

Note: To test the null hypothesis that the returns on any stock market i are normally distributed, the following system of equations is estimated by GMM for every stock market i:

$$e_{1,it} = r_{it} - \mu_i$$

$$e_{2,it} = \left(r_{it} - \mu_i\right)^2 - v_i$$

$$e_{3,it} = \frac{\left(r_{it} - \mu_i\right)^3}{v_i^{3/2}}$$

$$e_{4,it} = \frac{\left(r_{it} - \mu_i\right)^4}{v_i^2} - 3$$

All returns are denominated in Swiss francs. The parameters to be estimated are μ_i and v_i, the sample mean and the sample variance, respectively. The null hypothesis of normality imposes the restriction that the coefficients of skewness and excess kurtosis are jointly equal to zero. The chi-square (χ^2) test statistic has two degrees of freedom. The probability value from the test statistic is reported in the final column.
*Denotes rejection of the null hypothesis at the 5 percent level of significance.
**Denotes rejection of the null hypothesis at the 1 percent level of significance.

returns are normally distributed, skewness should be zero and kurtosis equal to 3. Returns are skewed to the left in all MSCI markets—they have a negative third moment around the mean (except the United Kingdom). Both negative and positive skewness show up in the emerging markets' sample. The kurtosis of most stock market returns deviates considerably from the theoretical level implied by a normal distribution. This empirical observation has become known as *fat tails* in the literature. Extreme return realizations (in both directions) are more likely than one would expect if returns were normally distributed. To formally test for normality, the following system of equations for each time-series of stock returns is estimated:[6]

$$e_{1,\,it} = r_{it} - \mu_i$$

$$e_{2,\,it} = \left(r_{it} - \mu_i\right)^2 - v_i$$

$$e_{3,\,it} = \frac{\left(r_{it} - \mu_i\right)^3}{v_i^{3/2}}$$

$$e_{4,\,it} = \frac{\left(r_{it} - \mu_i\right)^4}{v_i^2} - 3$$

where r_{it} stands for the return on the i th stock market index in month t, $t = 1, \ldots, T$, measured in Swiss francs. μ_i and v_i denote the parameters to be estimated, sample mean and sample variance, respectively. $e_t = \{e_{1it}, e_{2it}, e_{3it}, e_{3it}\}$ represents the vector of disturbances, and normality commands that $E(e_t) = 0$. The first two equations estimate sample mean and sample variance, respectively. The last two equations reflect the empirical assumption of normality. The test statistic results from setting the coefficients of skewness (in the third equation) and excess kurtosis (in the fourth equation) equal to zero. The system of equations is estimated using the Generalized Method of Moments (GMM), with a constant as the only instrument. Accordingly, the two parameters are estimated on the basis of four orthogonality conditions. In his famous paper, Hansen (1982) suggests a test of whether all sample moments represented by the four orthogonality conditions are as close to zero as would be expected under normality.

The test statistic is distributed chi-square (χ^2) with two degrees of freedom. The values of the test statistic and the associated p-values are reported in the two right-hand columns of Table 7.3.

The null hypothesis of normally distributed returns is rejected on the 5 percent level of significance in only two of the seven MSCI countries (Japan and United Kingdom). Again, this is in sharp contrast to emerging markets. At the 5 percent significance level, the null hypothesis of normally distributed returns can be rejected for nine of the IFC markets (Argentina, Colombia, Indonesia, Korea, Malaysia, Pakistan, Philippines, Taiwan, and Thailand). Applying the 10 percent level of significance leads to a rejection of normality for all emerging markets in the sample, except Mexico and Venezuela.

Non-normality in emerging stock market returns imposes severe problems for the traditional mean-variance approach. In the classical portfolio theory, we search for the portfolio with smallest volatility, given some target level of expected return. This paradigm might no longer be appropriate when there is significant skewness and kurtosis, as in emerging market data. It is reasonable to assume that investors have preferences over skewness and prefer positively skewed distributions to negatively skewed distributions. Intuitively, risk avoiders can be assumed to prefer return distributions with likely small negative surprises and less likely large positive surprises.[7] This expresses the notion that risk is defined by the possibility of disaster. The distributional characteristics—excessive volatility, combined with significant skewness and kurtosis—can therefore be expected to pose a great challenge for the standard mean-variance framework. The empirical results in later sections confirm this intuition.

Overall, the summary statistics reveal several contrasts between emerging stock markets and developed stock markets. Emerging markets have higher average returns and volatility than developed markets. The autocorrelations of emerging stock market returns can be considerably higher than those of developed stock markets. In addition, the correlations between the MSCI and the IFC stock market returns are lower than the correlations between the MSCI markets themselves, although correlations tend to increase over time. Finally, returns in emerging stock markets depart from the normal distribution. Given these observations, it is fair to view emerging stock markets as a distinctive, stand-alone asset class. In a portfolio context, their risk-return menu seems attractive and designed to potentially enhance portfolio performance.

EMERGING MARKETS AND DIVERSIFICATION

The addition of low correlation assets can enhance the reward-to-risk profile by shifting the efficient frontier to the upper-left. Many fund managers simply plug emerging market returns into the standard mean-variance framework and argue that the combination of high expected returns and low correlations pushes the efficient frontier to the upper-left. Figure 7.1 shows the unconditional efficient frontier for the seven MSCI markets (Canada, France, Germany, Japan, Switzerland, the United Kingdom, and the United States) and the efficient frontier that results from the addition of the seven IFC countries (Argentina, Brazil, Chile, India, Korea, Mexico, Thailand) from 1976.01 to 1998.07.[8] The dotted curve is based on the seven MSCI indices; the solid line shows the effect of adding the seven IFC indices. We refer to this latter parabola as the *global efficient frontier*. At the global minimum variance portfolio, the volatility is reduced from 14.4 percent to 13.2 percent.

Although comparing the two frontiers suggests that an increased risk-return spectrum is available to a global investor, stock returns are so volatile that it is hard to measure average returns with sufficient statistical significance. Therefore, estimation error turns out to be a major concern for asset allocation. A simple example can demonstrate the problem. Even with 20 years of data, if we measure an annual average return of 10 percent with a standard deviation of 20 percent, the 95 percent confidence interval implies that the true mean return is (roughly) between 1 percent (=10% − 2·4.5%) and 19 percent (= 10% + 2·4.5%). All returns in this probability range are indistinguishable from a purely statistical point of view. The entries for average returns and volatility in Table 7.1 indicate that the problems associated with estimation error might be even more severe

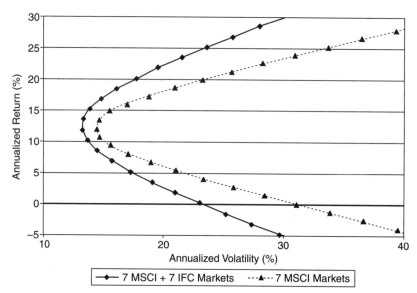

FIGURE 7.1 Shifting the efficient frontier by adding emerging markets. The dotted line displays the risk-return menu attainable by investing in seven developed stock markets (Canada, France, Germany, Japan, Switzerland, the United Kingdom, and the United States). The solid line shifts leftward because seven emerging stock markets are added to the portfolio of MSCI stocks (Argentina, Brazil, Chile, India, Korea, Mexico, and Thailand). No short-sale restrictions are imposed. The sample covers the period from 1976.01 to 1998.07.

than this simple example suggests. Therefore, the graphical analysis in Figure 7.1 cannot answer the question: Does the efficient frontier shift significantly when emerging markets are added to a portfolio of developed stock markets?

Following Huberman and Kandel (1987) and Ferson, Foerster, and Keim (1993), let $R = \{R_1, R_2\}$, where R_1 is the matrix of returns in the seven developed markets, and R_2 denotes the return matrix of the seven emerging stock markets. Spanning tests ask whether one can significantly improve the risk-return spectrum by adding additional "test" assets (IFC markets) to a portfolio of "spanning" assets (MSCI assets). Hence, the test is whether the set of developed stock market returns spans the frontier of both developed and emerging markets by estimating the following moment conditions:

$$E\left[\left(R_2 - C \cdot R_1\right) \otimes R_1\right] \text{ subject to } \underline{1}^T \cdot C = \underline{1} \qquad (7.1)$$

for unconditional spanning and

$$E\left[\left(R_2 - C \cdot R_1\right) \otimes \left(R_1, Z\right)\right] \text{ subject to } \underline{1}^T \cdot C = \underline{1} \qquad (7.2)$$

for conditional spanning.[9] C denotes a $7 \cdot 7$ coefficient matrix, $\underline{1}$ is a vector of ones, and the superscript T stands for the transpose of a vector. Finally, Z refers to conditioning information variables. Because it is standard in the empirical finance literature, lagged values of the global dividend yield and a global term spread are used as instrument variables with potential predictive power for expected returns. In addition, we use a vector of ones as an instrument. Again, the Generalized Method of Moments (GMM) can be used to estimate the coefficients in the matrix C. The chi square (χ^2) test statistic for the overidentifying restrictions tests whether the null hypothesis of mean-variance spanning can be rejected. Table 7.4 reports the results . Given a specific target level of returns, modest investment in emerging stock markets leads to significantly lower portfolio risk. Equivalently, a significantly higher expected rate of return is attainable for a global investor, holding the level of risk constant. The p-values reject the null hypothesis of both unconditional and conditional mean-variance spanning at the 1 percent level of significance. Overall, these results lead to two main insights. First, the shift in the efficient frontier in Figure 7.1 is real, not a mere artifact of sampling data. Second, simple unconditional strategies suffice to realize the gains from global diversification. Conditioning information might help, but is not necessary.

Another aspect is noteworthy. Loosely speaking, spanning tests can be interpreted as unparametric tests of market integration. Integration refers to the consistent pricing of global systematic risk. It is well known from the standard asset pricing theory that any portfolio

TABLE 7.4   Test for Mean-Variance Spanning

	Degrees of Freedom	Chi-Square (χ^2) Test Statistic	p-Value
Unconditional			
	7	40.127	0.000*
Conditional			
Instrument			
iDivYield	14	44.924	0.000*
iTSpread	14	41.721	0.000*

Note: To test the null hypothesis of mean-variance spanning, that is, the assumption that the set of developed stock market returns spans the global efficient frontier (including emerging stock markets), the following systems of equations are estimated by GMM:

$$E\left[\left(R_2 - C \cdot R_1\right) \otimes R_1\right] \text{ subject to } \underline{1}^T \cdot C = \underline{1}$$

for unconditional spanning, and

$$E\left[\left(R_2 - C \cdot R_1\right) \otimes \left(R_1, Z\right)\right] \text{ subject to } \underline{1}^T \cdot C = \underline{1}$$

for conditional spanning. The spanning assets (in R_1) contain seven MSCI markets (Canada, France, Germany, Japan, Switzerland, the United Kingdom, and the United States), and the test assets (in R_2) contain seven IFC countries (Argentina, Brazil, Chile, India, Korea, Mexico, and Thailand). Monthly returns over the period from 1976.01 to 1998.07 are measured in Swiss francs. The coefficient matrix C contains the parameters to be estimated. Lagged values of a world dividend yield (iDivYield) and the G7 term spread of interest rates (iTSpread) are used as instrument variables to condition expected returns. Instrument variables are denoted as Z. A vector of ones is also used as an instrument.
*Indicates statistical significance at the 1 percent level.

on the mean-variance frontier carries all pricing information. In particular, it is possible to span the underlying discount factor as a linear combination of any mean-variance portfolio. Therefore, rejecting mean-variance spanning indicates that the discount factor that consistently prices payoffs in the MSCI stock markets is not able to price the payoffs that accrue to investors holding emerging market stocks.[10] A loose interpretation is that the reward-to-risk ratio is not unique across international stock markets. Because no asset pricing restrictions have been imposed, a spanning test does not offer a strict proof for either integration or segmentation. However, the analysis in Table 7.4 strengthens the notion that IFC stock markets are at least partially segmented.

We conclude that emerging stock markets constitute a distinctive asset class with a specific risk-return tradeoff. The practical implication is that international diversification should not be restricted to developed stock markets. Instead, emerging markets should become increasingly important in the asset allocation process. At this point, many asset managers may find confirmation for what they always knew. At the end, the "emerging market solution" is for real! However, this is not the end of the story—not yet.

THE MEAN-VARIANCE ANALYSIS REVISITED

In fact, the exercise in Figure 7.1 and Table 7.4 turns out to be misleading. Although estimation error seems negligible for the two efficient frontiers in Figure 7.1, they are based on ex post mean returns. Of course, ex post—when the entire set of sample information has become available—we all know which strategies would have worked. Financial markets do not reward this type of knowledge. Therefore, we analyze the performance of an asset allocation strategy that optimizes investment weights at the end of each month and requires holding the implied portfolio for the next month. The strategy assumes that the investor holds the tangency portfolio.[11] Investment professionals as well as academics usually follow a pragmatic approach: Expected returns, variances, and covariances are simply replaced with their ex post sample values. We use a moving window of 144 months to compute the required input parameters. At the end of each month, the optimal asset allocation is then derived as if the most recent estimates were the true parameters.

A major problem with this naïve approach is that ideally all the input parameters for mean-variance optimization should be forward-looking. In contrast to the analysis in Figure 7.1, at any point in time the investor does not have the entire sample-period information available to construct optimal portfolios. Instead, the investor possesses information about past returns only up to the actual portfolio formation date. Estimation error becomes a major concern. Given the highly volatile behavior of emerging stock market returns, the problem of estimation risk is particularly severe.

In a provocative paper, Jobson and Korkie (1981b) argue that mean variance optimizers are in fact estimation-error maximizers. Optimal portfolios tend to overweight (underweight) assets that have large (small) estimated returns, negative (positive) correlations, and small (large) variances. Intuitively, these securities should also be the ones most affected by estimation error. This defect of the traditional mean-variance analysis causes serious problems in the asset allocation process:

- *Deterioration of out-of-sample performance.* Optimal portfolios based on historical sample means usually exhibit considerable deterioration of performance measures outside the sample period used to calculate means. Sample means are efficient estimators only if expected returns and variances are constant through time. However, there is strong empirical evidence that both the expected returns and variances are time varying.
- *Highly unstable optimum weights.* Portfolio weights are extremely sensitive to variations in expected returns. Small changes in the input variables can cause dramatic changes in the optimal weights. Considering the high volatility on emerging stock markets, this problem may be particularly severe in our analysis.
- *Mismatched levels of information.* Optimizers generally do not differentiate between the levels of uncertainty associated with inputs parameters. To make the problem even worse, in many cases the differences in estimated means may not be statistically significant. This implies that every point on the efficient frontier has a neighborhood that includes an infinite number of statistically equivalent portfolios, but with completely different compositions.

To demonstrate the problem of unstable portfolio compositions, Figure 7.2 plots the time evolution of the portfolio weights for Switzerland, Germany, and Japan in the tangency portfolio. The portfolios are constructed from monthly stock returns of the seven developed

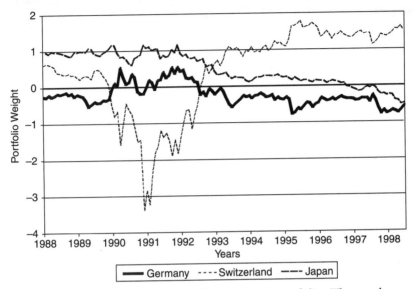

FIGURE 7.2 Evolution of weights in the tangency portfolio. The stock markets of the United States, Japan, the United Kingdom, Germany, France, Switzerland, and Canada are represented by the respective Morgan Stanley Capital International (MSCI) indices. Monthly returns over the period from 1988.01 to 1998.07 are calculated in Swiss francs. A moving window of 144 months is applied to estimate sample moments, which are then used to calculate the weights in the tangency portfolio. The figure shows the time evolution of the weights for Switzerland, Germany, and Japan.

markets in our sample. Sample moments are calculated using historical averages with moving windows that have 144 months of return data. With data starting in January 1976, the first portfolio is available in January 1988. The weights are extremely unstable. The optimal allocation is especially volatile for Swiss stocks and requires extreme long or short positions, depending on the time period. On the other hand, the weights for the German market fluctuate around zero in the early 1990s, and optimally would have been sold short since then.

One remedy would be to restrict short selling. Algorithms are available to account for all kinds of restrictions on the weights, but the calculations become tedious.[12] Another solution to alleviate extreme portfolio weights is to apply the so-called Stein-estimator, originally introduced by Jorion (1985, 1986). From a purely computational point of view, this approach is easier, and it has an appealing economic interpretation. Hence, the investor does not have to rely on complicated optimization techniques, which sometimes lead to non-intuitive results. Also, the allocation strategy just described is unconditional because of the way the investor chooses expected returns, variances, and covariances. Expected returns are the sample mean returns of the previous 144 monthly returns. Although the mean returns change through time as the moving window moves on, using average returns assumes that the best forecast of the equity return is its past average. This is consistent with a random walk model of stock prices with a constant drift. Although there is empirical evidence for modest predictability, the analysis in Table 7.4 shows that conditioning information can help, but is not necessary to realize the benefits of global diversification.[13] Instead of using conditioning information, our analysis accounts for estimation error in average returns. Shrinking expected return estimates toward a grand mean seems to be a worthwhile attempt to improve the efficiency of the traditional portfolio theory framework.

THE STEIN-ESTIMATOR

Jorion (1985, 1986) introduces a specific class of shrinkage estimators to portfolio theory. To get revised estimates for expected returns, the average return on every asset is shrunk toward a common mean. The ultimate goal is to reduce estimation risk associated with the sample mean. Denoting the expected return as $E(R)$, the general form of the Stein-estimator is:[14]

$$E(R) = (1 - \omega)Y + \omega \underline{1} Y_0 \qquad (7.3)$$

where ω is the shrinkage factor defined as $\omega = \lambda/(T + \lambda)$. Y is the vector of sample mean returns, defined as:

$$Y = \frac{1}{T}\sum_{t=1}^{T} y_t \qquad (7.4)$$

Y_0 denotes a grand mean.[15] This formula shrinks the country sample mean Y toward a grand mean Y_0. Intuitively, the efficiency gain of the estimator comes from the multivariate nature of portfolio choice. In a univariate setup, the sample mean is the optimal estimate. In contrast, shrinking implies that expected returns are estimated simultaneously for all countries. Therefore, the grand mean Y_0 must provide the missing link by pooling information over the entire set of returns.[16] λ is a precision parameter and can be estimated directly from the data. It is a function of the observed dispersion of sample averages around the grand mean Y_0, the number of assets N, and sample size T:

$$\lambda = \frac{(N+2)(T-1)}{(Y - Y_0 \underline{1})^T \Omega^{-1}(Y - Y_0 \underline{1})(T-N-2)} \qquad (7.5)$$

Ω denotes the variance-covariance matrix of returns. In this setup Jorion (1986) shows that Y_0 is the return on the minimum-variance portfolio. This implies that sample means are shrunk toward the return on the minimum-variance portfolio. The minimum-variance portfolio also suffers from estimation error. However, it is well known from portfolio theory that the optimal weights of the minimum-variance portfolio only depend on the sample covariance matrix. It is generally acknowledged that estimates of the covariance matrix are less affected by estimation error than expected returns. Therefore, estimation risk affects the minimum-variance portfolio the least among all portfolios on the efficient frontier.

The interpretation of the Stein-estimator is intuitive. As T becomes large, ω approaches zero, and $E(R)$ converges to Y. There is no estimation risk in this limiting case; the univariate sample mean is the most accurate estimate of expected returns. The precision factor λ indicates the degree of confidence an analyst puts in the estimates of sample means. For a very small λ (for high precision of the sample parameter estimates), ω tends to zero, and shrinkage becomes unnecessary as $E(R)$ reduces to Y. On the other hand, when the analyst puts very little confidence in the sample information (λ takes on a very large number), ω tends to one and $E(R)$ converges to Y_0.

Recall, traditional mean-variance optimizers overweight (underweight) securities that have large (small) estimated returns. Again, these securities should be the ones most affected by estimation error. The Stein-estimator tries to alleviate this problem. Expected returns of countries with extremely high or low sample mean returns are shrunk toward the (more realistic and more stable) average return of the minimum variance portfolio. Interestingly, shrinkage might be related to another puzzling observation in the empirical finance literature. Fama and French (1988) and Poterba and Summers (1988) find that stock returns are negatively correlated over holding periods of more than four quarters. International evidence is provided in Drobetz and Wegmann (1999). In another paper, Lakoniskok, Shleifer, and Vishny (1994) document that investors tend to extrapolate expected growth rates too long into the future and fail to account for mean-reversion in stock returns. Shrinking sample returns should avoid any misperception.[17]

To demonstrate the smoothing effect derived from shrinkage, Figure 7.3 shows the time evolution of the weights for Switzerland, Germany, and Japan in the minimum-variance portfolio. Comparison with the time variation of weights in the tangency portfolio in Figure 7.1 reveals striking differences. The composition of the minimum-variance portfolio remains remarkably stable over time, whereas the weights of the tangency portfolio fluctuate dramatically. A final observation is that the weights for all three markets no longer violate short-selling constraints.[18]

SIMULATING PORTFOLIO STRATEGIES WITH AND WITHOUT SHRINKAGE

Having set up the theoretical framework, we can apply the shrinkage estimator to return data from the seven developed and the seven

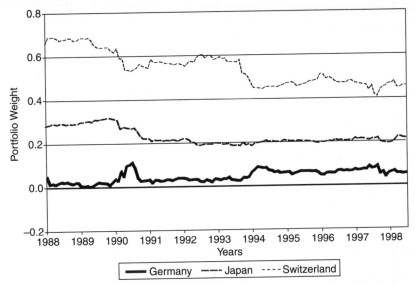

FIGURE 7.3   Evolution of weights in the minimum-variance portfolio. The stock markets of the United States, Japan, the United Kingdom, Germany, France, Switzerland, and Canada are represented by the respective Morgan Stanley Capital International (MSCI) indices. Monthly returns over the period from 1988.01 to 1998.07 are calculated in Swiss Francs. A moving window of 144 months is applied to estimate the sample covariance matrix, which is then used to calculate the weight of each country in the minimum-variance portfolio. The figure shows the time evolution of these weights for Switzerland, Germany, and Japan.

emerging stock markets. Investment weights are optimized at the end of each month, and the implied tangency portfolio is held for the next month. The sample has two subperiods of approximately equal length. A moving window of 144 months is used to estimate sample means and sample covariances. To calculate ex ante Sharpe ratios, these sample moments are then used to construct the classical tangency portfolio and the tangency portfolio based on the Stein-estimator. Knowing the actual returns in the following month, ex ante Sharpe ratios can be compared with their ex post values. Sharpe ratios are computed for a zero risk-free rate. The portfolio weights are reoptimized on the basis of the last rolling 144 months. The first portfolio return is available at the end of January 1989.

Jobson and Korkie (1981a) developed a test statistic for the difference in portfolio performance on the basis of Sharpe ratios. With their methodology, we test the hypothesis that ex post Sharpe ratios are equal in both strategies. Their test statistic is normally distributed and defined as follows:

$$z = \frac{s_n R_i - s_i R_n}{\sqrt{\dfrac{2\left(s_i^2 s_n^2 - s_i s_n s_{in}\right)}{T}}} \tag{7.6}$$

where R_i (R_n) and s_i (s_n) are the sample means and variances of two portfolios i and n, respectively. s_{in} denotes the sample covariance. This simple test allows us to determine whether shrinkage toward the minimum-variance portfolio helps to reduce estimation error and improve out-of-sample performance compared with the naïve strategy. Three cases have to be considered: simultaneous investment in MSCI and IFC markets, investment in MSCI markets, and investment in IFC markets.

Simultaneous Investment in MSCI and IFC Markets

Panel A of Table 7.5 shows the results for an asset allocation strategy that assumes an investor takes positions in both MSCI and IFC markets. Means and standard deviations are in percentages per month. On an ex ante basis, the classical tangency portfolio seems to be an excellent investment, as measured by a Sharpe ratio of 1.664. The classical strategy promises a return above 5 percent per month, with a standard deviation of 3.2 percent per month. However, this strategy is heavily tilted toward countries with high past returns. Therefore, the Stein-estimator shrinks the mean returns toward the return of the minimum-variance portfolio. The average shrinkage factor ω is 0.67, and the ex ante Sharpe ratio drops from 1.66 to (still impressive) 1.14. The most interesting point is the dramatic difference

TABLE 7.5 Performance of Portfolio Strategies for MSCI and IFC Stock Markets

	Mean (% Monthly)	SD (% Monthly)	Sharpe Ratio
Panel A: Investment in MSCI and IFC Stock Markets			
Classical Tangency Portfolio			
Ex ante	5.293	3.178	1.664
Ex post	0.907	9.205	0.096
Tangency Portfolio Based on Stein-Estimator for Expected Returns			
Ex ante	2.464	2.163	1.139
Ex post	1.219	5.428	0.225
p-Value (Jobson-Korkie test)			0.003**
Panel B: Investment in MSCI Stock Markets			
Classical Tangency Portfolio			
Ex ante	5.112	6.165	0.829
Ex post	1.789	9.272	0.193
Tangency Portfolio Based on Stein-Estimator for Expected Returns			
Ex ante	1.305	3.460	0.377
Ex post	1.415	5.434	0.260
p-Value (Jobson-Korkie test)			0.125
Panel C: Investment in IFC Stock Markets			
Classical Tangency Portfolio			
Ex ante	2.357	1.482	1.501
Ex post	0.712	14.488	0.049
Tangency Portfolio Based on Stein-Estimator for Expected Returns			
Ex ante	3.079	4.180	0.736
Ex post	2.023	9.100	0.222
p-Value (Jobson-Korkie test)			0.051*

Note: The table shows the summary statistics for two different portfolio strategies. The MSCI indices for the United States, Japan, the United Kingdom, Germany, France, Switzerland, as well as the IFC indices for Argentina, Brazil, Chile, Mexico, Korea, Thailand, and India are used to construct both the classical tangency portfolio and the tangency portfolio based on the Stein-estimator for expected returns. Returns are available over the period from 1976.01 to 1998.07. Portfolios are constructed at the end of each month, using sample moments computed on the basis of 144 months long moving windows. Means, standard deviations, and Sharpe-ratios are reported on an ex ante and an ex post basis. Sharpe-ratios are for a zero risk-free rate. The *p*-values measure the marginal significance of a Jobson-Korkie test statistic for equivalence of the ex post Sharpe-ratios.

*Denotes statistical significance at the 10 percent level.
**Denotes statistical significance at the 1 percent level.

between ex ante and ex post performance of global portfolios. Ex post, the Sharpe ratio for the classical tangency portfolio drops from 1.664 to only 0.096. Historical sample averages exhibit extremely poor forecasting ability. The Sharpe ratio of the tangency portfolio based on the Stein-estimator also drops from 1.14 to 0.23, but the difference is less pronounced. The p-values in Table 7.6 refer to the marginal significance level of a Jobson-Korkie (1981a) test statistic for the equivalence of ex post Sharpe ratios. The ex post performance measures are significantly different from each other at the 1 percent level of significance. This indicates that shrinkage leads to statistically improved results for an investor who invests globally.

Investment in MSCI Markets

In searching for an explanation for the dramatic deviations of ex post from ex ante performance, it is natural to examine the results for allocation strategies that look separately at developed and emerging stock markets. Panel B in Table 7.5 reports the results for a strategy with investments in the seven MSCI markets. Ex post, a portfolio that consists only of MSCI markets outperforms a portfolio of both MSCI and IFC markets under both optimization techniques. The average shrinkage factor ω is 0.66, which is almost identical to the shrinkage in the combined strategy. Again, ex post Sharpe ratios drop drastically. This time, however, they are not significantly different from each other. The p-value of 0.125 in Panel B indicates that an ex post Sharpe ratio of 0.193 for the naïve strategy is statistically indistinguishable from an ex post Sharpe ratio of 0.260 for the shrinkage strategy. This result is in contrast to the findings by Jorion (1985, 1991), who reports that shrinkage significantly affected portfolio choice among MSCI markets during an earlier sample period.

Investment in IFC Markets

The results so far show that the behavior of developed stock market returns does not account for the huge difference between ex ante and ex post Sharpe ratios in Panel A of Table 7.5. Therefore, we finally examine an allocation strategy that restricts investments to the seven emerging stock markets. Panel C of Table 7.5 shows the results. As could be expected, the difference in ex post performance is dramatic. The ex post Sharpe ratio for the tangency portfolio based on the Stein-estimator is 4.5 times larger than the corresponding Sharpe ratio for the classical portfolio. The difference is at the margin of being significant at the 5 percent level, as indicated by the p-value of the Jobson-Korkie test statistic. Thus, unlike for MSCI markets, shrinkage is very important for the asset allocation process in emerging stock markets. Accordingly, the average shrinkage factor ω increases to almost 0.8. We conclude that the results in Panel A of Table 7.5 are driven by the excessive volatility of IFC returns. Emerging stock markets are attractive ex ante, but they are responsible for any poor ex post portfolio performance. Shrinkage seems to be a useful and easy way to improve portfolio optimization with emerging stock market data. Even then, however, the ex post volatility of the tangency portfolio is 9 percent per month, which is hardly optimal.

CONCLUSION

Emerging stock markets are playing an increasingly important role in international asset allocation. The findings in this chapter suggest, however, that these markets cannot be treated like developed stock markets. Higher returns are coupled with higher volatility. In addition, emerging stock markets exhibit substantial deviations from normality. Traditional portfolio theory is unable to account for these distributional characteristics, and estimation error turns out to be a major issue in asset allocation for emerging stock markets.

A spanning test provides evidence that emerging markets constitute a stand-alone asset class with distinctive risk-return characteristics, but the behavior of emerging stock returns makes it difficult to realize these diversification benefits. The Stein-estimator, introduced by Jorion (1985, 1986) into the finance literature, is a simple remedy that alleviates estimation errors. It exploits the multivariate nature of the portfolio problem and shrinks sample means toward the mean return of the minimum-variance portfolio. Evidence from simulating a realistic portfolio strategy indicates that shrinkage improves the ex post performance of emerging stock market investments, but it is not useful when applied to developed stock markets.

The most important implication is that emerging stock markets are very attractive on the basis of ex ante Sharpe ratios. However, they are highly responsible for any poor ex post performance. This does not imply that emerging markets cannot help to diversify risk in global portfolio of stocks. Nevertheless, investors must keep in mind that emerging markets investments are inherently risky. At the end, free lunches are rare.

CHAPTER 8

The Structure of Sector and Market Returns

Implications for International Diversification

EXECUTIVE SUMMARY

- Should asset allocation strategies or financial analysis be based on countries or sectors? Many banks have adjusted their research departments as well as their benchmarks in asset management toward a global sector approach.
- Whether this is a more successful strategy than the traditional country-based investment approach depends on several factors. From a finance perspective, the correlation structure of the securities within the countries and sectors is typically most relevant when considering this question.
- In this chapter, we show that the correlation structure is an insufficient statistic to resolve this problem. The range of expected returns may be extremely different among countries and sectors; hence the structure of expected returns may be a better tool for answering the question.
- Economically, it is necessary to look at whether sector portfolios exhibit good diversification properties across countries, compared with the sector-diversification features of country portfolios.
- Empirical investigations of country and sector returns reveal that in the past sector diversification has produced slightly more efficient portfolios than country diversification.

- The country-diversification advantage of sector portfolios is particularly important if stock market downturns are country-specific, as in the 1980s and 1990s.

INTRODUCTION

Whether investors should diversify their international portfolios across countries or (global) sectors has long been debated in the academic literature and among investment professionals. With the emergence of the Euro as the single European currency, sector diversification has gained more practical significance. Many banks are now adjusting their financial analysis and research departments as well as their benchmarks in asset management toward a global sector approach. Whether this is a more successful strategy than the traditional country-based investment approach depends on several factors. From a finance perspective, the correlation structure of securities within countries and sectors is the key to answering this question.

The analysis of the correlation structure of international equity returns presents a puzzling picture. A common observation of several empirical studies—on different markets, sectors, and time periods—is that the correlation between individual stocks is stronger within countries than within (national or international) sectors.[1] For factor models, this implies that country factors are stronger than sector factors. This is unexpected in a global economy, where the sector characteristics seemingly should dominate the national characteristics of firms. There are, however, several possible explanations for this observation:

- During the time periods that have been analyzed in previous studies, most of the stocks (even international stocks) were traded only on their respective national exchanges.
- Corporate laws and many of the accounting principles for earnings disclosure and firm valuation were still national.
- Financial analysts, investment specialists, and trading departments of major banks and brokers have followed a country approach.

- Investment strategies, particularly benchmarks for institutional investors, were mostly defined in terms of country and currency weights.
- Sector-based mutual funds and derivative instruments, with few exceptions, have been virtually nonexistent.
- Finally, the country approach was facilitated by the diversity of currencies across countries.

Therefore, the strong country factor inherent in international stock returns primarily reflects how the investment community perceives the structure of the global stock market. However, this correlation pattern is likely to change in the next few years. In addition to the ongoing globalization process of the economy many historical structural characteristics will become less important. There is now a common currency across European stock markets, international accounting standards are adopted by most traded firms, global stock exchanges and trading platforms operate since several years, and sector-based mutual funds have attracted substantial interest within the investment community. Moreover, as mentioned, many of the financial analysis departments of banks and brokers now follow a sector approach.

This chapter addresses three basic issues on international diversification related to the country and sector approaches:

1. What determines whether a country or sector approach should be implemented for portfolio diversification? In general, the correlation structure does not provide sufficient information to answer this question. The issue is addressed both conceptionally (using simple numerical examples) and empirically (based on historical data).
2. Restricting our focus to volatility (abstracting from expected returns), we consider whether sector- or country-based portfolios are more robust during stock market turmoils.
3. In a mean-variance setting, we investigate whether a sector, country, or combined (two-dimensional) diversification approach

would have resulted in more efficient portfolios in the past, and whether the aggregation level of sectors or regions affects mean-variance efficiency.

This chapter also provides a detailed description of the Data-stream/Primark country and sector indices used throughout the empirical part of this chapter. A key advantage of this index family is that the same stock universe underlies the country and sector indices. Moreover, the indices are available on various aggregation levels: countries and global regions, sectors and subsectors (both global and country-wise). This represents a unique data set to investigate portfolio diversification topics.

THE SETUP OF THE PROBLEM: TWO NUMERICAL EXAMPLES

This section looks at whether it is relevant to diversify investments across sectors or countries if the underlying indices (or portfolios) cover the same stock universe. A fundamental separation theorem is related to efficient portfolios: Starting from the same universe of assets, the risk-return menu should be identical no matter whether investors invest in the individual assets or funds (portfolios) of them. However, this is true only if the funds themselves lie on the efficient frontier, which cannot be assumed for individual country or sector indices. Therefore, a crucial aspect is how assets are packed into indices.

The basic problem can be illustrated by a simple numerical example. Consider four stocks A, B, C, and D. Stocks A and B belong to the same country p, whereas stocks C and D are from country q. Moreover, stocks A and C belong to the same industrial sector x, and stocks B and D are from sector y. Table 8.1A provides illustrative statistics.

In the first example, we arbitrarily assume that correlations are stronger within countries than within sectors, which was empirically observable in the past. The two stocks of country p (country q)

TABLE 8.1A   Numerical Example I

	Classification		Capitalization			Expected		Correlation		
				Relative to		Return	Volatility			
	Country	Sector	Absolute in USD	Country (%)	Sector (%)	(%)	(%)	A	B	C
Stocks										
A	*p*	*x*	10	40.0	33.3	13.0	24.0	A 1		
B	*p*	*y*	15	60.0	75.0	20.0	32.0	B 0.8	1	
C	*q*	*x*	20	80.0	66.7	5.0	14.0	C 0.3	0.2	1
D	*q*	*y*	5	20.0	25.0	18.0	30.0	D 0.1	0.2	0.7
Countries								A+B	C+D	
A+B	*p*		25	50.0		17.2	27.5	A+B 1		
C+D	*q*		25	50.0		7.6	16.0	C+D 0.2	1	
Sectors								A+C	B+D	
A+C		*x*	30		60.0	7.7	14.0	A+C 1		
B+D		*y*	20		40.0	19.5	26.5	B+D 0.7	1	

exhibit a correlation of 0.8 (0.7), whereas the two stocks of sector x (sector y) exhibit a correlation of 0.3 (0.2) (see the bold numbers in Table 8.1A). Based on this assumption, country portfolios should be more efficient than sector portfolios. Our example, however, is constructed in such a way that this conclusion is wrong (see Figure 8.1).

To illustrate this effect, two capitalization-weighted country indices (p and q) and two sector indices (x and y) are constructed from

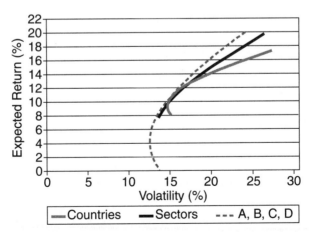

FIGURE 8.1   Efficient frontiers: Numerical example I.

the four assets. Table 8.1A also displays the statistical properties of these indices. It is apparent that the correlation between the two country indices is much smaller than the correlation between the two sector indices (0.2 vs. 0.7), which simply reflects our assumption of a strong country factor (and weak sector factor) in stock returns. Therefore, the benefits of diversification are more pronounced if portfolios are diversified across the two country indices.

Figure 8.1 shows that this suspicion is true: The risk reduction (reflected by the curvature of the efficient frontier) from country diversification is larger than from sector diversification. Generally, however, the sector portfolios exhibit more favorable risk-return characteristics. Comparing the two efficient frontiers for sectors and countries, country portfolios are more efficient than sector portfolios in only a small range of expected portfolio returns (9.7% to 12.4%). For both low- and high-risk strategies, however, country portfolios are inefficient. The dashed line in Figure 8.1 depicts the efficient frontier of all four stocks (A, B, C, and D), which is naturally more efficient than the frontiers for both the aggregated country and sector indices.

The predominance of the sector approach for most of the risk-return spectrum in Figure 8.1 shows that the correlation structure of country and sector indices (in Table 8.1A) is an incomplete guide to efficient diversification. Of course, expected returns and volatility for countries and sectors must also be taken into account. In our example, sector diversification is inferior to country diversification in terms of correlation (0.7 vs. 0.2), but superior in terms of expected return and volatility. The strong country factor has a side effect: It reduces correlation between country indices, but it also increases their volatility. Similarly, it raises the correlation of sector indices, but lowers their volatility. Consequently, sector indices exhibit a lower volatility than country indices in our example (14.0% and 26.5% vs. 16.0% and 27.5%). Moreover, the example is set up so that sector indices also exhibit higher expected returns, on average (7.7% and 19.5% vs. 7.6% and 17.2%). This effect stems from the different (market-capitalization) weights of the stocks in the underlying sector and country indices. Compared with the other stocks, stock C promises a very low return (5%; it also exhibits a slightly lower volatility and a moderate correlation). This stock is in sector x and in country

q, whereby its weight in country index q is relatively higher (80.01%) compared with its weight in sector index x (66.5%). In this respect, a diversification strategy across sectors is more suitable to avoid a high exposure in unattractive stock C.

Table 8.1B shows the characteristics of the 9.0 percent return level and the 25.0 percent volatility portfolios along the sector and country efficient frontiers. The first two columns show expected returns and volatility; the third and fourth column show the associated portfolio weights of a strategy. These weights can be translated into the implied portfolio weightings of the individual assets (A, B, C, and D). Alternatively, the country portfolios can be translated into implied sector portfolios, and vice versa (see columns 5 and 6). The entries in Table 8.1B confirm the graphical intuition from Figure 8.1. At the 9.0 percent return level, the sector portfolios exhibit a smaller volatility (14.6%) than country portfolios (15.1%). More important, the two approaches result in different portfolio compositions. To achieve a return of 9.0 percent, one must take a 14.6 percent position in country p (85.4% in country q) under the country approach. This implies sector weightings of 74.2 percent for unattractive sector x, and 25.8 percent for sector y. Following a sector approach, the 9.0 percent return portfolio exhibits a different structure—an 88.7 percent weighting of sector x (compared with 74.2%) and a 11.3 percent weighting of sector y (compared with

TABLE 8.1B Numerical Example I: Country and Sector Portfolios

Expected Return	Volatility	Portfolio Weights Countries		Implicit Portfolio Weights Sectors		Stocks			
		p	q	x	y	A	B	C	D
			Country Portfolio						
9.0	15.1	14.6	85.4	74.2	25.8	5.8	8.8	68.3	17.1
16.2	25.0	89.3	10.7	44.3	55.7	35.7	53.6	8.6	2.2

Expected	Volatility	Sectors		Implicit Portfolio Weights Countries		Stocks			
				Sector Portfolio					
9.0	14.6	88.7	11.3	38.0	62.0	29.6	8.5	59.1	2.8
18.4	25.0	9.2	90.8	71.2	28.8	3.1	68.1	6.1	22.7

25.8%). The effect is even more transparent when comparing two strategies that yield the same volatility of, say, 25.0 percent. Table 8.1B shows that this requires a 89.3 percent position in country p (and 10.7% country q), which corresponds to an implicit sector x weighting of 44.3 percent (and 55.7% in sector y). However, diversification across the two sectors requires a small holding of only 9.2 percent in unattractive sector x, compared with 44.3 percent.

Furthermore, Table 8.1C illustrates that the portfolio composition even differs at the intersection points of the two efficient frontiers (where country and sector diversification yield the same risk and return). Figure 8.1 shows two intersection points: one at 9.7 percent expected return and the other at 12.4 percent expected return. Table 8.1C gives a breakdown of the implicit country, sector, and stock weightings of the two intersection portfolios.

With a return of 12.4 percent, the country and sector strategies result in exactly the same portfolios: 50 percent is invested in each country p and q, or 60 percent in sector x and 40 percent in sector y, respectively. The two other intersection portfolios with a return of 9.7 percent differ in their composition. In this case, the implied weighting of country p (q) in the sector portfolio is 40.6 percent (59.4%), whereas the respective weight in the country portfolio is 22.2 percent (77.8%). In the underlying assets, for example, stock A receives a

TABLE 8.1C Numerical Example I: Intersecting Portfolios

Expected Return	Volatility	Portfolio Weights Countries		Implicit Portfolio Weights Sectors		Stocks			
		p	q	x	y	A	B	C	D
				Country Portfolio					
9.7	15.1	22.2	77.8	71.1	28.9	8.9	13.3	62.2	15.6
12.4	17.5	50.0	50.0	60.0	40.0	20.0	30.0	40.0	10.0

Expected Return	Volatility	Sectors		Implicit Portfolio Weights Countries		Stocks			
				Sector Portfolio					
9.7	15.1	82.6	17.4	40.6	59.4	27.5	13.1	55.1	4.4
12.4	17.5	60.0	40.0	50.0	50.0	20.0	30.0	40.0	10.0

TABLE 8.2 Numerical Example II

	Classification		Absolute in USD	Capitalization Relative to Country (%)	Relative to Sector (%)	Expected Return (%)	Volatility (%)	Correlation	A	B	C
	Country	Sector									
Stocks											
A	*p*	*x*	10	40.0	33.3	13.0	24.0	A	1		
B	*p*	*y*	15	60.0	75.0	20.0	32.0	B	0.3	1	
C	*q*	*x*	20	80.0	66.7	5.0	14.0	C	0.8	0.2	1
D	*q*	*y*	5	20.0	25.0	18.0	30.0	D	0.1	0.7	0.2
Countries									A+B	C+D	
A+B	*p*		25	50.0		17.2	23.9	A+B	1		
C+D	*q*		25	50.0		7.6	13.7	C+D	0.7	1	
Sectors									A+C	B+D	
A+C		*x*	30		60.0	7.7	16.4	A+C	1		
B+D		*y*	12		40.0	19.5	29.7	B+D	0.3	1	

weight of 8.9 percent under the country approach and 27.5 percent under the sector approach. This illustrates that the two diversification strategies fundamentally differ in their underlying weightings of sectors, countries, and individual stocks.

Does reversing the correlation structure affect diversification? Table 8.2 shows a different set of assumptions, and Figure 8.2 shows the resulting portfolio frontiers. The two stocks within country *p*

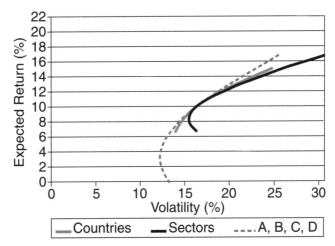

FIGURE 8.2 Efficient frontiers: Numerical example II.

(country q) now exhibit a correlation of 0.3 (0.2), whereas the two stocks within sector x (sector y) exhibit a correlation of 0.8 (0.7). This may be the setup in a world where countries have become less important for global asset allocation. The correlation between the two country indices is now 0.7, whereas the correlation between the sectors has dropped to 0.3. In this case, the diversification potential of the sector approach seems superior. However, the efficient frontiers in Figure 8.2 reveal that this intuition is misleading. Except for the high risk, high-return scenario, country portfolios are more efficient. On average, the sector indices still have a higher return. But now they have a lower correlation and an increased volatility (from 14.0% to 16.4% for sector x and from 26.5% to 29.7% for sector y).

This numerical exercise has the following implications:

■ Diversification along asset classes instead of single assets inevitably leads to a loss of efficiency because the asset structure within asset classes remains fixed and cannot be optimized (see the solid and the dashed lines of Figures 8.1 and 8.2).

■ It matters how assets are grouped into asset classes. Country and sector diversification not only can lead to different risk and return tradeoffs, they also fundamentally differ with respect to the underlying weightings of sectors, countries, and individual stocks (see the intersection portfolios in Table 8.1B).

■ The correlation structure of asset classes is an incomplete guide to efficient diversification. Our first numerical example shows that sector portfolios can be more efficient than country portfolios even if there is a strong country factor and a weak sector factor (a low correlation among countries and a high correlation among sectors).

STRUCTURE OF THE INDICES

Characteristics of the Datastream Index Family

Using stock market indices for the analysis of international portfolio decisions is only a natural procedure. Assuming that approximately

5,000 liquid stocks are traded on the major international stock markets, tremendous quantities of data are necessary to compute efficient portfolio frontiers. It would require information on approximately 25 million pairwise correlation coefficients, which is hardly feasible.

The stock indices used in this study are those of the Datastream/Primark index family. A major advantage of these indices is that they represent a closed asset universe of approximately 5,500 stocks. *Closed* means that the 41 country indices cover exactly the same stocks as the 38 sector indices. This important property makes it possible to get an unbiased comparison between sector- and country-based diversification strategies.

Table 8.3 gives a brief characterization of the Datastream index family. The universe is split into 10 industrial sectors and 38 subsectors, as well as 4 geographic regions and 41 countries. In the most detailed case, the index family provides information about 990 subsectors in 41 countries. However, to keep things as simple as possible, the most detailed country-sector breakdowns we use are the 10 sectors in the 4 geographic regions (40 two-dimensional country/sector indices).

Statistical Properties of the Index Returns

Our empirical study is based on time series of continuously compounded index returns in U.S. dollars from May 1991 to April 2001. This 10-year period covers major ups and downs in the major stock markets, although the overall trend was a bull market. The average annual return on the world market index was 8.8 percent over the

TABLE 8.3 Structure of the Datastream Index Family, April 2001

Number of Indices within the Various Categories			
	World	Regions (4)	Countries (41)
Total market	1	4*	41
10 sectors	10	40	377
38 subsectors	38	152	990

* Excluding India and South Africa.

TABLE 8.4A   Descriptive Statistics of the Datastream Country Indices

Regions Countries	Number of Observations	Number of Assets	Market Capitalization as of 2001.04 (in million USD)	World Market Share as of 2001.04 (%)	Average Annual Return (%)	Average Annual Volatility (%)	Jarque-Bera Test Statistic
United Kingdom	120	546	2,225,079	8.97	10.57	14.77	0.4
Europe excluding U.K.				21.06			
Austria	120	50	23,556	0.09	−1.65	16.86	13.2
Belgium	120	89	152,593	0.62	8.65	14.83	42.4
Denmark	120	48	89,588	0.36	10.13	16.61	6.3
Finland	120	50	168,809	0.68	19.01	32.47	11.0
France	120	200	1,137,021	4.58	12.25	17.49	0.1
Germany	120	200	899,408	3.63	8.97	15.80	9.0
Greece	120	49	62,042	0.25	7.00	30.61	4.5
Ireland	120	50	69,547	0.28	13.33	18.03	36.1
Italy	120	156	620,838	2.50	6.87	24.72	1.1
Luxembourg	110	35	22,850	0.09	13.20	18.71	47.0
Netherlands	120	130	573,263	2.31	14.21	15.21	5.5
Norway	120	48	55,761	0.22	6.82	24.81	82.0
Poland	85	50	24,264	0.10	−10.89	47.81	5.5
Portugal	120	50	59,208	0.24	7.98	21.06	25.9
Spain	120	120	362,628	1.46	9.21	21.42	9.4
Sweden	120	69	217,272	0.88	10.26	24.99	4.4
Switzerland	120	149	651,822	2.63	14.35	16.68	30.6
Turkey	120	50	32,029	0.13	3.89	65.18	6.0
Pacific				17.84			
Australia	120	158	315,194	1.27	8.37	18.74	0.7
China	82	100	170,099	0.69	23.03	40.70	307.1
Hong Kong	120	130	495,576	2.00	14.66	29.88	6.4
Indonesia	120	100	17,616	0.07	3.18	39.92	20.0
Japan	120	997	2,794,068	11.27	−1.10	23.68	6.4
Korea	120	99	129,464	0.52	−1.50	43.76	31.5
Malaysia	120	90	81,249	0.33	1.64	39.32	36.9
New Zealand	120	51	17,466	0.07	7.96	21.68	1.4
Philippines	120	50	21,388	0.09	2.23	34.71	40.0
Singapore	120	100	110,978	0.45	2.40	24.54	31.2
Taiwan	120	70	243,850	0.98	4.02	35.57	29.5
Thailand	120	50	24,231	0.10	−6.34	44.07	21.0
Americas				51.36			
Argentine	92	50	34,461	0.14	6.46	31.85	2.2
Brazil	80	100	176,975	0.71	2.41	39.43	4.0
Canada	120	245	552,167	2.23	10.14	17.73	65.0
Chile	120	50	43,590	0.18	10.13	24.55	1.8
Colombia	108	50	4,214	0.02	−6.56	28.51	2.9
Mexico	120	89	120,892	0.49	10.19	36.53	61.1
Peru	87	50	5,316	0.02	1.88	27.63	74.4
United States	120	994	11,797,544	47.57	13.95	13.63	12.4
India	120	50	93,172	0.38	−16.47	46.90	30.8
South Africa	120	69	102,308	0.41	3.92	27.43	239.6
Total market	120	5881	24,808,415	100.00	8.85	13.61	6.09

Note: All numbers are based on continuously compounded monthly returns in U.S. dollars. The sample covers the period from 1991.05 to 2001.04.

entire time period, and the annual volatility was 13.6 percent. Mean returns as well as the volatility differ substantially across countries, as shown in Table 8.4A. Several countries even exhibit negative average returns over the sample period (Japan, Korea, Austria, Poland, Thailand, Colombia, and India), and about one third of the countries exhibit two digit returns. The volatility of returns in less developed stock markets is generally higher than in developed stock markets: China (40.7%), Thailand (44.7%), Indonesia (39.2%), Poland (47.8%), Turkey (65.2%), to mention a few.

In comparing the country statistics with those for the sectors in Table 8.4B, it is immediately apparent that the mean returns and volatility are much more uniform across sectors. The least performing sectors are construction (−0.1%), steel (−2.5%), and distributors (−2.8%), but the average returns are substantially less negative than those of the worst performing countries. The same observation applies to the volatility. Although there are more volatile sectors (e.g., information technology hardware, software and computer services, mining, and specialty and other finance), they are substantially less risky than the most volatile countries.

Figure 8.3 displays the risk-return characteristics of the 38 subsectors and the 41 countries in a return-volatility diagram. Throughout the study, the risk of an investment is measured by its (annualized) volatility. We perform tests for the distributional characteristics of returns and reject normality for 28 countries and 24 subsectors (at a 95% confidence level), based on the Jarque-Bera test statistic.[2] Nevertheless, we use mean-variance analysis throughout this chapter, despite the well-known problems in the standard portfolio optimization model for coping with non-normal distributions. The analysis in Figure 8.3 already allows drawing some preliminary conclusions. First, sectors are much better diversified (across countries) than countries (across sectors). Second, we confirm the finding in other studies that the correlations between stocks within sectors are lower (and hence, the diversification potential is larger) than the correlations between stocks within countries.

The specification of sectors and subsectors is not without problems. Intuitively, the definition of sectors is more arbitrary than the

TABLE 8.4B Descriptive Statistics of the Datastream Sector Indices

Sectors Subsectors	Number of Observations	Number of Assets	Market Capitalization as of 2001.04 (in million USD)	World Market Share as of 2001.04 (%)	Average Annual Return (%)	Average Annual Volatility (%)	Jarque-Bera Test Statistic
Resources				6.53			
Mining	120	n/a	160,317	0.65	4.25	24.22	10.4
Oil and gas	120	n/a	1,459,414	5.88	10.78	15.60	5.5
Basic Industries				4.19			
Chemicals	120	n/a	434,345	1.75	6.89	14.28	2.5
Construction and building material	120	n/a	304,611	1.23	−0.14	15.58	7.8
Forestry and paper	120	n/a	122,726	0.49	2.95	18.13	12.6
Steel and other metals	120	n/a	176,488	0.71	−2.55	19.44	3.4
General Industries				8.67			
Aerospace and defense	120	n/a	264,017	1.06	12.60	16.50	24.8
Diversified industrials	120	n/a	852,620	3.44	8.23	15.14	12.8
Electronic and electronic equipment	120	n/a	705,185	2.84	11.86	18.55	8.8
Engineering and machinery	120	n/a	327,196	1.32	2.50	17.00	3.2
Cyclical Consumer Goods				3.49			
Automobiles and parts	120	n/a	572,152	2.31	7.23	16.19	1.8
Household goods and textiles	120	n/a	293,037	1.18	4.04	17.05	6.9
Noncyclical Consumer Goods				15.38			
Beverages	120	n/a	405,171	1.63	9.84	15.48	65.3
Food producers and processors	120	n/a	459,417	1.85	7.40	12.14	5.0
Health	120	n/a	442,022	1.78	12.36	15.29	33.6
Packaging	120	n/a	31,031	0.13	4.80	16.60	50.8
Personal care and household products	120	n/a	325,984	1.31	12.26	15.55	85.3
Pharmaceuticals	120	n/a	1,976,097	7.97	14.74	14.84	0.1
Tobacco	120	n/a	175,231	0.71	10.02	20.44	14.6
Cyclical Services				12.15			
Distributors	120	n/a	110,795	0.45	−2.82	20.16	2.6
Retailers, general	120	n/a	839,195	3.38	10.23	16.07	3.7
Leisure, entertainment and hotels	120	n/a	625,943	2.52	7.73	15.25	18.5
Media and photography	120	n/a	791,289	3.19	12.20	15.34	8.6
Support services	120	n/a	236,119	0.95	9.21	14.02	4.7
Transport	120	n/a	410,064	1.65	2.55	14.07	9.3
Noncyclical Services				10.51			
Food and drug retailers	120	n/a	354,298	1.43	10.62	12.01	8.3
Telecom services	120	n/a	2,251,184	9.08	10.09	18.45	7.6
Utilities				4.07			
Electricity	120	n/a	732,657	2.95	7.86	9.51	0.5
Gas distribution	120	n/a	233,735	0.94	10.59	14.44	5.4
Water	120	n/a	42,672	0.17	11.24	19.18	22.2

TABLE 8.4B *(Continued)*

Sectors	Number of Observations	Number of Assets	Market Capitalization as of 2001.04 (in million USD)	World Market Share as of 2001.04 (%)	Average Annual Return (%)	Average Annual Volatility (%)	Jarque-Bera Test Statistic
Financials				22.54			
Banks	120	n/a	2,806,316	11.32	7.47	17.71	46.4
Insurance	120	n/a	1,011,745	4.08	11.95	15.27	44.4
Investment companies	120	n/a	210,951	0.85	9.11	13.94	30.6
Life assurance	120	n/a	341,857	1.38	13.58	14.73	2.0
Real estate	120	n/a	292,698	1.18	5.49	18.72	4.7
Specialty and other finance	120	n/a	926,422	3.74	7.95	21.85	7.3
Information Technology				12.51			
Information technology hardware	120	n/a	2,080,645	8.39	15.00	28.17	54.8
Software and computer services	120	n/a	1,022,770	4.12	20.37	27.43	9.8
Total Market	120	5,881	24,799,396	100.00	8.85	13.61	6.09

Note: All numbers are based on monthly returns in U.S. dollars. The sample covers the period from 1991.05 to 2001.04.

definition of countries. The more global that industries become, the more difficult it is to assign stocks to specific sectors and subsectors. The problem is more pronounced with a highly detailed sector structure. In addition, the industry structure has undergone substantial changes over the past decade (e.g., the relative market capitalizations

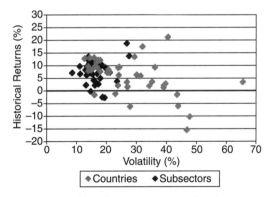

FIGURE 8.3 Risk-return profiles for countries and subsectors. Based on continuously compounded monthly returns in U.S. dollars over the period from 1991.05 to 2001.04.

of microelectronics, healthcare, financial services, and telecommunication have grown steadily). These changes resulted in an index reclassification of some major index providers. The sector indices in our empirical illustration were reclassified in April 1999 (along with the reclassification of the *Financial Times* sector indices).

The Temporal Behavior of Index Volatility and Correlations

It is well known from the empirical literature that correlations and volatility of financial assets are time varying (Chapter 4 discusses this observation in detail). We are not interested in the time-series characteristics of these temporal patterns. The purpose of this section is to compare the structural characteristics of the volatility and correlations between countries and sectors. For this purpose, we compute the sample volatility for and correlations between the 38 subsector and 41 country return series over a moving 12-month time window from January 1986 to April 2001. This results in 38 volatility and 703 correlation series for the subsectors, and 41 volatility and 820 correlation series for the countries (with 184 monthly observations each). At each point in time, we compute simple (unweighted) arithmetic means representing the average temporal behavior of correlations among countries and subsectors (Figure 8.4) and volatility of countries and subsectors (Figure 8.5). The number of underlying stocks varies during the sample period; the number of country indices was 19 at the beginning of the sample period and gradually increased over time. In contrast, the number of subsector indices was constant over the entire sample period.[3]

Figure 8.4 shows that, except during a short period in the second half of 2000, the average correlation between the subsectors has been substantially higher than the correlation between the countries. This confirms our preliminary conclusion in the previous section. The correlation between the sector indices is higher because the correlation between individual stocks within the sectors is lower. Conversely, the correlation between the country indices is lower because the individual stocks within the countries are more highly correlated.

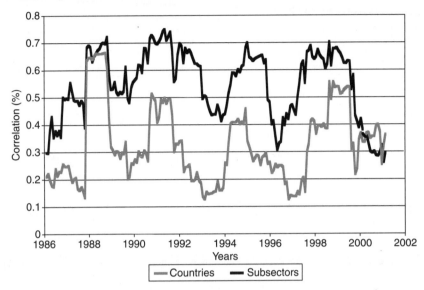

FIGURE 8.4 Temporal behavior of average correlations among 38 subsectors and among 41 countries. Based on continuously compounded monthly returns in U.S. dollars over the period from 1986.01 to 2001.04; 12-month moving time window.

Therefore, the conclusion from older studies, which find country factors to be more important than industry factors in stock returns, still seems to be valid.

    In 2000, however, a reversal of this pattern seemed to occur. The correlations of sectors dropped below those of countries over the second half of 2000. This picture might reflect the growing importance of a sector factor. Possibly, investors have started classifying stocks in terms of their sector characteristics (e.g., into old- and new-economy stocks). Alternatively, the globalization of the industrial structure, the Euro, and the internationalization of shareholdership may be exerting a greater effect on security returns.

    Figure 8.5 displays the temporal behavior of volatility confirming the overall picture from the previous analysis. Country indices exhibit a substantially larger volatility than sector indices, particularly in turbulent times such as the global stock market crash in 1987, the emerging market crisis in July 1997, or the Russian crisis in the fall

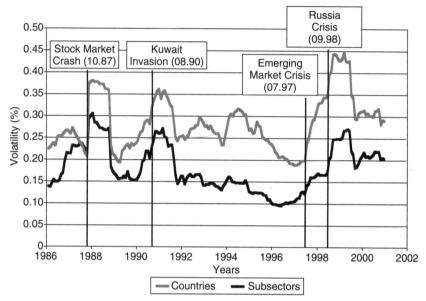

FIGURE 8.5   Temporal behavior of average volatilities of 38 subsectors and 41 countries. Based on monthly returns in U.S. dollars over the period from 1986.01 to 2001.04; moving time window.

of 1998. Because this finding is extremely relevant for international investors, who seek downside protection in their portfolios, we analyze this issue in detail in the next section.

MARKETS, SECTORS, AND EXTREME MARKET EVENTS

The observation that sector indices exhibit a smaller volatility than country indices seems to remain viable for extreme market environments. Figure 8.6 provides a comparison of the cross-sectional distribution of sector and country returns in five especially turbulent market periods:

1. The first episode is the stock market crash in October 1987. Panel 1 depicts the frequency distribution of the October returns across countries and sectors. Despite an overall market correction of

roughly 30 percent, country indices generally exhibit a much worse performance. The continuously compounded October returns of the stock markets in the Far East (Hong Kong, Malaysia, and Singapore) and Australia are all below the worst performing sector (mining). No other sector performs substantially worse than the overall average.

2. The Kuwait crisis in August 1990 confirms this picture (see Panel 2 in Figure 8.6). Again, the outliers are five country indices (Taiwan, Philippines, Singapore, Thailand, and Austria). Sector indices are negatively affected as well, but react much more uniform.

3. In the emerging market crisis in May 1998, again, no sector performs worse than the worst country. Instead, the sectors are all distributed around the mean, and Panel 3 in Figure 8.6 shows no sector is particularly affected by the bad performance of the stock markets in the Far East (Indonesia, Thailand, Korea, Malaysia, Singapore, and Hong Kong).

4. The stock market pattern during the September 1998 Russia Crisis is another example. Several countries experience dramatic losses (Turkey, Poland, Mexico, South Africa, and others), whereas the sectors are much more stable again.

5. The stock market downturn in 2000 is represented in Panel 5 of Figure 8.6. In this case, there was a gradual decrease in stock prices over time, rather than a sudden jump within a specific month. Therefore, we compared the return distribution of sectors and countries based on average monthly returns over the time period from April 2000 to April 2001. The graph shows that, for the first time, sectors seem to be less robust than countries in a market downturn. Although the worst performing index is a country index (Turkey), several sectors are poor performers as well (information technology, software, and computer services).

Given the earlier numerical examples (see Table 8.1), we can interpret these observations as a structural movement away from viewing the world as having a weak sector (strong country) factor (Table 8.1A, Example I), toward viewing the world as having a strong sector (weak country) factor (Table 8.1B, Example II). Sector factors have

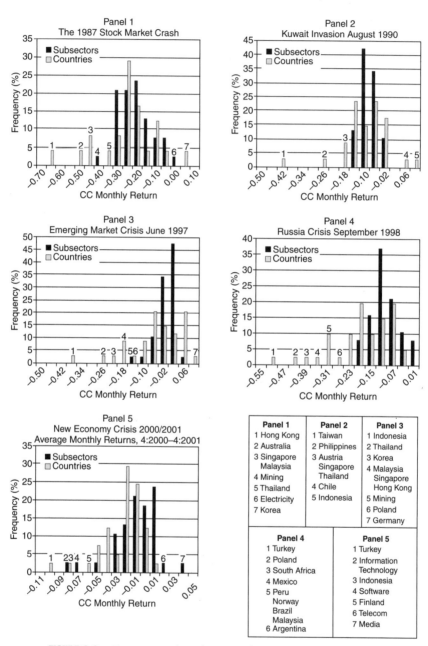

FIGURE 8.6 Frequency distribution of countries and sectors.

become more important, reducing the correlation between sector indices (see Figure 8.4) and simultaneously raising their risk (Panel 5 in Figure 8.6).

Not surprisingly, the worst performing sector indices in our final example are the new economy sectors: information technology, software, and computer services. Turkey and Finland are among the countries performing poorly. Whereas Turkey had to cope with a homemade financial crisis, the Finish index reflects the poor performance of the information technology sector. Finland is one of the least diversified country indices, heavily exposed to the information technology sector (Nokia shares account for more than 50% of the Finnish stock market index).

In general, however, the results of Figure 8.6 confirm the conclusion of the previous section. Global subsector indices represent better diversified portfolios than country indices because country factors are (still) more relevant in explaining variances of individual stock returns than global sector factors (see Drummen & Zimmermann, 1992, among others). This implies that diversification effects are more pronounced if portfolios are diversified across countries instead of across sectors. Global sector indices are apparently better able to exploit the overall benefits of global diversification. However, the sector diversification of country indices is limited.

EFFICIENT FRONTIERS

How do country- and sector-based portfolio strategies affect the efficient diversification of risk? Is a mixed strategy superior to simple diversification strategies? In this section, we analyze simple static portfolio diversification strategies to provide empirical content for the numerical examples at the beginning of the chapter.

Simple Diversification Strategies

The first step is to analyze simple diversification strategies. By *simple,* we mean that portfolios are explicitly diversified across geographic or

TABLE 8.5 Index Categories

Geographical Indices	Sector Indices	2-Dimensional Indices
Countries (34)	Subsectors (38)	4 Regions—10 Sectors (40)
Regions (4)	Sectors (10)	

sector indices, but not both at the same time. Table 8.5 gives an overview of the index categories for our analysis. The geographic and sector indices are available on two aggregation levels: 41 countries and 38 subsectors, as well as 4 regions and 10 sectors, respectively. As the second column of the descriptive statistics in Table 8.4A indicates, some of the 41 country indices did not yet exist in 1991. Therefore, they are excluded from the sample, which reduces the number of country indices to 34.[4]

The efficient frontiers for portfolios diversified across subsectors and individual countries (i.e., the low aggregation level) are analyzed in Figure 8.7. This comparison is likely to produce reliable results because the stock universe underlying the two index families is identical, and the number of assets classes (34 countries, 38 subsectors) is approximately equal.

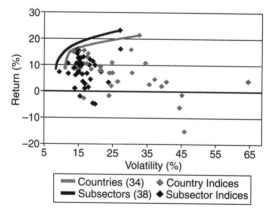

FIGURE 8.7 Efficient frontiers for subsectors and countries. Based on simple monthly returns in U.S. dollars over the period from 1991.05 to 2001.04.

It is assumed that negative portfolio weights are not allowed, which seems reasonable for most investors. An algorithm is used to minimize the portfolio variance under the non-negativity constraint for each mean return level. The results are similar for both approaches. The efficient frontier based on the 38 subsectors even offers, on average, a slightly better risk-return tradeoff than the frontier based on the 34 countries although correlation has been lower between countries (see Figure 8.4). The magnitude of the improvement is difficult to characterize in general. But for the portfolios in the medium-risk range (between 15% and 20%), the increase of average return is approximately 2 percent (for the same level of risk), and the risk reduction is between 2 percent and 8 percent (for the same level of average return). This result may be influenced by the number of subsectors (38), which is slightly higher than the number of countries (34). It might also depend on the time period chosen. Whether the sector approach is consistently and, more important, significantly (in a statistical sense) superior to the country approach is an empirical matter not addressed here. The results based on the highly aggregated indices (4 geographic regions and 10 sectors) are disappointing, as can be seen in Figure 8.8. Although country diversification is superior to the sector approach from a purely empirical standpoint, the risk-return menu of the resulting frontiers is not particularly attractive.

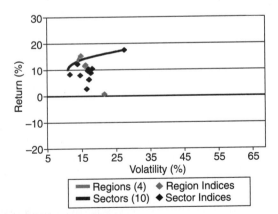

FIGURE 8.8 Efficient frontiers for sectors and regions. Based on simple monthly returns in U.S. dollars over the period from 1991.05 to 2001.04.

A practical implication of this section is that the aggregation level of the indices underlying diversification strategies has a substantial impact on the risk-return menu available to investors. This is particularly important when taking portfolio constraints into account.

Two-Dimensional Diversification Strategies

The next step is to investigate the diversification effects if portfolios are diversified across countries as well as across sectors. Our analysis is based on a set of 10 sector indices in 4 geographic regions; hence the portfolio strategies are referred to as "two-dimensional." Performing the same analysis with all the subsectors in the 34 countries would provide an even more complete picture of the two-dimensional diversification effects. But to keep things simple, we restrict ourselves to the 4 geographic regions.

Figure 8.9 shows the contrast between the efficient frontier of the two-dimensional diversification strategy and two purely one-dimensional strategies. It is apparent that a two-dimensional approach improves the risk-return menu even further, especially

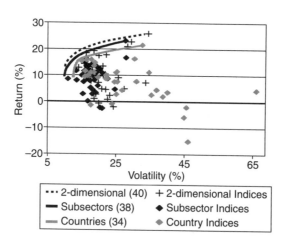

FIGURE 8.9   Efficient frontiers for 2-dimensional indices, subsectors, and countries. Based on simple monthly returns in U.S. dollars over the period from 1991.05 to 2001.04.

compared with the country approach. Again, one might argue that this comparison is somehow biased because the aggregation level of the one-dimensional strategies is different from the two-dimensional strategy (40 indices as opposed to 34 countries and 38 sectors). On the other hand, the figure also reveals that there are more two-dimensional indices with high returns than country or sector indices. In the high-risk, high-return area, one country index, Finland (with an average return of 20.9%), primarily makes up the efficient frontier for the countries (this is also shown in the portfolio composition in Table 8.7). The second-best country return, the United States with 15.8 percent, is substantially lower. The same applies to the sector frontier, whose upper-right-hand side consists mainly of the software sector due its high return of 22.6 percent. The second-best sector, information technology, exhibits an average return of 16.2 percent.[5] The two-dimensional world, however, includes 6 indices with a return higher than 17 percent: information technology in the United Kingdom (25.3%), information technology in continental Europe (22.2%), information technology in the Americas (20.4%), finance in the Americas (18.7%), general industries in the Americas (17.9%), and noncyclical services in continental Europe (17.2%). Over the sample period, the information technology sector has shown a good performance, irrespective of the global region (with the exception of the Pacific markets). The other three sectors, finance, general industries, and noncyclical services are not attractive as a whole, but are acceptable for specific global regions (the Americas and Europe). This finding indicates that high-performing investment opportunities emerge in sectors within specific global regions, but are less pronounced in individual countries or subsectors.

Analyzing Specific Portfolios

Analyzing the composition of specific portfolios optimized under the different approaches can provide a better understanding of the results in the previous subsections. Looking at Figure 8.9, it is interesting to compare the various 15 percent return portfolios and the 20 percent volatility portfolios. Consider the 15 percent return portfolios first. It

TABLE 8.6 15 Percent Return Portfolio*

						Portfolio Structure (Portfolio Shares in Percent)				
	Return (%)	Volatility (%)	General Industrials, Americas	Noncyclical Construction Goods, Americas	Cyclical Services, Americas	Utilities, Americas	Information Technology, Americas	Noncyclical Construction Goods, Europe Except United Kingdom	Noncyclical Services, Europe Except United Kingdom	Utilities, United Kingdom	Information Technology, United Kingdom
2-Dimensional	15.00	9.52	12.38	2.36	5.99	39.85	0.30	21.47	5.71	4.76	7.19
Subsectors	15.00	10.95	Aerospace and Defense 10.21	Electricity 14.09	Life Assurance 17.46	Pharmacy 29.85	Software 17.00	Water 11.39			
Countries	15.00	12.68	Chile 3.12	Finland 0.49	Ireland 1.39	Netherlands 23.41	Switzerland 16.30	United States 55.29			
Sectors	15.00	16.68	Noncyclical Construction Goods 47.8	Utilities 52.2							
Regions	15.00	13.00	Americas 89.53	Europe Except United Kingdom 6.90	United Kingdom 3.56						

* Holding period: 1991.05 to 2001.04.

is obvious from Figure 8.9 that the volatility differences between the three portfolios are rather small. However, Table 8.6 shows that the subsector and two-dimensional portfolios exhibit the smallest volatility.

Although all strategies yield the same return and a similar volatility, the portfolio composition of the five approaches is fundamentally different. Figure 8.10 depicts the implied country weighting of all strategies. For example, neither the two geographic approaches nor the two-dimensional approach assigns a weight to the Japanese index. In the sector and subsector portfolios, on the other hand, Japan accounts for 5.1 percent and 8.5 percent respectively. Thus, different diversification approaches can provide extremely different portfolios.

Consider the 20 percent volatility portfolios next. Again, the two-dimensional approach provides a higher return than the portfolios diversified along subsectors or countries. In the high-risk, high-return zone shown in Table 8.7, portfolio weights become more

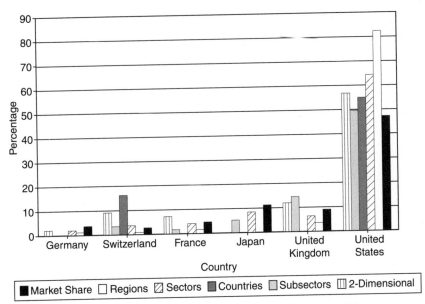

FIGURE 8.10 Implied country weights: 15 percent return portfolio, 1991.05. Values for Market Share are based on Table 8.4a (Datastream Country Indices, 2001.04).

TABLE 8.7 20 Percent Volatility Portfolio*

			Portfolio Structure (Portfolio Shares in Percent)		
	Return (%)	Volatility (%)	Financials, Americas	Information Technology, Europe Except United Kingdom	Information Technology, United Kingdom
2-Dimensional	22.00	20.00	48.93	5.30	45.77
			Pharmacy	Software	
Subsectors	20.00	20.00	34.93	65.07	
			Finland	Switzerland	United States
Countries	18.00	20.00	47.08	32.50	20.42
			Noncyclical Construction Goods	Information Technology	
Sectors	16.00	20.00	30.81	69.19	
Regions			n/a		

*Holding period: 1991.05 to 2001.04.

extreme. In fact, the portfolios are invested in only two to three indices. Furthermore, the portfolio structure is more diverse across the different strategies. Figure 8.11 reveals that the implied country compositions of portfolios differ substantially. The main differences between the portfolios are the Swiss, the U.K., and the U.S. stock market shares. The country approach heavily overweighs the Swiss market (32.5%, opposed to 2.6% market share in the world market). The two-dimensional approach, on the other hand, strongly overweighs the U.K. stock market with 45.7 percent portfolio share (compared with less than 10% in the other approaches).

What explains the superior performance of the two-dimensional approach? Notice that a specific (global) sector with a specific exposure in the U.K. stock market is attractive, not the U.K. stock market as a whole. Thus the two-dimensional approach provides a more

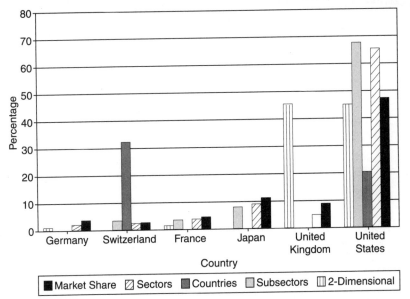

FIGURE 8.11   Implied country weightings: 20 percent volatility portfolio, 1991.05. Values for Market Share are based on Table 8.4a (Datastream Country Indices, 2001.04).

efficient separation of an attractive part of the U.K. stock market (the information technology sector) than the country and subsector approaches. Ignoring diversification effects, no comparable sector in another country has a return as high as 25.3 percent. Therefore, the possibility of separating sectors (even global) and countries increases the diversification potential. This implies that the structure of funds, and not primarily their number, is highly relevant for exploiting attractive diversification opportunities.

CONCLUSION

This chapter can be summarized as follows:

- Correlations between the stocks within countries are substantially larger than the correlations within sectors. This finding is consistent with the empirical literature. The interesting observation is that this pattern emerges consistently over the entire time period. Only recently the correlation of sectors fell below the correlation of countries (see Figure 8.4). The prevalence of a strong country factor is surprising in our globalized economy.

■ The volatility of sector and subsector returns is substantially smaller than the respective country or regional returns. This is particularly true in highly turbulent markets such as the October 1987 stock market crash, the 1990 Kuwait stock market turmoil, or the 1998 emerging markets crisis. It is not true for the stock market crisis in the second half of 2000, which was caused by a sector-specific revaluation of new economy stocks.

■ Whether a country or sector approach should be implemented in international diversification strategies crucially depends on the country structure of global sectors or, alternatively, the sector structure of countries. No general recommendation about an adequate approach is possible without the specification of expected returns. No conclusions can be drawn from the correlation structure of country and sector indices without further information.

■ The range of efficient portfolios (the risk-return menu derived from efficient diversification strategies) crucially depends on the selection of the underlying indices. As a pragmatic rule, diversification strategies should not be based on indices that are too broad; excluding short sales, the resulting range of efficient portfolios is extremely limited in most cases.

■ The new economy turndown in 2000/2001 is the first and only occasion where sector and country hedges had a similar effect. From a hedging perspective, however, the new economy turndown is less severe than previous market turmoils because it is a gradual market correction.

■ Overall, country diversification effects can be exploited in sector portfolios, whereas the potential to reduce sector risk in country portfolios is less pronounced.

CHAPTER 9

The Value-Growth Enigma

Time-Varying Risk Premiums and Active Portfolio Strategies

EXECUTIVE SUMMARY

- In this chapter, we investigate the dynamics of value-growth spreads on global equity markets and discuss ways to exploit them with active style rotation strategies.
- We explore global economic forces driving the performance of value stocks relative to growth stocks in 18 markets and identify observable instrumental variables that can predict the value-growth spreads on international markets. Finally, we examine the conditional covariation between value premiums across international markets.
- Our results show that value premiums reveal a time variation similar to the movements of global economic risk premiums. Part of this time variation is related to the global business cycle and the market climate. Moreover, expected (ex ante) value premiums are more highly correlated than ex post observed value premiums, supporting our hypothesis that the pricing of global risk is related to a value premium.
- We conclude that return spreads between value and growth stocks are driven by expectations about global economic conditions, which is a key feature of the reward for systematic risk on global capital markets. Therefore, the widely documented superior returns of value investment strategies result from a fundamental valuation of systematic risk and not from market inefficiencies.

- Finally, we show how investors can exploit value-growth cycles by using a tactical asset allocation strategy.

INTRODUCTION

Exploration of a Phenomenon

Many empirical studies document that value stocks earn higher returns than growth stocks. In the universe of equity investments, high earnings-to-price (EP) ratios, dividend yields (DY), or book-to-market (BM) ratios can identify value stocks. The expected growth rates of corporate revenues implied by the prices of value stocks are below the overall market level of expected growth opportunities. The opposite is true for growth stocks.

In the early 1980s, the superior performance of stocks with high EP or BM ratios over those with low EP or BM ratios, even after adjusting for market risk, was considered a pricing anomaly. In the meantime, several explanations appeared in the literature for the exceptional returns of value investments (often referred to as "value premiums"). Some authors invoke market inefficiency to justify the phenomenon. De Bondt and Thaler (1985) and Lakonishok, Shleifer, and Vishny (1994) argue that the value premium is due to market overreaction and mispricing of stocks. Others identify problems with research databases and test design. Banz and Breen (1986) discuss look-ahead bias as a possible explanation for superior returns of value stocks. Lo and MacKinlay (1990) address problems associated with data snooping. Davis (1995) argues that the high returns of value stocks may suffer from a survivorship bias. In contrast, the higher average returns of value stocks could be attributed to the higher systematic risk of such investments. Using multibeta pricing models, Chan (1988), Ball and Kothari (1989), and Fama and French (1992, 1996, 1998) forcefully argue that the observed differences between the returns on value and growth portfolios mirror a compensation for bearing systematic risk. Fama and French (1996) test an ad hoc modification of the Capital Asset Pricing Model with a value-growth spread (high-minus-low BM factor, HML) and the return differential between small and large capitalization stocks (small-minus-big factor, SMB) to support their notion that the value premium reflects a compensation for financial distress. Liew and Vassalou (1999) show that the performance of HML or SMB portfolios is a leading indicator of future economic growth.

Most of the empirical research on the value-growth phenomenon is based on stock market data from the United States. Fama and French (1998) and Arshanapalli, Coggin, and Doukas (1998), however, document the existence of value premiums on stock markets outside the United States as well. Their tests use a broad cross-section of international stock market returns. There is empirical evidence that investors around the world could benefit from the superior rewards of value investment strategies.

Open Questions for Value Investors

Value premiums are still a phenomenon on global equity markets. Although the notion that the return differential between value and growth stocks is related to differences in risk profiles has been gaining acceptance throughout the academic community, the lack of plausible economic explanations is obvious. In a review paper, Cochrane (1999a) casts doubt on the line of reasoning originated by Fama and French (1996). He argues that financial distress, as an idiosyncratic risk factor, should be diversifiable in a portfolio context.

Despite deficiencies in the understanding of the fundamentals of the value-growth spread, most investment professionals recognize that value stocks reveal attractive performance characteristics. In accordance with extensive empirical work, value investing might indeed be favorable in the long run. But on the other hand, such strategies are far from being secure investments over short horizons. Arshanapalli, Coggin, and Doukas (1998) show that the value-growth spreads on international stock markets vary substantially from year to year in both sign and magnitude. The reasons for this cyclical behavior of value premiums are still unexplored.

Even less is known about the comovement of international value premiums. The correlation analyses of Arshanapalli, Coggin, and

Doukas (1998) and Fama and French (1998) indicate that value-growth spreads are not highly synchronized across countries. Finally, links between global economic conditions and the magnitudes of value premiums on international markets are largely unexplored. This chapter investigates these open issues.

Insights from the Empirical Analysis

By investigating the dynamics of value premiums on 18 stock markets in three global regions from January 1980 to June 1999, we explore the global economic forces driving the performance of value stocks relative to growth stocks. We also identify observable instrumental variables that can predict the value-growth spreads on international stock markets. Finally, we examine the conditional covariation between value premiums across international stock markets.

Our results indicate that value premiums reveal a time variation similar to the movements of global economic risk premiums. Part of this time variation is related to the global business cycle and the market sentiment. Moreover, expected (predicted) value premiums are more highly correlated than ex post historical value premiums. This supports the proposition of global stock market integration—that the risk related to value stocks is consistently priced across international stock markets.

Our results can be summarized as follows:

- Value-growth return spreads vary considerably over time. Over the past 20 years, value stocks produced higher returns than growth stocks on most equity markets around the world. Over short investment horizons, however, value strategies are not reliable because periods of value stock superiority alternate with periods of growth stock superiority in a cyclical fashion. Econometric analyses of the dynamics of value-growth return spreads indicate that value stocks tend to outperform growth stocks when business conditions and market sentiment improve.
- Value-growth return spreads reflect risk premiums. Return spreads between value and growth stocks are notably driven by

expectations about global economic conditions, which is a characteristic feature of the rewards for systematic risk on capital markets. Hence, the widely documented superior returns of value investment strategies might result from a fundamental valuation of systematic risk rather than from market inefficiencies. The international correlations of expected value-growth spreads indicate that an unobservable global risk factor is priced consistently across stock markets.

■ To some extent, the value-growth return spreads on equity markets are predictable on the basis of indicators for expected economic conditions. Active style rotation strategies, using signals from a well-specified instrumental regression model with carefully selected indicator variables, outperform passive value or growth investments. The extra returns are economically significant.

Our findings contribute to the understanding of the dynamics of value-related returns. We also point out strategies for exploiting the value-growth cycles by model-based tactical asset allocation. The following section in this chapter briefly describes the database. Next, we document statistics on international value-growth spreads and their dynamic behavior. There is then an empirical analysis of the fundamentals of value premiums, providing evidence and discussion on economic driving forces, risk stories, and global integration. Finally, we examine active style rotation strategies, exploiting the time-varying behavior of value premiums.

DATA DESCRIPTION

Our sample covers 18 stock markets located in Europe, North America, and the Pacific Rim over the period from January 1980 to June 1999. Country-specific value-growth spreads are calculated on the basis of the style indices provided by Morgan Stanley Capital International (MSCI). These are total return subindices of the MSCI country indices, all denominated in local currencies. The segmentation into value stocks and growth stocks is based on a country-specific ranking of the companies with respect to their previous month-end price-to-book (PB) ratios, which are equal to the inverse of the BM ratios. The value index includes the companies with the lowest PB ratios, covering half of the market capitalization of the country. The remaining stocks make up the growth index. The style indices are rebalanced semiannually. Both indices are market capitalization weighted on the basis of the stocks in the MSCI universe and, hence, represent investable strategies. Due to the construction of the indices there is no look-ahead or survivorship bias in the data.

EMPIRICAL FACTS ON INTERNATIONAL VALUE-GROWTH SPREADS

Long-Horizon Value Premiums

Table 9.1 documents statistics on style-related returns and premiums across the countries and regions in our sample. From January 1980 to June 1999, the average annual return spread between value and growth stocks in the MSCI global universe was 1.88 percent (all returns are denominated in local currencies). This value premium results from a rebalanced portfolio including long positions in the value stocks and short positions in the growth stocks of each country. The value-growth spread was 1.79 percent per annum in Europe, 5.17 percent in the Pacific Rim, and a negative −0.43 percent in North America. Evidently, there are substantial differences across global regions. Differences in value-growth spreads are even more pronounced on the individual country level. Long-horizon annual value premiums vary between minus 2.76 percent for Denmark and 12.84 percent for Norway, with an arithmetic mean of 2.47 percent across countries. In more than two thirds of the countries, however, value stocks earn higher returns than growth stocks. In addition, the ratio of return and volatility is higher for value stocks in most of the countries.

TABLE 9.1 Statistics on Value and Growth Stock Returns

Individual Countries	Growth Stocks Mean (%)	Growth Stocks SD (%)	Value Stocks Mean (%)	Value Stocks SD (%)	Value-Growth Spread Mean (%)	Value-Growth Spread SD (%)	Value-Growth Spread Min. (%)	Value-Growth Spread Max. (%)	V>G (%)
Europe									
Austria	8.39	24.57	8.35	24.65	−0.04	18.49	−30.68	20.59	51.28
Belgium	14.25	18.60	22.80	18.46	7.48	10.38	−10.48	12.59	56.41
Denmark	17.84	21.53	14.59	19.49	−2.76	17.77	−14.71	20.53	43.16
France	15.35	21.33	17.88	21.75	2.20	12.19	−12.52	11.71	54.70
Germany	13.69	21.32	14.57	19.45	0.77	10.09	−9.95	9.91	48.72
Italy	20.82	25.39	18.95	27.51	−1.55	13.31	−14.04	15.06	50.00
Netherlands	17.29	18.98	23.49	19.31	5.29	16.22	−15.72	19.89	54.27
Norway	5.01	28.15	18.49	26.94	12.84	21.72	−14.44	24.77	57.69
Spain	21.61	24.86	24.15	23.30	2.08	18.03	−20.89	16.57	50.00
Sweden	27.75	23.61	25.40	26.30	−1.84	17.95	−15.86	16.44	50.43
Switzerland	12.89	17.02	16.17	19.86	2.90	12.24	−21.06	11.12	55.13
United Kingdom	17.36	18.03	19.90	17.77	2.17	9.28	−9.08	10.33	54.27
North America									
Canada	9.15	20.06	12.15	16.81	2.75	12.74	−17.30	17.21	53.42
United States	18.38	16.49	17.60	14.37	−0.66	7.98	−6.46	9.97	53.42
Pacific Rim									
Australia	11.44	25.09	16.62	20.08	4.65	12.12	−10.10	15.91	55.13
Hong Kong	18.07	32.19	18.53	36.56	0.39	14.60	−12.52	26.36	49.57
Japan	5.06	22.04	10.82	19.05	5.48	11.74	−17.18	11.15	57.69
Singapore	8.01	26.64	10.44	29.50	2.25	16.49	−21.91	27.63	48.72
Global Regions									
World	13.86	14.40	16.00	13.49	1.88	5.82	−5.55	7.91	52.99
North America	17.78	16.28	17.27	14.31	−0.43	7.57	−6.11	9.82	52.99
Europe	16.62	15.50	18.71	15.79	1.79	5.98	−5.65	7.71	55.98
Pacific Rim	5.79	20.45	11.26	17.77	5.17	10.55	−15.96	10.56	57.69

Note: Value and growth stocks are represented by the style-specific total return indices provided by MSCI for countries and regions over the time period from 1980.01 to 1999.06. Returns are denominated in local currencies. Means and standard deviations (SD) are reported on an annual basis. Min. = Smallest monthly value-growth spread; Max. = Largest monthly value-growth spread; % V>G = Percentage of months in which the return of value stocks exceeds the return of growth stocks.

TABLE 9.2 Year-to-Year Value-Growth Spreads

Countries	1980	1981	1982	1983	1984	1985	1986	1987	1988	1989	1990	1991	1992	1993	1994	1995	1996	1997	1998	1999
Europe																				
Austria	8.2%	−16.1%	10.6%	1.0%	−1.8%	−165.8%	7.9%	25.8%	−13.3%	−28.7%	8.9%	1.2%	−29.3%	36.4%	14.7%	−1.9%	21.4%	15.5%	5.6%	4.5%
Belgium	−4.3	11.4	12.8	10.0	1.5	18.9	−11.9	5.6	19.1	2.8	10.4	0.0	16.3	9.9	6.2	19.2	0.9	9.3	20.2	11.5
Denmark	−34.7	−45.9	−22.3	50.8	24.2	21.7	2.9	−4.8	−27.2	−32.5	4.3	−15.5	−13.6	−10.8	6.0	8.0	−6.6	−33.2	46.5	−12.3
France	−9.9	14.9	−0.8	23.1	0.8	3.6	26.0	5.2	0.9	−3.0	−2.4	2.3	−2.1	9.2	1.2	−12.2	−27.9	28.2	−19.8	19.4
Germany	−12.1	−5.5	−4.2	−10.5	−2.7	−3.1	−13.0	20.5	−0.3	1.2	−8.8	8.7	0.2	10.8	1.1	−13.3	11.2	11.2	−12.2	28.5
Italy	−47.6	−7.1	10.7	−1.0	5.4	3.2	−56.7	−9.7	10.6	11.6	−8.5	−6.7	−1.4	25.8	6.3	−15.4	6.1	16.1	12.7	−1.5
Netherlands	−45.4	31.1	17.5	31.2	10.7	−35.3	3.1	14.5	4.3	5.0	−11.6	3.1	−9.3	22.6	−2.9	21.4	−6.7	9.4	18.1	40.8
Norway	24.3	44.6	13.9	−9.6	17.7	21.2	15.3	10.3	32.9	28.1	17.2	−31.7	31.7	67.6	−25.9	−12.2	19.2	15.4	−8.0	15.8
Spain	7.2	−12.9	14.3	−2.5	70.2	6.4	−95.6	−22.6	−6.5	16.2	14.3	15.4	31.7	−7.7	3.1	−6.6	24.0	2.7	3.5	5.2
Sweden	13.9	3.5	9.1	34.8	17.5	12.9	−20.5	−5.0	16.2	−9.9	−5.5	16.1	−50.0	28.3	0.1	−20.3	−10.5	4.2	−39.5	−14.3
Switzerland	−10.0	5.0	12.1	22.4	−0.3	2.1	−24.4	15.5	21.3	−4.3	−2.4	8.9	−15.7	24.9	−5.6	−7.9	−1.4	15.7	1.7	12.5
United Kingdom	−19.4	12.7	−25.3	24.5	−0.5	7.0	23.1	7.7	7.5	4.6	−1.9	−23.3	−0.6	26.4	6.7	−4.9	2.0	3.7	−14.0	11.3
North America																				
Canada	18.2	0.3	23.3	23.0	1.9	1.1	4.8	3.8	6.1	1.8	0.5	5.5	−8.0	9.4	2.3	0.9	11.6	−11.3	−12.5	−16.2
United States	−1.3	10.3	−3.4	10.9	5.9	−4.3	4.4	−5.0	11.3	−13.9	−7.4	−18.6	5.6	16.7	−2.8	0.6	−4.7	−0.8	−32.4	4.0
Pacific Rim																				
Australia	−3.8	22.0	4.9	38.0	−4.5	15.3	−35.3	6.5	12.8	−4.3	−15.0	12.9	9.8	15.2	−8.0	10.2	7.7	17.9	−9.7	12.7
Hong Kong	−33.1	18.7	4.3	−16.3	6.4	−7.9	1.2	−0.9	−8.8	20.9	−23.2	16.0	23.0	55.8	−4.5	7.8	20.2	−23.6	−5.3	−13.0
Japan	8.3	30.8	15.4	−8.0	−23.2	16.5	−1.7	5.4	3.7	12.4	7.5	−2.3	5.2	7.1	15.4	6.3	13.3	−10.3	5.2	−0.7
Singapore	−28.0	15.7	5.0	−1.2	−8.5	−9.5	41.3	7.4	−1.9	16.3	1.5	5.6	−3.7	−18.2	−2.2	−6.4	0.2	3.9	−2.3	54.6
Regions																				
World	−2.3%	13.1%	0.0%	9.1%	−0.3%	2.3%	1.3%	3.7%	7.0%	2.3%	−0.6%	−8.1%	3.2%	16.0%	2.8%	0.3%	1.9%	−0.5%	−17.4%	6.8%
North America	0.4	9.3	−1.7	11.7	5.5	−4.1	4.3	−4.4	11.0	−12.6	−6.7	−16.6	4.7	16.3	−2.6	0.6	−3.9	−1.3	−31.3	3.3
Europe	−15.2	8.5	−8.0	16.0	3.7	1.7	−1.8	9.7	7.0	2.0	−2.7	−6.6	−3.3	19.9	2.3	−5.7	−0.7	9.3	−7.9	14.1
Pacific Rim	4.5	27.9	13.1	−4.4	−20.0	14.9	−2.0	6.0	3.6	12.2	6.3	−1.4	5.8	10.7	9.5	5.5	12.8	−8.0	3.6	1.6

Note: The table shows the annual returns of value stocks relative to the annual returns of growth stocks. Value and growth stocks over the time period from 1980.01 to 1999.06 are represented by the style-specific total return indices provided by MSCI for countries and regions.

Our results deviate somewhat from the findings in other studies. The international value-growth return spreads documented by Arshanapalli, Coggin, and Doukas (1998) for the period from 1975 to 1995 are generally larger. For example, they report a long-horizon value premium of 13.07 percent per year in North America. This is because their sample includes the 11.8 percent value premium of 1975 and the 22.9 percent value premium of 1976 for this region, but does not yet include the negative −31.1 percent value premium of 1998. Hence, figures on long-horizon return spreads between value and growth stocks seem to be extremely sensitive to the time window chosen for calculation.

Short-Horizon Value Premiums

Year-to-year value-growth spreads vary considerably in both signs and magnitudes. Table 9.2 documents the value premiums in the 18 countries and global regions on a yearly basis from 1980 to 1999. Table 9.3 provides a statistical description of these premiums. The annual value growth spread for the global MSCI aggregate of stocks varies between minus 17.4 percent and plus 16.0 percent, with a standard deviation of 7.04 percent. There are 6 years with negative and 12 years with positive value premiums.

Figures 9.1 and 9.2 display year-to-year value-growth spreads for the global and the regional aggregates. There is no country or region in which the yearly value premium is consistently positive or negative. Often the overall picture is influenced by outlier observations. The year-to-year value-growth spread varies over a broad range of values in Austria, Denmark, the Netherlands, Norway, Spain, Sweden, and Hong Kong; in these countries the standard deviation of the spread measured on the basis of calendar years is higher than 20 percent. Countries with relatively stable value premiums are Belgium and Canada.

Figure 9.3 shows the return differences between value and growth stocks across the global MSCI universe for a one-year investment horizon, determined on the basis of a moving 12-month data window. Apparently, the performance of value stocks relative to

TABLE 9.3   Statistics on Year-to-Year Value-Growth Spreads

	Mean	SD	t-statistic	Minimum	Maximum	Number of Positive Years	Number of Negative Years
Europe							
Austria	−4.8%	41.33%	−0.52	−165.8%	36.4%	13	7
Belgium	8.5	8.53	4.45	−11.9	20.2	17	3
Denmark	−4.7	26.10	−0.81	−45.9	50.8	8	12
France	2.8	14.53	0.87	−27.9	28.2	12	8
Germany	0.4	11.63	0.15	−13.3	28.5	9	11
Italy	−2.3	19.78	−0.53	−56.7	25.8	10	10
Netherlands	6.1	21.18	1.29	−45.4	40.8	14	6
Norway	14.4	23.29	2.76	−31.7	67.6	15	5
Spain	0.9	29.57	0.14	−95.6	70.2	12	8
Sweden	−0.9	21.34	−0.20	−50.0	34.8	11	9
Switzerland	3.5	13.16	1.19	−24.4	24.9	11	9
United Kingdom	2.4	14.59	0.73	−25.3	26.4	12	8
North America							
Canada	3.3	10.60	1.40	−16.2	23.3	16	4
United States	−1.2	11.32	−0.49	−32.4	16.7	9	11
Pacific Rim							
Australia	5.3	15.67	1.50	−35.3	38.0	13	7
Hong Kong	1.9	20.47	0.41	−33.1	55.8	10	10
Japan	5.3	11.44	2.08	−23.2	30.8	14	6
Singapore	3.5	18.40	0.84	−28.0	54.6	10	10
Global Regions							
World	2.0	7.04	1.29	−17.4	16.0	13	7
North America	−0.9	10.77	−0.38	−31.3	16.3	10	10
Europe	2.1	9.02	1.06	−15.2	19.9	11	9
Pacific Rim	5.1	9.85	2.32	−20.0	27.9	15	5

Note: Mean and standard deviations (SD) are based on the return differences between value stocks and growth stocks calculated over the calendar years. The *t*-statistic measures the statistical significance of the yearly mean. Min. = Smallest yearly value-growth spread; Max. = Largest value-growth spread; No. of Pos. Years = Number of years with positive value-growth spreads; No. of Neg. Years = Number of years with negative value-growth spreads. Value and growth stocks are represented by the style-specific total return indices provided by MSCI for countries and regions over the period from 1980.01 to 1999.06. Returns are denominated in local currencies.

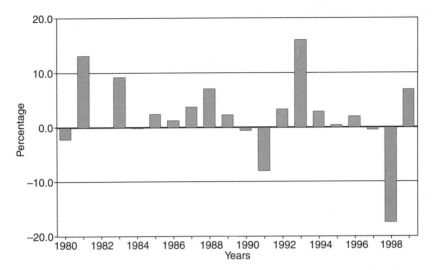

FIGURE 9.1   Year-to-year value-growth spreads in the MSCI global stock universe. The figure shows the annual returns of value stocks relative to annual returns of growth stocks in the MSCI stock universe. Value-growth return differences are denominated in local currencies, respectively.

growth stocks follows distinct cycles. Such a pattern is fairly representative for all regions and countries. Over short investment horizons, value investing is not a reliable strategy to enhance portfolio performance.

International Correlations of Value Premiums

The correlations of value premiums across global markets are typically low. Measured on a monthly basis, the average correlation coefficient is 0.036 across the 18 countries in our sample. On a year-to-year basis, cross-country correlations are larger with an average of 0.092. This is an important result: Higher correlations of yearly value premiums imply that the common performance characteristics of value and growth stocks across international markets are reflected in medium-term cycles, not short-term return differences.

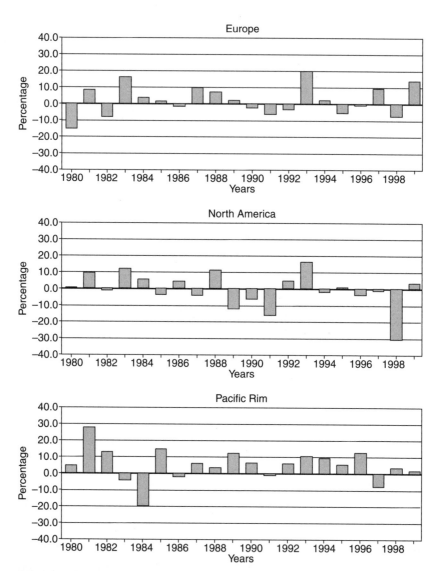

FIGURE 9.2 Year-to-year value-growth spreads in the 3 global regions. The figure shows the annual returns of value stocks relative to the annual returns of growth stocks in global regions. Value-growth return differences are denominated in local currencies.

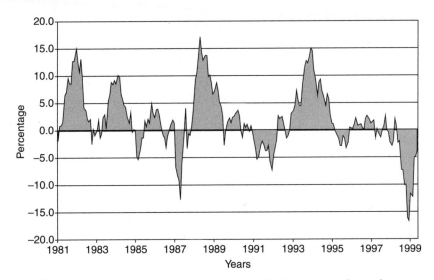

FIGURE 9.3 Cumulated return of value stocks relative to growth stocks (MSCI universe). The figure shows the return difference between value and growth stocks in the MSCI stock universe, determined on the basis of a moving 12-month data window. Example: The 1989 entry represents the time period from January 1, 1988, to January 1, 1989. Value-growth return differences are denominated in local currencies.

Table 9.4 shows the correlations between annual value premiums across countries and regions. The comovement of value premiums is notably more pronounced across economically linked countries. Examples of such pairs of countries include France and United Kingdom (0.57), Switzerland and Germany (0.46), Switzerland and Italy (0.63), and the United Kingdom and the United States (0.63). Value-growth spreads on European and Asian stock markets are often negatively correlated.

In general, the patterns of value premiums in the Pacific Rim deviate significantly from the patterns in the other two regions. The correlations of the Pacific Rim with Europe and North America are −0.04 and −0.01, respectively. This is in contrast with the remarkably high correlation of 0.56 between the value premiums across Europe and North America. However, correlations are not stable over time. Figure 9.4 depicts the correlations across the regional

TABLE 9.4 International Correlations of Year-to-Year Value-Growth Spreads

Countries	Belgium	Denmark	France	Germany	Italy	Netherlands	Norway	Spain	Sweden	Switzerland	United Kingdom	Canada	United States	Australia	Hong Kong	Japan	Singapore
Austria	-0.348	-0.145	0.001	0.188	-0.041	0.430	-0.079	-0.068	-0.014	0.154	-0.024	0.131	0.065	-0.165	0.094	-0.245	0.091
Belgium		0.193	-0.164	-0.034	0.578	0.233	0.053	0.200	-0.159	0.371	-0.056	-0.312	-0.012	0.477	0.002	0.230	-0.205
Denmark			-0.107	-0.309	0.065	0.103	-0.459	0.079	-0.039	-0.018	0.151	0.004	-0.212	-0.058	-0.155	-0.374	-0.132
France				0.195	-0.114	0.374	0.122	-0.427	0.321	0.286	0.571	-0.103	0.498	0.211	-0.153	-0.295	0.479
Germany					0.386	0.284	0.135	0.147	0.050	0.468	0.175	-0.320	0.081	0.301	0.207	-0.102	0.359
Italy						0.340	0.144	0.544	0.163	0.623	0.049	-0.183	-0.051	0.466	0.355	0.016	-0.196
Netherlands							-0.037	-0.078	0.005	0.480	0.333	-0.182	0.202	0.330	0.290	-0.160	0.494
Norway								-0.079	0.100	0.142	0.390	0.013	0.538	0.087	0.379	0.236	-0.069
Spain									0.280	0.251	-0.438	0.025	-0.190	0.270	-0.017	-0.191	-0.414
Sweden										0.619	0.165	0.612	0.400	0.436	-0.061	-0.152	-0.322
Switzerland											0.186	0.158	0.226	0.696	0.051	-0.126	-0.090
United Kingdom												-0.078	0.627	0.163	0.215	-0.059	0.295
Canada													0.255	0.137	0.044	0.124	-0.391
United States														0.358	0.176	-0.084	-0.001
Australia															0.115	0.034	-0.196
Hong Kong																0.229	-0.044
Japan																	-0.035
Singapore																	

Regions	North America	Europe	Pacific Rim
World	0.873	0.738	0.319
North America		0.564	-0.012
Europe			-0.044

Note: Correlation coefficients are calculated on the basis of yearly differences between the returns on value stocks and the returns on growth stocks across countries. Correlation coefficients larger than 0.3 are underlined. Value and growth stocks are represented by the style-specific total return indices provided by MSCI for countries and regions over the period from 1980.01 to 1999.06.

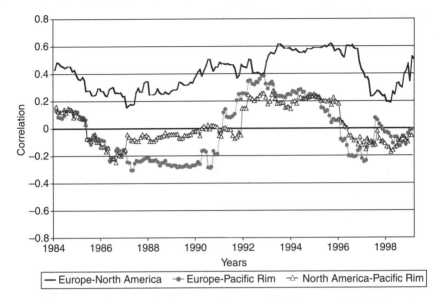

FIGURE 9.4 Correlation of value-growth spreads in Europe, North America, and the Pacific Rim. The figure shows the correlations across the regional value-growth spreads, determined on the basis of a moving 48-month data window. Example: The 1989 entry represents the time period from January 1, 1985, to January 1, 1989. Value-growth return differences are denominated in local currencies.

value-growth spreads, calculated on the basis of a moving 48-month data window. There is a weak positive trend in the patterns of Europe and North America. The R-square of a trend regression is 0.152.

To sum up, the dynamics of value premiums have two major characteristics: First, short-horizon value premiums—the year-to-year return differences between value and growth stocks—vary substantially over time. Characteristic value-growth patterns exist on each stock market. Second, the correlations of value premiums across countries and global regions seem to be affected by the degree of economic interaction between the countries and global regions. But what do these findings of our empirical analysis imply for the investor? The low correlations between the value premiums on international stock markets call for a country-specific style management. The lack of synchronicity in the relative performance of value and growth stocks across markets makes it almost impossible to enhance portfolio performance by simply holding a globally diversified portfolio with a tilt toward either value or growth stocks.

ECONOMICS OF INTERNATIONAL VALUE-GROWTH SPREADS

Instrumental Regression Framework

The forces driving the magnitudes of value premiums on global equity markets and, hence, the cross-market correlations of value premiums are largely unexplored. A commonly held view is that the spread between the returns on value and growth stocks, when measured over long horizons, represents a compensation for taking on systematic risk. Fama and French (1998) posit the most prominent view—that the risk inherent in value stocks is related to financial distress. We contribute to this line of reasoning by linking the variation of value premiums to instrumental variables that are commonly used to explain the variation of systematic risk premiums. Our main proposition is that value premiums are in fact risk premiums; they vary over time, depending on changes in the economic conditions and the market sentiment. Accordingly, value premiums mirror the conditional time variation of risk premiums.

We examine the variation of value premiums on the basis of global instrumental variables in the following regression framework:

$$R_{V,t} - R_{G,t} = C_0 + C_1 \cdot Z_{1,t-1} + C_2 \cdot Z_{2,t-1} + \cdots + C_k \cdot Z_{k,t-1} + \varepsilon_t \quad (9.1)$$

where $R_{v,t} - R_{G,t}$ denotes the difference between the returns on value and growth stocks in period t, and $Z_{j,t-1}$, $j = 1,\ldots,k$, stands for the level of the jth instrumental variable at the beginning of the period, at time $t-1$. C_0 is a constant, C_j, $j = 1,\ldots,k$, captures the influence of the jth instrument, observed at time $t-1$, on the value-growth spread in period t. Finally, ε_t is a mean-zero residual.

Our approach is to regress the time series of ex post measured value-growth spreads on time series of lagged instrumental variables. This allows the exploration of the predictable variation of value premiums on a country-by-country basis. The model decomposes value premiums into (1) a constant component, (2) a time-varying component related to the levels of the lagged instruments, and (3) an unsystematic component. This methodology is commonly applied in research on the predictable variation in stock returns and conditional asset pricing.

We implement our model on the basis of eight instrumental variables $Z_{j,t-1}$, $j = 1, \ldots, 8$. In accordance with economic theory and former empirical work on the variation of risk premiums on capital markets, the variables employed are proxies for the global business conditions and the stock market sentiment. Our eight variables are:

1. *U.S. purchasing manager index* (BUSCLI). Index proxying for expected business conditions, provided by the U.S. National Association of Purchasing Management. Risk premiums on capital market should be negatively related to the level of a leading business indicator.
2. *Global stock market volatility* (GLVOLA). Standard deviation of the daily returns of the Datastream global stock market index, calculated over the preceding month. Global volatility increases when the level of uncertainty on equity markets increases. Accordingly, global risk premiums should be positively related to global volatility.
3. *Inverse relative global wealth* (INRELW). Weighted sum of the MSCI global stock market index levels, measured at the beginning of each of the preceding 12 months, relative to the current index level. Increasing relative wealth—mirrored by a decreasing inverse ratio—implies a decreasing risk aversion of the market participants and leads to decreasing risk premiums.
4. *Global real interest rate* (GLREAL). GDP-weighted aggregate of long-term interest rates in the G7 countries minus the countries' inflation rates for the previous month. Increasing global real interest rates reflect increasing premiums for taking on risks in bond investments. Under the assumption of integrated financial

markets, bond market risk premiums should be positively correlated to stock market risk premiums.

5. *Moody's U.S. credit spread* (CREDSP). Spread between interest rates for BAA corporate bonds and AAA corporate bonds in the United States, as provided by Moody's. The spread decreases when the economic situation improves and increases when conditions worsen. Therefore, the credit spread should be positively related to risk premiums on capital markets.

6. *Treasury-Eurodollar spread* (TEDSPR). Spread between the interest rate for 90-day U.S. Treasury bills and the 3-month Eurodollar interest rate. Because the spread is a proxy for the current and expected health of the global financial system, it ought to be negatively related to global risk premiums.

7. *Global term spread* (TERMSP). GDP-weighted aggregate of the spreads between the yields of long-term government bonds and 3-month interest rates in the G7 countries. The term spread is positively related to the expected economic conditions and, therefore, one can expect a negative relation to global risk premiums.

8. *Global dividend yield* (GLDIVY). GDP-weighted aggregate of the dividend yields on the stock markets in the G7 countries. On

TABLE 9.5   Correlations of Instrumental Variables

	GLDIVY	TERMSP	TEDSPR	CREDSP	GLREAL	INRELW	GLVOLA	BUSCLI
GLDIVY	1.000	−0.304	0.333	−0.005	0.567	0.398	−0.059	−0.082
TERMSP		1.000	−0.391	−0.214	0.171	−0.050	−0.041	0.478
TEDSPR			1.000	0.197	0.324	0.103	0.193	0.207
CREDSP				1.000	−0.073	0.077	0.235	−0.103
GLREAL					1.000	0.211	−0.098	0.353
INRELW						1.000	0.482	−0.089
GLVOLA							1.000	0.044
BUSCLI								1.000

Note: The table shows the correlation coefficients for the levels of instrumental variables over the period from 1986.01 to 1999.06. BUSCLI = U.S. purchasing manager index; GLVOLA = Global stock market volatility; INRELW = Inverse relative wealth; GLREAL = Global real interest rate; CREDSP = U.S. credit spread (Moody's); TEDSPR = Treasury-Eurodollar spread; TERMSP = Global term spread; GLDIVY = Global dividend yield.

the basis of the simple dividend discount model, the level of the dividend yield corresponds to risk-adjusted expected returns and should, thus be positively related to risk premiums.

Table 9.5 documents the correlations between the eight instruments. Table 9.6 shows the results of our instrumental regressions.

TABLE 9.6 Estimation Results of Instrumental Regressions

Countries	Instrumental Variables								R^2 (%)
	BUSCLI	GLVOLA	INRELW	GLREAL	CREDSP	TEDSPR	TERMSP	GLDIVY	
Europe									
Austria	0.147	1.486	−0.988	−0.062	0.283	0.144	0.170	−0.280	2.94
Belgium	−0.036	1.737	2.511	−1.245	−0.857	1.464	1.221	0.472	16.19
Denmark	−0.490	−1.775	2.788	1.266	0.899	0.351	−0.395	−3.391	9.57
France	1.238	0.452	−1.265	0.139	−0.117	−0.833	−1.214	0.959	3.46
Germany	−0.902	0.871	−1.955	0.284	−0.132	1.796	1.362	−0.284	6.22
Italy	2.104	−0.005	−1.340	−3.072	−0.320	−0.617	0.641	2.017	10.59
Netherlands	−1.111	0.678	−2.085	0.280	−0.342	1.194	0.510	−0.467	5.43
Norway	0.252	−0.898	−0.343	0.650	1.322	−0.170	−0.369	−0.095	2.66
Spain	0.105	0.209	0.052	−2.164	−2.060	0.819	0.602	0.522	6.25
Sweden	−0.834	0.790	−2.468	−1.342	−0.380	0.819	1.126	1.799	6.01
Switzerland	0.646	0.016	−0.893	−0.123	−0.681	0.654	0.340	0.166	2.64
United Kingdom	1.429	0.131	−0.850	0.285	1.697	−0.505	0.053	1.010	5.13
North America									
Canada	−0.494	−1.546	1.066	−0.417	−1.733	1.187	1.055	1.164	8.21
United States	1.538	0.752	−1.289	−0.768	1.531	−0.847	1.541	2.590	9.51
Pacific Rim									
Australia	1.784	−1.158	−0.077	−2.035	0.223	0.490	1.322	0.982	7.24
Hong Kong	0.493	1.140	−0.941	−0.755	1.004	−1.754	−0.344	1.939	5.09
Japan	0.637	0.474	−0.692	−1.684	−0.981	0.788	0.615	1.230	3.30
Singapore	−0.074	1.441	−1.330	0.862	0.967	−0.572	−0.728	0.474	3.62
Regions									
World	1.799	0.911	−2.054	−2.068	−0.208	0.442	1.476	3.021	10.32
North America	1.457	0.598	−1.190	−0.821	1.344	−0.683	1.628	2.676	9.34
Europe	1.255	0.581	−2.087	−0.513	0.444	0.518	0.596	1.112	6.33
Pacific Rim	0.799	0.686	−0.859	−1.876	−0.931	0.752	0.620	1.466	4.05

Note: The table shows the t-statistics of the coefficients and the associated R-squares in regressions of country-specific value-growth return spreads on global instrumental variables over the period from 1986.01 to 1999.03:

$$R_{v,t} - R_{G,t} = C_0 + C_1 \cdot Z_{1,t-1} + C_2 \cdot Z_{2,t-1} + \ldots + C_k \cdot Z_{k,t-1} + \varepsilon_t$$

BUSCLI = U.S. purchasing manager index; GLVOLA = Global stock market volatility; INRELW = Inverse relative wealth; GLREAL = Global real interest rate; CREDSP = U.S. credit spread (Moody's); TEDSPR = Treasury-Eurodollar spread; TERMSP = Global term spread; GLDIVY = Global dividend yield. Value and growth stocks are represented by the style-specific total return indices provided by MSCI for countries and regions. Returns are denominated in local currencies.

Global Forces Driving Value Premiums

The estimation period starts in January 1986 and ends in March 1999 due to data restrictions for the instrumental variables. The model explains between 2.94 percent (Austria) and 10.59 percent (Italy) of the monthly variation of the value-growth spreads across countries, with a mean R-square of 6.34 percent. Our instruments account for 6.33 percent of the variance of the value premium in Europe, 9.34 percent in North America, 4.05 percent in the Pacific Rim, and 10.32 percent of the value-growth spread changes across the global MSCI global aggregate. The R-square values, although low, are in a range typical for such instrumental regressions. Nevertheless, the regression results indicate that there is predictable variation in the value premiums on international equity markets.

Signs and significance levels of the regression coefficients vary considerably across the countries. Results are more stable across the global regions; six instruments uniformly drive the regional value-growth spreads: BUSCLI (positive), GLVOLA (positive), INRELW (negative), GLREAL (negative), TERMSP (positive), and GLDIVY (positive). Figure 9.5 shows the t-statistics of the instrument coefficients describing the value-growth spread in the global MSCI aggregate.

BUSCLI, TERMSP, GLDIVY, INRELW, and GLREAL show up with a reliable influence. The global value premium expands when the purchasing manager index (BUSCLI) increases, global term spreads (TERMSP) widen, aggregate risk aversion declines due to high relative wealth (INRELW), global real interest rates (GLREAL) decrease, and the global dividend yield (GLDIVY) goes up. All signs of the regression coefficients, except the sign for the dividend yield, indicate that value stocks are likely to outperform growth stocks when investors expect business conditions to improve.

We document that the value premiums on international stock markets are driven by changes in the global economic outlook. This is consistent with the findings of Liew and Vassalou (2000). They study the economics of value premiums from the opposite direction, showing that value premiums include information about future economic growth. We contribute to that issue documenting that the variation of

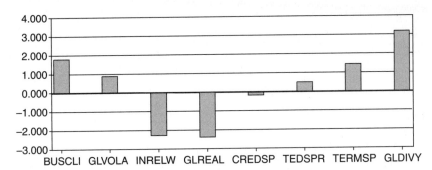

FIGURE 9.5   Forces driving value premiums. The figure shows the *t*-statistics testing for significance of the coefficients in the regression of the value-growth return spread in the MSCI stock universe on global instrumental variables over the period from 1986.01 to 1999.03. BUSCLI = U.S. purchasing manager index, GLVOLA = Global stock market volatility, INRELW = Inverse relative wealth, GLREAL = Global real interest rate, CREDSP = U.S. credit spread (as provided by Moody's), TEDSPR = Treasury-Eurodollar spread, TERMSP = Global term spread, and GLDIVY = Global dividend yield.

value-growth spreads is to some extent predictable by lagged indicators of expected business conditions and market sentiment. There is no strict consistency across individual countries for the interaction between instruments and the magnitudes of the value premiums. Nevertheless, the regression results for global regions show that value stocks tend to outperform growth stocks when the outlook is good and the risk premiums on capital markets are low.

Our findings are also consistent with the explanation of Fama and French (1998) for the value-growth performance differential. They argue that the long-horizon value premium is a compensation for taking on higher risk of financial distress. When the business climate improves, the premium for financial distress declines—if any such premium exists. The prices of stocks with a high exposure to that source of risk should rise, because the shareholders are discounting expected cash flows on the basis of lower distress premiums. Our empirical results support this notion. Value stocks tend to deliver higher returns than growth stocks when our instrumental variables indicate improving economic conditions. In contrast, when the economic situation is expected to deteriorate, growth stocks outperform value stocks, which might be a result of applying higher distress premiums to discount the cash flows of value stocks.

Global Integration of Value Premiums

Our analysis suggests that the value premiums on international equity markets mirror a compensation for systematic risk, presumably a premium for the peril of financial distress. Furthermore, the magnitudes of value premiums seem to correspond to the business cycle, suggesting that the reward for the underlying risk is not stable over time. In accordance with our understanding of asset pricing, this is a characteristic feature of risk premiums on capital markets. Instrumental variables representing global or U.S. information on the economic climate can explain a reasonable portion of the variation of value-growth spreads. It is a natural extension of our approach to examine whether comovement of expected value premiums exists across international equity markets. Any such covariation would indicate globally integrated pricing of the underlying risk factor.

We model month-to-month expected value premiums using the following time series of fitted values from our instrumental regression model: (1) the regression coefficients estimated for an individual stock market or a region, and (2) the time series of global instruments to calculate expected value premiums for the stock market or the region over the sample period. The focus of our examination is the comovement between these time series of predicted value-growth spreads.

The average correlation of predicted value premiums across the 18 countries is 0.078, which is twice as large as the average correlation measured for ex post value premiums (0.036). For example, correlation between conditional value premiums in Switzerland and Germany is 0.68 relative to 0.46 in the case of ex post measurement; for the United Kingdom and the United States it is 0.82 (conditional) relative to 0.63 (ex post). Figure 9.6 shows the comovement of the predicted value premiums in these countries.

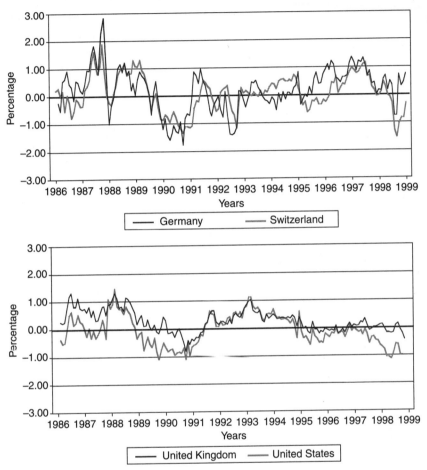

FIGURE 9.6 Comovement of expected value-growth return spreads in different countries. The figure shows the comovement of predicted (conditional) value premiums across countries. Predicted value premiums are generated on a month-to-month basis using the time series of fitted values from the instrumental regression model. Entries represent January-to-January time periods.

Figure 9.7 compares the correlations between the value-growth spreads on individual stock markets and the MSCI world aggregate ex post (historical measurement) and ex ante (regression-based prediction). It shows that the correlations of predicted value premiums are substantially larger. The mean correlation between countries and the world aggregate is 0.33 for the predicted spreads and 0.19 for the spreads measured ex post. For some countries, including Germany, Italy, Sweden, Switzerland, and Australia, that difference is remarkable.

The correlations of expected value premiums between the global regions are likewise notably larger than the correlations of ex post value premiums. The correlation between expected value premiums

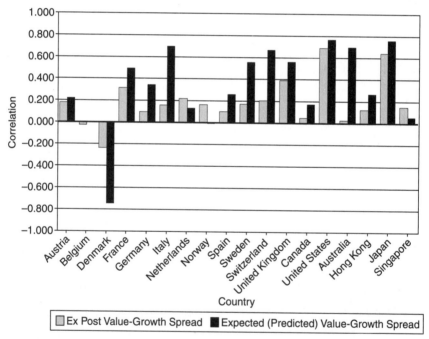

FIGURE 9.7 Global integration of value premiums. The figure shows the correlations between value-growth return spreads on individual stock markets and in the MSCI global stock universe. Value premiums measured ex post are compared to predicted value premiums over the period from 1986.01 to 1999.03. Value-growth return spreads are denominated in local currencies.

in Europe and North America is 0.62, compared with 0.48 for ex post premiums. The corresponding figures are 0.54 and minus 0.06 for Europe and the Pacific Rim, and 0.31 and 0.03 for North America and the Pacific Rim. Again, these are tremendous differences. Overall, our correlation results indicate notable common variation of expected value-growth spreads. This implies that international value growth-spreads are related to a common (but unobservable) global risk factor, which is consistently priced across major stock markets.

TACTICAL STYLE ROTATION STRATEGIES

Devising a Simple Switching Strategy

The preceding empirical evidence indicates that the return difference between value and growth stocks is to some extent predictable on the basis of lagged information about the economic outlook and the market sentiment. To test whether this predictability can be exploited by active style rotation strategies, we examine the significance of our findings from the viewpoint of an investor.

Active style rotation strategies are compared with passive value as well as growth strategies on a country-by-country basis. The signals for style switching within a country are determined on the basis of the fitted values of the instrument regression models. If the value-growth spread predicted at the beginning of a month is positive, the funds are entirely allocated to value stocks over the following month; otherwise growth stocks are held. The asset allocation is revised on a monthly basis. This active style rotation procedure and both passive benchmarks represent investable strategies because the MSCI indices (the basis for our simulations) include the most liquid stocks in each country.

Performance of Active Value-Growth Strategies

Table 9.7 documents the risk and return figures for the tactical style rotation strategy and the two alternative passive investments, measured

TABLE 9.7 Risk and Return of Tactical-Style Rotation versus Passive-Style Investment

Countries	Tactical Style Rotation				Growth Investing			Value Investing		
	Mean (%)	Volatility (%)	RR Ratio	No. TA	Mean (%)	Volatility (%)	RR Ratio	Mean (%)	Volatility (%)	RR Ratio
Europe										
Austria	6.78	26.71	0.254	36	3.18	25.00	0.127	9.00	28.02	0.321
Belgium	23.06	18.46	1.249	42	14.20	18.76	0.757	22.54	18.29	1.232
Denmark	19.23	19.90	0.967	28	13.61	20.57	0.662	10.13	19.42	0.521
France	16.48	22.54	0.731	25	14.66	21.82	0.672	14.74	22.33	0.660
Germany	13.04	21.70	0.601	30	8.42	23.59	0.357	11.39	20.61	0.553
Italy	19.99	26.55	0.753	26	13.85	24.97	0.555	11.76	27.46	0.428
Netherlands	22.82	19.37	1.178	21	14.42	18.44	0.782	19.55	19.07	1.025
Norway	16.28	28.61	0.569	25	3.88	26.42	0.147	13.39	28.98	0.462
Spain	27.02	25.95	1.041	22	22.93	27.87	0.823	20.80	24.25	0.858
Sweden	28.34	25.33	1.119	32	24.79	24.52	1.011	16.20	27.03	0.599
Switzerland	18.91	18.77	1.007	25	13.60	19.03	0.715	15.10	22.28	0.678
United Kingdom	17.78	18.02	0.987	21	14.26	17.90	0.797	16.78	18.04	0.930
North America										
Canada	12.80	16.34	0.783	31	9.65	17.01	0.567	9.83	15.93	0.617
United States	21.98	16.40	1.340	14	19.42	16.80	1.156	16.36	14.91	1.098
Pacific Rim										
Australia	19.16	20.69	0.926	20	12.65	24.74	0.511	14.24	19.93	0.715
Hong Kong	22.47	34.10	0.659	34	15.54	30.56	0.509	17.09	35.61	0.480
Japan	5.34	23.06	0.231	17	−0.36	24.58	−0.015	4.87	20.81	0.234
Singapore	17.55	29.06	0.604	35	7.25	26.97	0.269	10.34	31.19	0.331
Regions										
World	15.88	14.73	1.078	16	12.47	15.19	0.821	13.40	14.35	0.934
North America	20.68	15.86	1.304	14	18.81	16.48	1.141	16.01	14.76	1.084
Europe	16.69	16.64	1.003	19	13.88	16.71	0.830	15.44	16.99	0.909
Pacific Rim	6.11	20.93	0.292	17	1.10	22.60	0.049	5.98	19.30	0.310

Note: Tactical-style rotation is based on monthly switching between value stocks and growth stocks, using the signals from country-specific instrumental regressions. Mean and volatility are given as annualized values, denominated in local currencies. RR ratio = Ratio of mean return to volatility; No. TA = Number of transactions to implement the active strategy. Value and growth stocks are represented by the style-specific total return indices provided by MSCI for countries and regions over the period from 1986.01 to 1999.03. Returns are denominated in local currencies.

from January 1986 to March 1999. Figure 9.8 displays the return differences between the tactical style portfolio and the respective passive investment with the highest return in the different countries. It shows that active style rotation beats passive value or growth investments in terms of absolute returns in all countries, with the exception of Austria. The return differences are between 0.47 percent (in Japan) and 7.21 percent (in Singapore) per year. In 16 of the 18 countries, the return-to-risk ratio, defined as average return over volatility, is also superior for the active portfolio strategy.

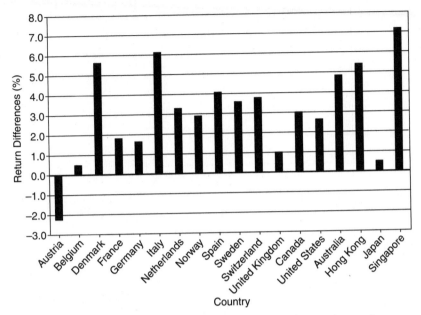

FIGURE 9.8 Tactical style rotation strategies (I). The figure shows the return differences between the actively managed style rotation portfolio and the passive benchmark with the highest return in each country. Return differences are denominated in local currencies. The signals for style switching within a country are determined on the basis of the fitted values of the instrument regression model over the period from 1986.01 to 1999.03.

Figure 9.9 shows the cumulated return differences relative to the passive benchmarks on the basis of the initially invested funds for a reduced sample of countries. For example, the style rotation strategies in Switzerland and the United States show that in Switzerland, the value portfolio has been the best performing passive investment and, therefore, the benchmark for the active investment. In contrast, in the United States it has been the growth portfolio. In Switzerland, the additional return of active style rotation over 159 months sums to 293.7 percent; in the United States it cumulates to 294.9 percent, including round-trip transaction costs of 0.4 percent. To implement the style

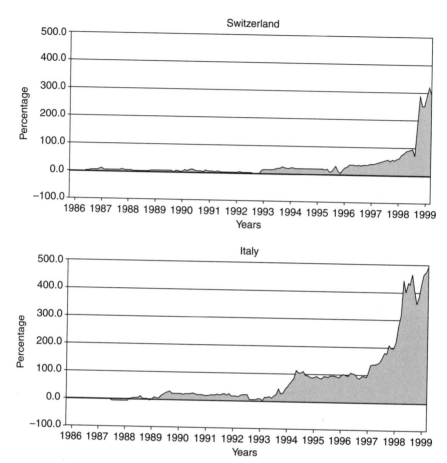

FIGURE 9.9 Tactical style rotation strategies (II). The figure shows the cumulated return difference between the actively managed style rotation portfolio and the best performing passive investment, relative to the initial investment over the period from 1986.01 to 1999.03. In Switzerland, the best performing passive investment and, hence, the benchmark for the active investment strategy is the value portfolio; Italy: growth; Netherlands: value; United States: growth; Japan: value; Australia: value.

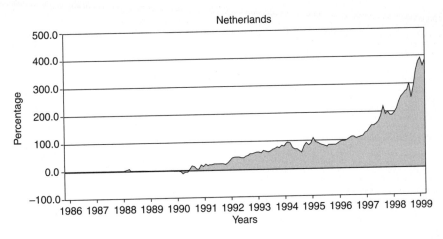

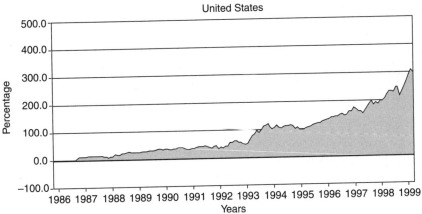

FIGURE 9.9A *(continued)*

rotation strategy in Switzerland, 25 transactions had to be executed (on average, the style of investments is altered after 6 months). In the United States, the number of transactions was only 14, implying a change of market segments after 10 months on average.

Our simulations show that active style management on the basis of a quantitative model can significantly add value to a portfolio. In most countries, tactical switching between value and growth stocks outperforms the risk and return of passive value and growth strategies. At the same time, the number of transactions required is not

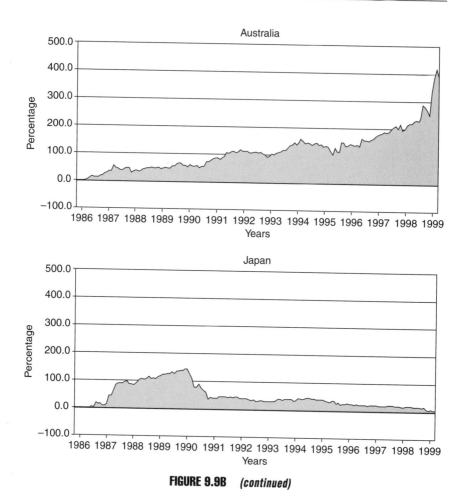

FIGURE 9.9B   *(continued)*

prohibitive. Yet, the results presented here only suggest the performance potential of style rotation. The sets of instruments in our regression models are not individually fitted to the specific value-growth cycles in the different countries; we simply apply the same eight instruments for each stock market. Moreover, a more frequent reestimation of the regression model parameters could have a positive impact on the performance of the strategy. On the other hand, the analysis presented here is in-sample; even though the instrument variables are lagged in the regression, the parameters are estimated on the basis of the entire sample period. The stability of the results for out-of-sample style rotation strategies—where the parameters are estimated using only data up to the portfolio formation date—would be another important empirical question.

CONCLUSION

To explore the dynamics as well as the economics of value-growth spreads on international equity markets, our sample covers 3 global regions and 18 countries over the 1980s and 1990s. Several major results are documented. Over the past 20 years, value stocks outperformed growth stocks on most international equity markets. Across the globe, however, year-to-year value-growth return spreads vary considerably in both sign and magnitude. In addition, the performance of value stocks relative to growth stocks reveals characteristic cycles in all regions and countries. Also, the correlations of value-growth return spreads across the globe are typically low. There is some comovement of the value-growth spreads across countries that are economically linked. Most important, our analysis shows that expected business conditions and market sentiment drive value-growth return spreads. Value stocks tend to outperform growth stocks when the outlook improves and premiums for systematic risk decrease. Reasonable portions of the value-growth return spreads on international markets are ex ante predictable by indicators of expected global economic conditions. The predictable variation of value-growth return spreads is economically significant and active style rotation strategies can exploit it. Finally, there is notable common variation of the expected value-growth spreads across international countries and regions. In particular, the correlations of expected value-growth return spreads are substantially higher than the correlations of the ex post spreads.

Overall, our findings support the notion that value-growth return spreads on equity markets reflect a compensation for systematic risk. Most important, we document evidence that value-growth spreads are driven by global economic conditions—a characteristic feature of risk premiums on global capital markets. Our analyses of the correlations between the expected value-growth spreads in different countries can be interpreted as indicating the existence of an underlying (but unobservable) risk factor that determines the consistent pricing of value stocks around the globe. The specific patterns in our predicted value-growth spreads are compatible with the prevalent view in the literature that the latent risk factor priced in value stock returns is related to financial distress.

CHAPTER 10

Integrating Tactical and Equilibrium Portfolio Management

Putting the Black-Litterman Model to Work

EXECUTIVE SUMMARY

■ The traditional mean-variance approach has several potential drawbacks. Among other things, it requires a complete set of expected returns to generate optimal portfolio weights. Most analysts, however, do not have return expectations for the entire asset class universe.

■ Moreover, mean-variance optimization frequently leads to extreme and implausible portfolio weights in either direction. Even more disturbing, these weights are excessively sensitive to changes in the expected returns. Finally, the traditional approach does not differentiate between the levels of uncertainty associated with input variables (estimation error).

■ Black and Litterman's approach (1992) is an elegant and intuitive way to alleviate many of these problems; it combines the market equilibrium (with all positive weights) with an investor's subjective views of the market. Depending on the asset manager's confidence in those views, the Black-Litterman technique tilts the optimal portfolio away from the equilibrium toward the assets he or she likes best.

■ In this chapter, we apply the Black-Litterman portfolio approach to a portfolio of European sectors in the Dow Jones STOXX universe. We give a simple road map for the implementation of the Black-Litterman approach in practice.

■ We demonstrate that the Black-Litterman approach—compared with the traditional Markowitz approach—helps users to arrive at more reasonable, less extreme, and less sensitive portfolio weighting schemes.

INTRODUCTION

The Markowitz (1952) formulation of modern portfolio theory combines the two basic objectives of investing: maximizing expected return while minimizing risk. In a portfolio context, risk is measured as the standard deviation (or volatility) of returns around their expected value. Traditional portfolio optimization leads to a parabolic efficient frontier indicating the compositions of portfolios with the highest expected return given a certain level of risk.

Even though modern portfolio theory has stood the test of time within the academic community and generations of business students have encountered mean-variance portfolio selection as a core concept of modern investment theory, it has had surprisingly little impact in the investment community.

He and Litterman (1999) state two reasons for this observation. First, asset managers typically focus on a small segment of the investment universe. They look at fundamental ratios, momentum, and styles to find stocks they feel are undervalued. In contrast, the Markowitz approach requires inputting expected returns for all assets in the universe. Second, mean-variance optimization implies a trade-off between risk and expected returns along the efficient frontier. Portfolio weights are the mere result of a mathematical optimization exercise. In contrast, asset managers usually think directly in terms of portfolio weights, deviating from their benchmark in the tactical asset allocation. They find that the weights returned by an optimizer are extreme, not intuitive, and thus inappropriate for being implemented in a client's portfolio. Much of this discomfort with the standard approach occurs because historical returns are generally used instead of expected returns and estimation errors are not taken into account.

These observations were the motivation for the work by Fisher Black and Robert Litterman (1992). The goal was to enhance modern portfolio theory to make it more applicable for investment professionals. Their approach is flexible enough to combine the market equilibrium with subjective views and an investor's economic reasoning. Because the Black-Litterman model starts with neutral portfolio weights that are consistent with market equilibrium, the revised weighting schemes tend to be much less extreme than the results from traditional mean-variance optimization.

Even though their paper brings academic finance a major step closer to the investment community, the number of professional users still seems small. This chapter presents a road map to put the Black-Litterman approach to work. Our exposition emphasizes simple examples instead of the underlying mathematics. First, we describe the pitfalls of traditional portfolio optimization in detail. Then we introduce the reverse-optimization technique. The resulting implicit returns serve as the neutral starting point for the Black-Litterman approach. The main contribution of Black and Litterman—how to combine equilibrium expected returns with an investor's subjective views in a consistent way—is demonstrated next. Our simple examples use historical returns from European sectors.

THE DEFICIENCIES OF STANDARD PORTFOLIO THEORY

As described in the following subsections, standard portfolio theory has several major deficiencies that discourage its more frequent use by investment professionals.

Amount of Required Input Data

Traditional Markowitz optimization requires as inputs the expected returns and the expected variance-covariance structure for all assets in the investment universe. Yet, portfolio managers typically have reliable return forecasts for only a small subset of assets. Proper forecasts for the variance-covariance structure are even harder to obtain.[1] The ex post performance of the resulting weighting schemes, however, depends heavily on the quality of input data, especially the vector of expected returns (see Merton, 1980).

Extreme Portfolio Weights

Optimized allocations tend to include large short positions that the portfolio manager cannot justify in a client's portfolio. In the following example, we use monthly returns in Swiss francs from the Dow Jones STOXX indices for European sectors from June 1993 to November 2000. Descriptive statistics of our data set are shown in the appendix at the end of this chapter. As discussed, the investor usually does not have a complete set of expected returns for all sectors in the Dow Jones STOXX family. Therefore, we start by setting the expected return for all sectors equal to 13.93 percent, which is the value-weighted average annual return over the sample period.

The results appear as black bars in Figure 10.1.[2] Equal returns compensate for the different levels of risk across our sample, but they

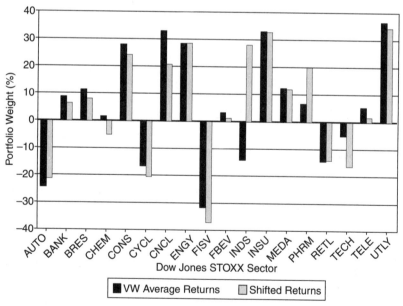

FIGURE 10.1 Optimal weights starting from equal expected returns.

tend to generate extreme portfolio holdings. For example, mean-variance maximization yields an optimal weight of 36 percent for utilities (UTLY) because they had a low volatility of 18.1 percent per year. In contrast, the much larger bank sector (BANK) receives a weight of only 9 percent because banks were more volatile with an annual standard deviation of 22 percent. Some of the most volatile European sectors—automobiles (AUTO), cyclical consumption goods (CYCL), financial services (FISV), and the retail sector (RETL)—even have substantial negative weights. Financial services (FISV) receive the largest negative weight with −31.5 percent. Also, some sectors with small capitalizations, such as the construction sector (CONS), get unreasonably large weights, whereas some of the larger sectors, such as tech stocks (TECH), have small (or even negative) weights. Overall, the resulting portfolio hardly constitutes a realistic strategy for an asset manager.

Instead of using equal returns (as we do in Figure 10.1 for the sake of simplicity), investors might consider using historical returns as inputs for expected returns. However, both the vector of expected returns and the covariance structure required for mean-variance optimization must be forward-looking. Merton (1980) demonstrates that historical returns are poor proxies for future expected returns and that estimation error is a crucial issue for putting portfolio theory into practice. Michaud (1989) even argues that mean-variance optimizers are estimation error maximizers. Optimized portfolios tend to overweight (underweight) assets with large (small) expected returns, negative (positive) correlations, and small (large) variances. Intuitively, assets with extreme returns tend to be most affected by estimation error. Jorion (1985) suggests a Bayes-Stein shrinkage estimator to alleviate the problem associated with estimation errors.

A remedy often proposed to avoid extreme weights is to introduce constraints in the optimization problem (e.g., non-negativity constraints). Constraints may come from client-specific and/or legal restrictions. However, with too many restrictions, "optimized" results may merely reflect the prespecified views, which are not always economically intuitive. Even worse, short sale constraints typically lead to corner solutions and the dropping of some assets from the optimized portfolios. These constrained weighting schemes are again hard to implement in a client's portfolio because they often imply unreasonable weights in only a small subset of (possibly small-capitalization) assets.

Sensitivity of Portfolio Weights

Optimal allocations are particularly sensitive to changes in expected returns. Small changes in input variables can cause dramatic changes in the weighting schemes. A major concern of asset managers is that mean-variance optimization leads to extremely unstable portfolio weights.

This property can be demonstrated by extending the previous example involving European sectors. For the moment, we assume that an investor has only a single view about European sectors: Pharmaceuticals (PHRM) and industrials (INDS) outperform telecom (TELE) and technology (TECH) stocks by 3 percent per year. To incorporate this view in a simplistic manner, the expected returns for both industrials and pharmaceuticals are shifted up by 1.5 percent and the expected returns for telecom and technology stocks are shifted down by 1.5 percent (starting from the value-weighted average of 13.93%).

The grey bars in Figure 10.1 show that this small shift in expected returns causes huge swings in the weights for the sectors involved in the investor's view. The weight for industrials soars from −14 percent to almost 30 percent. Similarly, the weight for pharmaceuticals jumps from 7 percent to roughly 20 percent. In contrast, technology stocks' weight is further reduced from −5 percent to −16 percent; the telecom sector goes down from 5 percent to 1.5 percent.

An even more uncomfortable observation is that weights can change considerably even for sectors without a particular view. For example, the weight for chemicals (CHEM) decreases from 1.5 percent to −5 percent, noncyclical goods (CNCL) from 33 percent to 20 percent. Yet, the investor has not expressed any views about these sectors. Accordingly, strong correlations between European sectors hinder fine-tuning of portfolio weights. Even a small change in the expected return of only one asset can lead to perplexing changes in the weights for all other assets (for which the investor has no specific view).

Mismatch in Levels of Information

Standard mean-variance optimization does not distinguish strongly held views from vague assumptions. Optimizers generally do not differentiate between the levels of uncertainty associated with input variables. Therefore, the optimal weights associated with revised expected returns often bear no intuitive relation to the view the investor actually wishes to express. Again, one way to alleviate this problem is to apply Bayes-Stein estimators, which shrink expected returns toward a common mean (see Jorion, 1985).

To make the problem even worse, in many cases the differences in estimated means may not be statistically significant. This implies that every point on the efficient frontier has a neighborhood that includes an infinite number of statistically equivalent portfolios. Though equivalently optimal, these portfolios may have completely different compositions.[3]

NEUTRAL VIEWS AS THE STARTING POINT

The approach suggested by Black and Litterman (1992) is an attempt to alleviate the deficiencies of standard portfolio theory. Their goal was to make mean-variance theory more applicable for investment professionals. The approach allows combining an investor's views about the outlook for his or her investment universe with some kind of equilibrium returns. Equilibrium returns provide a neutral reference point, leading to more reasonable and more stable portfolio compositions than the traditional mean-standard deviation optimization.

Black and Litterman argue that the only sensible definition of *neutral* means is the set of expected returns that would clear the market if all investors had identical views.[4] Hence, the natural choice for neutral expected returns is to use the equilibrium expected returns derived from reverse optimization. The Black-Litterman model gravitates toward a neutral market capitalization weighted portfolio that tilts in the direction of assets favored in the views the investor has expressed. The extent of this deviation from equilibrium depends on the degree of confidence the investor has in each view. Alternatively, any strategic asset allocation could serve as a possible starting point in the Black-Litterman approach.

It is well known that given the coefficient of relative risk aversion, γ, the n-dimensional vector of expected returns, Π, and the covariance matrix, Ω, the unconstrained maximization problem faced by an investor with quadratic utility function or assuming normally distributed returns

$$\max_{\omega} \omega'\Pi - \frac{\gamma\omega'\Omega\omega}{2} \qquad (10.1)$$

has a solution of optimal portfolio weights

$$\omega^* = (\gamma\Omega)^{-1}\Pi \qquad (10.2)$$

The reverse optimization technique suggests working backward. Assume that a set of portfolio weights ω is optimal and solve this equation for the vector of implied returns:

$$\Pi = \gamma\Omega\omega \qquad (10.3)$$

By construction, optimization using the implied returns yields the portfolio weights that were used to compute the implied returns. Intuitively, this approach is closely linked to the Capital Asset Pricing Model (CAPM). The model predicts that prices will adjust until, in market equilibrium, the expected returns will be such that the demand for these assets will exactly match the available supply.

Using the relative market capitalizations as the weights, the grey bars in Figure 10.2 show the implied expected returns for our sample of European sector indices. These implied returns serve as a neutral starting point to incorporate an investor's view about future returns. The black bars in Figure 10.2 depict the historical returns over the sample period from June 1993 to November 2000.

Figure 10.3 shows the resulting optimal portfolio weights, using unconstrained mean-variance optimization. By construction, the grey

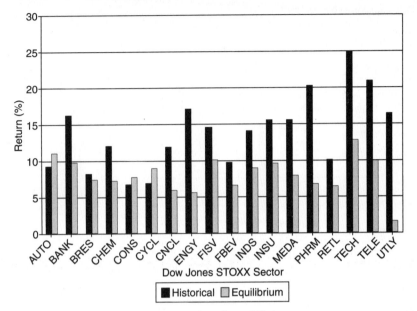

FIGURE 10.2 Historical and equilibrium returns.

bars represent the (all positive) relative market capitalizations of the different sectors. In contrast, when the historical returns are used, the resulting weights are even more extreme than when we used equal returns for all sectors. Needless to say, an asset manager would find it impossible to implement the portfolio represented by the black bars in Figure 10.3.

Again, error maximization seems to be a problem. Unconstrained optimization leads to extreme short positions in assets with very low past returns, such as cyclical goods (CYCL) and retail companies (RETL), and extreme long positions in assets with very high past returns, such as energy companies (ENGY). On the other hand, the plausible weight for the technology sector (TECH) indicates that mean-variance optimization to some extent trades off mean against standard deviation. Tech stocks had the highest historical return over the sample period (25.0% per year), but also the highest volatility (31.3% per year).

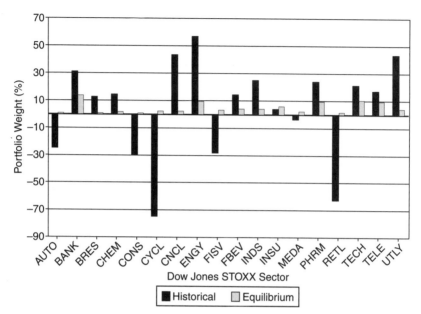

FIGURE 10.3   Optimal portfolio weights based on historical returns and equilibrium returns from reverse optimization.

In contrast, having equilibrium expected returns in the back of the mind, the market portfolio weights are all positive, and they are close to what might be called normal investment behavior of an average investors. For this reason, they reflect a hypothetical passive manager who tracks the benchmark portfolio. Alternatively, strategic target portfolio weights could represent the benchmark from which asset managers can deviate according to their economic reasoning in the tactical asset allocation. The major contribution of Black and Litterman, however, is to combine the equilibrium returns with uncertain views about expected returns in a consistent way to derive realistic portfolio holdings. As Black and Litterman state it, the equilibrium concept is interesting but not particularly useful. Its real value is to provide a neutral framework the investor can adjust according to subjective views and constraints.[5] In particular, the market capitalization weights are tilted in the direction of assets most favored by the investor.

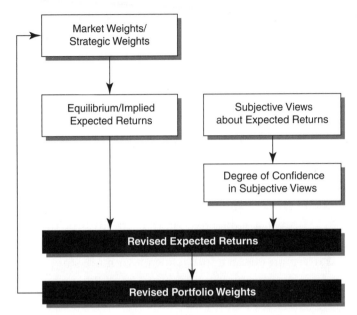

FIGURE 10.4 Major steps behind the Black-Litterman model.

THE BLACK-LITTERMAN APPROACH

The major steps in the Black-Litterman model are visualized in Figure 10.4. As stated, Black and Litterman start with a set of market weights. Alternatively, a set of strategic, or long-term, weights can be used. These weights represent the normal investment behavior of an average investor. In market equilibrium, these weighting schemes imply a corresponding vector of expected returns for the asset universe. Given the current economic conditions, however, an asset manager's expectations about short-term returns may differ from those implied by long-term market clearing conditions. The Black-Litterman approach is flexible enough to incorporate many different views, and it offers a method for combining the equilibrium (or neutral) view with an investor's subjective views in a consistent way.

In addition to the return expectations, investors must specify the degree of confidence they put in the stated views. All information is translated into symmetric confidence bands around normally distributed returns. The most important contribution of Black and Litterman is to devise a consistent weighting scheme between the subjective view and the equilibrium view. Intuitively, the higher (lower) the degree of confidence, the more (less) the revised expected returns are tilted toward the investor's views.

The vector of revised expected returns is then handed over to a portfolio optimizer. As shown later, even though the views spread across all asset classes and, hence, imply changes for the entire vector of expected returns, the optimal weights change only for those asset classes with explicit views. For all other assets, the equilibrium/strategic weights are applied. In contrast to the ad hoc methods discussed earlier, this reflects the subjective views of an investor in a consistent way. Equally important, and in contrast to the Markowitz approach, the Black-Litterman model approach leads to more stable and less extreme portfolio weights.

Long-Term Equilibrium

The following derivation of the Black-Litterman approach closely follows their original paper, He and Litterman (1999), and the textbook treatment by Lee (2000).[6] The vector of equilibrium returns backed out from reverse optimization is again denoted as Π. To keep things simple, Black and Litterman posit that the covariance matrix of expected returns is proportional to the historical one, rescaled only by a shrinkage factor τ. Because statistical uncertainty of the mean is lower than the uncertainty of the returns themselves, the value of τ should be close to zero. Hence, a complete specification of the equilibrium distribution of expected returns is

$$E(R) \sim N(\Pi, \tau\Omega) \qquad (10.4)$$

where Ω is an $n \cdot n$ covariance matrix of realized historical returns, and $E(R)$ is an $n \cdot 1$ vector of expected returns. An investor who does not hold a subjective view about expected returns should simply hold the market portfolio. This reflects the equilibrium state at which supply equals demand. When the investor has some views about expected returns, the difficult task is to combine these views with the market equilibrium in a consistent way.

The Black-Litterman model requires the investor to express a degree of confidence about subjective views. Accordingly, both sources of information—the equilibrium expected returns and the views—are expressed in terms of probability distributions. Intuition suggests that the relative weights put on the equilibrium and the views depend on the degree of confidence in both sources of information. The less certain the investor's subjective views, the more the resulting portfolio becomes tilted toward the equilibrium. In contrast, the deviations of weights from the market portfolio will be more pronounced in a portfolio of an investor who is highly confident in his or her views.[7] This notion of the Black-Litterman approach is similar to the shrinkage suggested by Jorion (1985).

Expressing Views

To implement the Black-Litterman approach, the asset manager has to express views in terms of a probability distribution. Black and Litterman assume that the investor has relative views of the form: "I expect that sector A outperforms sector B by V," where V is a given value. Absolute views of the form: "I expect that sector C has an expected return of 10 percent over the next year," can also be incorporated in the analysis, as shown in a later example.

For the moment, assume that the investor has k different views on linear combinations of expected returns of the n assets. These are written in matrix form as

$$P \cdot E(R) = V + e \qquad (10.5)$$

where P is a $k \cdot n$ matrix, V is a $k \cdot 1$ vector, and e is a $k \cdot 1$ vector with error terms of the views. The first view is represented as a linear combination of expected returns in the first row of P. The value of this first view is given by the first element of V (the expected value), plus an error term as the first element of e. The error term measures the degree of uncertainty about a particular view. More uncertainty is reflected in a higher value of the entry in e. Finally, let the covariance matrix of error terms be denoted as Σ. Black and Litterman assume that all views are independently drawn from the future return distribution, implying that Σ is a diagonal matrix. Accordingly, its diagonal elements are the elements in the vector e.

Initially, assume the investor has only a single view. As before, the investor expects that a value-weighted portfolio of pharmaceuticals and industrials outperforms a value-weighted portfolio of telecom and tech stocks by 3 percent. This view is represented in matrix form as

$$P \cdot \begin{pmatrix} E(R_{\text{AUTO}}) \\ E(R_{\text{BANK}}) \\ \vdots \\ E(R_{\text{UTLY}}) \end{pmatrix} = (3\%) + (0.61\%^2) \tag{10.6}$$

with $P = \begin{pmatrix} 0 & \cdots & 0 & 0.34 & 0 & \cdots & 0 & 0.66 & 0 & -0.51 & -0.49 & 0 \end{pmatrix}$

where the single entry in the error vector e indicates the degree of confidence in the view. This requires being a little more precise about the specification of the view. For example, the investor could state being 90 percent sure that the spread in expected returns between the two portfolios is between 2 percent and 4 percent over the next year. Following Pitts (1997a, 1997b), we interpret this statement as a 90 percent confidence interval for the return spread with half-width 1 percent and centered at 3 percent.[8] Assuming normality, the 90 percent confidence interval implies a standard deviation of 0.61 percent. The greater the degree of confidence, the smaller is the half-width of the interval and/or the greater is the probability mass for an interval. The intuition is shown in Figure 10.5.

The bell-shaped curve in Figure 10.5 indicates the distribution of return spreads. A normal distribution is completely described by the first two moments, mean and standard deviation. A 90 percent interval implies going 1.664 times the standard deviation to the left side and the right side of the mean spread at 3 percent. This results in a confidence interval from 2 percent to 4 percent.

Because the investor expresses the view as a value-weighted spread, the P vector has 0.34 for industrials and 0.66 for pharmaceuticals (both weights summing to one) and −0.51 for tech and −0.49

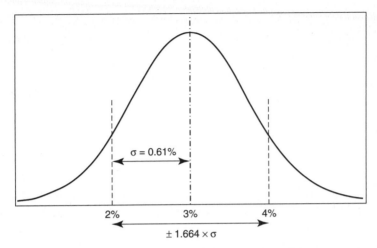

FIGURE 10.5 Interpreting the degree of confidence.

for telecom stocks (the weights summing to one again). Hence, the nonzero elements in *P* are the relative market capitalization weights of long and short portfolios, according to the relative view. The remaining entries in *P* for all other sectors are zero.

This setup for specifying subjective views is extremely flexible. Virtually all possible (relative and absolute) views can be incorporated into the model. The number of opinions can be smaller or larger than the number of assets in the investment universe. If the asset manager has consistently expected return forecasts for all asset classes, the *P* vector has as many rows as there are asset classes. In contrast, if the asset manager has useful views for only a small set of assets (which might be the case in the investment practice), the *P* vector has fewer rows than there are assets. After the equilibrium distribution of expected returns and the views have been specified, the task is to combine these two sources of information. Intuition suggests that the more certain are the investor's views, the more the resulting portfolio should be tilted toward the favored assets.

Combining Certain Views

For certain views on behalf of the asset manager, the matrix Σ contains only zeros. The distribution of expected returns conditional on the equilibrium and views can be derived as the solution to the following problem:[9]

$$\min_{E(R)} \left[E(R) - \Pi \right]^T \tau \Omega^{-1} \left[E(R) - \Pi \right]$$

subject to $P \cdot E(R) = V$

(10.7)

This is a constrained least-squares minimization problem. The sum of squares of deviations of expected returns from equilibrium, $[E(R) - \Pi]$, weighted by the covariance matrix, $\tau \Omega$, is minimized, taking the restrictions on expected returns expressed by the asset manager into account. T denotes the transpose of a vector or a matrix. The solution of this problem is given as

$$\text{Mean of } E(R) = \Pi + \tau \Omega P^T \left(P \tau \Omega P^T \right)^{-1} (V - P\Pi)$$

(10.8)

Combining Uncertain Views

If the investor is not perfectly sure about his or her view (which is the more realistic case), the error terms in the vector e will not be zero. Black and Litterman show that the conditional distribution of returns can be derived using Bayes' Law.[10] Without going into the details, the Bayesian approach posits that views about the state of the world are subjective. Instead of estimating paramaters as if they were fixed (as in classical statistical analysis), observed data are used to sequentially update the subjective prior beliefs about the current state. In the Black-Litterman approach, the investor's views about expected returns are used to adjust the deviation of expected returns away from equilibrium. The magnitude of the revision depends on the degree of certainty expressed in the investor's views.

Again, without going into the details of the derivation, the conditional distribution of $E(R)$ is normal with[11]

$$\text{Mean of } E(R) = \left[(\tau\Omega)^{-1} + P^T \Sigma^{-1} P \right]^{-1} \left[(\tau\Omega)^{-1} \Pi + P^T \Sigma^{-1} V \right]$$

(10.9)

Hence, given the values for P, V, Π, τ, Ω, and Σ, we can derive the posterior means, which can then be handed over to a portfolio optimizer. This procedure results in optimal weights based on revised expected returns and the degree of confidence in the views. They are tilted toward the assets most favored by the investor.

A SIMPLE EXAMPLE

Incorporating a Relative View

An investor who does not have any views on expected returns should use the equilibrium distribution of returns. In fact, the vector of CAPM-related equilibrium returns Π results when all entries in the P vector (and the Σ matrix) are set equal to zero.

The Black-Litterman approach does not require the investor to hold views about expected returns on all sectors or asset classes. We continue with the earlier example, assuming that a value-weighted portfolio of pharmaceutical and industrial stocks outperforms a portfolio of telecom and technology stocks by 3 percent per year. The investor is 90 percent sure about this 3 percent return spread with half-width 1 percent (assuming normality). As demonstrated, this view is expressed as an expected return of 3 percent for a value-weighted portfolio with long positions in pharmaceuticals and industrials and short positions in telecom and tech stocks.

The equilibrium expected returns from Figure 10.2 serve as the reference point. These long-term returns are now combined with the single view on European sectors. Depending on the confidence in the investor's view, the optimal portfolio is tilted away from the market portfolio in the direction of the view. Figure 10.6 shows the resulting monthly expected returns for our sample of European sectors.[12]

In contrast to the Markowitz approach, the Black-Litterman model adjusts the expected returns for all STOXX sectors away from their equilibrium value toward the view. Because the opinion is expressed as a long position in industrial and pharmaceutical stocks and short positions in telecom and technology stocks, the expected

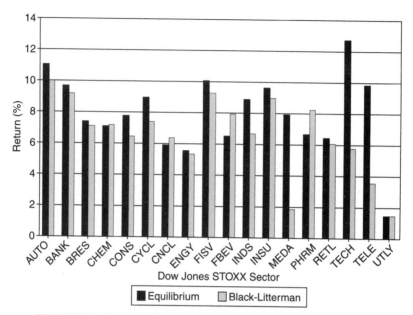

FIGURE 10.6   Expected returns in the Black-Litterman model.

return on this long-short portfolio is substantially raised from an equilibrium value of −3.9 percent to slightly below the stated 3 percent. This should come as no surprise, given the investor's high degree of confidence in this view (compared with the much wider confidence intervals for equilibrium returns).

Based on the view, decreasing returns for telecom and technology stocks are intuitive. On the other hand, although the expected return for pharmaceutical stocks increases, the expected return for industrials decreases. This is perfectly consistent with the investor's view. Nothing has been said about whether the expected return of a particular sector increases or decreases. All that has been assumed is a 3 percent spread between the four sectors involved. The view is not that industrial stocks go up; it says only that they outperform telecom and tech stocks.

The most interesting observation in Figure 10.6 is that, without explicit views, the expected returns change for all other sectors as well. Because all European sectors are highly correlated, the investor takes an implicit view on all other sectors. This effect occurs because of the matrix multiplications involving P, $\tau\Omega$, and Σ, expressing the views as a linear combination of expected returns, the covariance matrix of equilibrium expected returns, and the covariance matrix of views. Hence, the Black-Litterman model spreads the errors inherent in the input values for expected returns through the covariance matrix. This effect might reduce the error maximization problem proposed by Michaud (1989).

It is easy to show an example for the effect of spreading errors through the covariance matrix. Telecom and technology stocks have been the major drivers of European stock markets over recent years. The correlation structure implies that decreasing returns for these sectors lead to decreasing returns for most other sectors as well. The changes for those markets without explicit views, however, are generally much smaller than for the markets with stated explicit opinions. The sharply decreasing expected return for the media sector can be explained on the basis of its high correlation with the telecom sector. On the other hand, the slightly higher expected return for chemicals is attributed to their close relationship with the pharmaceutical sector. Overall, the implied changes displayed in Figure 10.6 seem consistent with common sense.

Finally, the revised vector of expected returns in Figure 10.6 is handed over to a portfolio optimizer. Figure 10.7 displays the resulting weighting scheme (again without short-sale restrictions). Compared with the equilibrium weights, the optimal portfolio increases the weights in industrial and pharmaceutical stocks and decreases the weights in technology and telecom stocks. This exactly represents the investor's view, going long in a value-weighted portfolio of industrials and pharmaceuticals and short in a value-weighted portfolio of tech and telecom stocks.

In contrast to standard mean-variance optimization, the weights for sectors without stated views remain unchanged at their relative market capitalization level. Hence, the optimal portfolio weights become much less sensitive to changes in the input variables. Even in unconstrained portfolios, extreme positions (both negative and positive) seldom occur (unless the spread itself becomes extreme) because

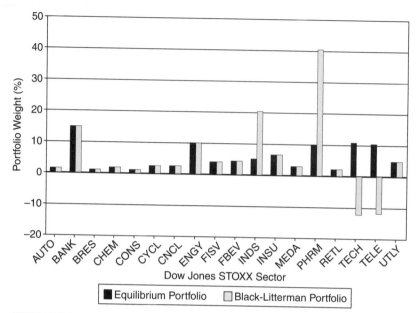

FIGURE 10.7 Optimal portfolio weights in the Black-Litterman model.

neutral weights serve as the starting point. Admittedly, increasing the tactical exposure in pharmaceuticals from roughly 10 percent to 40 percent might not be possible within an asset manager's prespecified strategic bandwidths. On the other hand, the relatively small short positions in technology and telecom stocks seem reasonable for an actively managed portfolio. In addition, short positions can be avoided by increasing uncertainty in the stated views.

Incorporating an Absolute View

So far, we have assumed that the investor has only one view. The Black-Litterman approach is flexible enough to incorporate many views. For example, in addition to the (relative) view on industrials and pharmaceuticals versus telecom and technology stocks, we assume the investor believes that noncyclical consumption goods perform better than implied by equilibrium conditions. In particular, the expected return for this sector is revised upward from 5.94 percent to

7.5 percent per year. Again, the investor is reasonably certain about this view, expressing a 90 percent confidence band between 6 percent and 9 percent. As explained earlier, this implies a volatility of 0.91 percent (assuming normality). The resulting matrix representation of the two views is

$$P \cdot \begin{pmatrix} E(R_{\text{AUTO}}) \\ E(R_{\text{BANK}}) \\ \vdots \\ E(R_{\text{UTLY}}) \end{pmatrix} = \begin{pmatrix} 3\% \\ 7.5\% \end{pmatrix} + \begin{pmatrix} 0.61\%^2 \\ 0.91\%^2 \end{pmatrix} \tag{10.10}$$

with

$$P = \begin{pmatrix} 0 & \cdots & 0 & 0.34 & 0 & \cdots & 0 & 0.66 & 0 & -0.51 & -0.49 & 0 \\ 0 & 0 & 0 & \cdots & 0 & 0 & 1 & 0 & 0 & \cdots & 0 & 0 \end{pmatrix} \tag{10.11}$$

The first row of the P matrix expresses the first view on pharmaceuticals and industrials versus telecom and technology stocks. The second row has all zeros except the "1" for noncyclical consumption goods, representing a long position in this sector.

Again, the uncertainty associated with the view is reflected in the magnitude of the corresponding error term. The higher the value of the error term, the more uncertainty the investor puts into the view. It has been assumed that the views represent independent draws from the future return distributions. Therefore, the covariance matrix of error terms, denoted as Σ, is a diagonal matrix. The two elements along the diagonal in Σ are collected in the e vector, which is the second part on the right-hand side of the matrix representation of the views.

Figure 10.8 shows the revised expected returns of European sectors, incorporating both views as stated in the P matrix. Again, the expected returns change for all assets, not just those sectors for which the investor has expressed explicit views. The implicit views (e.g., the strong increase in expected returns for food and beverages) are caused by the correlation between the sectors. As expected, since the

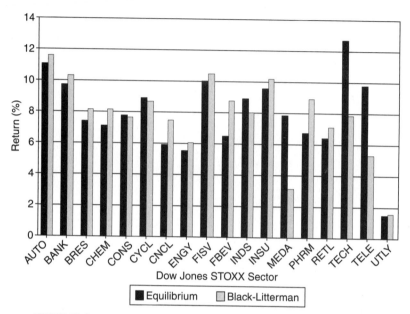

FIGURE 10.8 Expected returns in the Black-Litterman model.

view is again quite certain, the expected return for noncyclical consumption goods increases to just below 7.5 percent. Intuitively, the less confidence the investor had put in this view (e.g., if the confidence level was lower than 90 percent or τ smaller than 0.3), the more the revised expected return would end up below 7.5 percent.

The vector of revised expected returns is again handed over to an optimizer. Figure 10.9 shows the resulting weights for each sector in the optimal portfolio. Even though the expected returns are revised for the entire set of assets, the optimal weights change only for those sectors with specific views. Starting from neutral weights, this feature of the Black-Litterman approach implies much more stable portfolio compositions. In our example with two views, the optimal weight in noncyclical consumption goods changes from 2.9 percent in equilibrium to 16.9 percent. Compared with Figure 10.6, the weights for all four sectors incorporated in the first view (pharmaceutical, industrial, technology, and telecom) decrease slightly.

The overall lesson for asset managers is that the portfolio weights in the Black-Litterman setup are much less sensitive to changes in

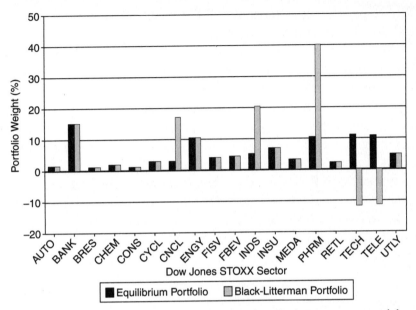

FIGURE 10.9 Optimal portfolio weights in the Black-Litterman model.

expected returns. They change, but in a consistent way and only to the degree the change is intuitive and ultimately embedded in an investor's view. The approach also incorporates uncertainty about individual views. As mentioned, it is unclear why the optimal weights should change for all sectors, when a view has only been specified for some sectors. In our example, it is not particularly intuitive why increasing the expected return for noncyclical consumption should affect the optimal weight in, say, automobiles. Consistent with this critique of standard mean-variance optimization, the weights displayed in Figure 10.9 differ from those in Figure 10.7 only for those sectors with explicit opinions.

CONCLUSION

In this chapter, we have demonstrated the intuition behind the portfolio optimization model presented by Black and Litterman (1992).

Their approach helps to alleviate many problems associated with the traditional mean-variance approach.

Their advice is intuitive and consistent with the normal investment behavior of an average investor. The asset manager starts from the market portfolio, or some strategic weighting scheme, constituting a neutral point of reference. Starting from all positive weights, the asset manager then deviates toward the most favored asset classes by taking appropriate long and short positions. Using the technique allows investors to distinguish between strong views and vague assumptions, as reflected by the optimal amount of deviation from the equilibrium weighting scheme. This technique reduces the problem associated with estimation errors and leads to more intuitive and less sensitive portfolio compositions. In addition, the Black-Litterman approach is flexible in expressing many possible views.

APPENDIX

TABLE 10A.1 Annualized Volatilities and Market-Capitalization Weights

		Historical Returns	Equilibrium Expected Returns	Market Capitalization Weights
AUTO	Automobiles	9.29%	11.07%	1.65%
BANK	Banks	16.34	9.73	15.04
BRES	Basic resources	8.17	7.38	1.22
CHEM	Chemicals	12.14	7.12	1.80
CONS	Construction	6.76	7.78	1.26
CYCL	Cyclical goods and services	6.95	8.94	2.85
CNCL	Noncyclical goods and services	11.96	5.94	2.90
ENGY	Energy	17.06	5.55	10.30
FISV	Financial services	14.53	10.04	4.12
FBEV	Food and beverages	9.65	6.50	4.59
INDS	Industrial goods and services	14.04	8.88	5.19
INSU	Insurance	15.51	9.61	6.89
MEDA	Media	15.52	7.89	3.27
PHRM	Pharmaceutical	20.32	6.70	10.24
RETL	Retail	10.12	6.43	2.27
TECH	Technology	25.01	12.73	11.03
TELE	Telecommunication	20.97	9.84	10.56
UTLY	Utilities	16.47	1.52	4.83

TABLE 10A.2 Correlation Structure between Dow Jones STOXX Sectors

	AUTO	BANK	BRES	CHEM	CONS	CYCL	CNCL	ENGY	FISV	FBEV	INDS	INSU	MEDA	PHRM	RETL	TECH	TELE	UTLY
AUTO	1.0000																	
BANK	0.7901	1.0000																
BRES	0.6921	0.5261	1.0000															
CHEM	0.8162	0.6756	0.7961	1.0000														
CONS	0.8289	0.7211	0.7865	0.8126	1.0000													
CYCL	0.8381	0.7759	0.7517	0.7904	0.9219	1.0000												
CNCL	0.7273	0.6569	0.5789	0.6911	0.7177	0.6995	1.0000											
ENGY	0.5582	0.5690	0.6043	0.7458	0.6801	0.6453	0.5558	1.0000										
FISV	0.8140	0.9449	0.5757	0.6866	0.7807	0.8345	0.6875	0.5689	1.0000									
FBEV	0.7632	0.7459	0.5994	0.7432	0.7263	0.7104	0.7947	0.5729	0.7504	1.0000								
INDS	0.7999	0.7456	0.7245	0.7579	0.8954	0.9002	0.6928	0.6367	0.7921	0.6066	1.0000							
INSU	0.8093	0.9279	0.4848	0.6528	0.6869	0.7411	0.6890	0.4898	0.9012	0.7240	0.7203	1.0000						
MEDA	0.2674	0.2656	0.1631	0.2309	0.4358	0.4828	0.1622	0.2196	0.3315	0.0335	0.5744	0.2739	1.0000					
PHRM	0.5555	0.6723	0.2979	0.4843	0.4426	0.5206	0.6521	0.3495	0.6859	0.6544	0.4654	0.7346	0.1522	1.0000				
RETL	0.7127	0.7064	0.5407	0.6880	0.7173	0.7282	0.8159	0.6250	0.7041	0.7149	0.7242	0.7039	0.2822	0.5981	1.0000			
TECH	0.5884	0.5744	0.4513	0.4536	0.6488	0.6996	0.3980	0.3970	0.6162	0.2706	0.7896	0.5980	0.7243	0.3627	0.5010	1.0000		
TELE	0.4579	0.4768	0.1772	0.2946	0.5009	0.5529	0.3536	0.2484	0.5213	0.1886	0.6289	0.5296	0.7618	0.3427	0.4602	0.7867	1.0000	
UTLY	0.0945	0.0841	0.0200	0.0387	0.0792	0.1298	0.0780	-0.027	0.1271	0.1135	0.1093	0.0330	0.1501	0.1552	0.2259	0.0645	0.1408	1.0000

bibliography

Adler, M., and B. Dumas. (1983). International Portfolio Choice and Corporation Finance: A Synthesis, *Journal of Finance, 38*, 925–984.

Adler, M., and P. Jorion. (1992). Universal Currency Hedges for Global Portfolios, *Journal of Portfolio Management, 18*, 28–35.

Adler, M., and B. Prasad. (1990). On Universal Currency Hedges, *Journal of Financial and Quantitative Analysis, 27*, 9–38.

Arshanapalli, B., T. D. Coggin, and J. Doukas. (1998). Multifactor Asset Pricing Analysis of International Value Investment Strategies, *Journal of Portfolio Management*, 10–23.

Ball, R., and S. P. Kothari. (1989). Non-Stationary Expected Returns: Implications for Tests of Market Efficiency and Serial Correlation of Returns, *Journal of Financial Economics, 25*, 51–74.

Banz, R. W., and W. Breen. (1986). Sample Dependent Results Using Accounting and Market Data: Some Evidence, *Journal of Finance, 41*, 779–793.

Beckers, S., R. Grinold, A. Rudd, and D. Stefek. (1992). The Relative Importance of Common Factors across the European Equity Markets, *Journal of Banking and Finance, 16*, 75–95.

Bekaert, G., and C. R. Harvey. (1995). Time-Varying World Market Integration, *Journal of Finance, 50*, 403–444.

Bekaert, G., and R. Hodrick. (1992). Characterizing Predictable Components in Excess Returns on Equity and Foreign Exchange Markets, *Journal of Finance, 47*, 467–509.

Black, F. (1972). Capital Market Equilibrium with Restricted Borrowing, *Journal of Business, 45*, 444–454.

Black, F. (1974). International Capital Markets with Investment Barriers, *Journal of Financial Economics, 1*, 337–352.

Black, F. (1989). Universal Hedging: Optimizing Currency Risk and Reward in International Equity Portfolio, *Financial Analysts Journal, 45,* 16–22.

Black, F. (1990). Equilibrium Exchange Rate Hedging, *Journal of Finance, 45,* 899–908.

Black, F., and R. Litterman. (1992). Global Portfolio Optimization, *Financial Analysts Journal* (September–October), 28–43.

Bollerslev, T., R. Chou, and K. Kroner. (1992). ARCH Modeling in Finance: A Review of the Theory and Empirical Evidence, *Journal of Econometrics, 52,* 5–59.

Boyer, B. H., M. S. Gibson, and M. Loretan. (1997). Pitfalls in Tests for Changes in Correlations, International Finance Discussion Papers No. 597, Board of Governors of the Federal Reserve System (First version, December 1997; revised, March 1999).

Brandenberger, S. (1995). Universal Currency Hedging, *Journal of Financial Markets and Portfolio Management, 9,* 458–481.

Breeden, D. (1979). An Intertemporal Asset Pricing Model with Stochastic Consumption and Investment Opportunities, *Journal of Financial Economics, 7,* 265–296.

Brown, S. J., and T. Otsuki. (1993). Risk Premia in Pacific-Basin Capital Markets, *Pacific-Basin Finance Journal, 1,* 235–261.

Burmeister, E., and M. B. McElroy. (1988). Joint Estimation of Factor Sensitivities and Risk Premia for the Arbitrage Pricing Theory, *Journal of Finance, 43,* 721–735.

Campbell, J. Y. (2001). Consumption-Based Asset Pricing, in G. Constantinides, M. Harris, and R. Stulz (Eds.), *Handbook of the Economics of Finance* (North Holland: Amsterdam).

Campbell, J. Y., and J. H. Cochrane. (1999). By Force of Habit: A Consumption-Based Explanation of Aggregate Stock Market Behavior, *Journal of Political Economy,* 205–251.

Campbell, J. Y., and Y. Hamao. (1992). Predictable Stock Returns in the United States and Japan: A Study of Long-Term Market Integration, *Journal of Finance, 37,* 43–69.

Campbell, J. Y., A. Lo, and A. C. MacKinley. (1997). *The Econometrics of Financial Markets* (Princeton, NJ: Princeton University Press).

Cassel, G. (1916). The Present Situation on the Foreign Exchanges, *Economic Journal,* 62–65.

Chamberlain, G. (1983). Funds, Factors and Diversification in Arbitrage Pricing Models, *Econometrica, 51,* 1305–1323.

Chamberlain, G., and M. Rothschild. (1983). Arbitrage, Factor Structure, and Mean Variance Analysis on Large Asset Markets, *Econometrica, 51,* 1281–1304.

Chan, K. C. (1988). On the Contrarian Investment Strategy, *Journal of Business, 61,* 147–163.

Chan, K. C., A. Karolyi, and R. Stulz. (1992). Global Financial Markets and the Risk Premium on U.S. Equity, *Journal of Financial Economics, 32,* 137–167.

Chan, L., J. Karceski, and J. Lakonishok. (1999). On Portfolio Optimization: Forecasting Covariances and Choosing the Risk Model, *Review of Financial Studies, 12,* 937–974.

Chen, N. F., R. Roll, and S. A. Ross. (1986). Economic Forces and the Stock Market, *Journal of Business, 59,* 383–403.

Cho, D. C., C. S. Eun, and L. W. Senbet. (1986). International Arbitrage Pricing Theory: An Empirical Investigation, *Journal of Finance, 41,* 313–329.

Chow, G., E. Jacquier, M. Kritzman, and K. Lowry. (1999). Optimal Portfolios in Good Times and Bad, *Financial Analysts Journal* (May–June), 65–73.

Cochrane, J. H. (1999a). New Facts in Finance, *Economic Perspectives,* 36–58.

Cochrane, J. H. (1999b). Portfolio Advice in a Multifactor World, *Economic Perspectives,* 59–78.

Cochrane, J. H. (2001). *Asset Pricing* (Princeton, NJ: Princeton University Press).

Cooper, I., and E. Kaplanis. (1995). Home Bias in Equity Portfolios and the Cost of Capital for Multinational Firms, *Journal of Applied Corporate Finance, 8,* 3, Fall, 95–102.

Cox, J., and S. Ross. (1976). The Valuation of Options for Alternative Stochastic Processes, *Journal of Financial Economics,* 145–166.

Davis, J. (1994). The Cross-Section of Realized Stock Returns: The Pre-Compustat Evidence, *Journal of Finance, 49,* 1579–1593.

De Bondt, W. F. M., and R. H. Thaler. (1985). Does the Stock Market Overreact? *Journal of Finance, 40,* 793–805.

De Santis, G., and B. Gerard. (1997). International Asset Pricing and Portfolio Diversification with Time-Varying Risk, *Journal of Finance, 52,* 1881–1912.

De Santis, G., and B. Gerard. (1998). How Big Is the Premium for Currency Risk? *Journal of Financial Economics,* 375–412.

Divecha, A., J. Drach, and D. Stefek. (1992). Emerging Markets: A Quantitative Perspective, *Journal of Portfolio Management,* 41–50.

Drobetz, W. (2000). Volatility Bounds for Stochastic Discount Factors on Global Stock Markets, Working paper, Swiss Institute of Banking and Finance (s/bf), University of St. Gallen.

Drobetz, W., and P. Wegmann. (1999). Mean-Reversion on Global Stock Markets, Working paper, Swiss Institute of Banking and Finance (s/bf), University of St. Gallen.

Drummen, M., and H. Zimmermann. (1992). The Structure of European Stock Returns, *Financial Analysts Journal* (July–August), 15–26.

Dumas, B. (1994). Partial Equilibrium versus General Equilibrium Models of the International Capital Market, in *The Handbook of International Macroeconomics* (London: Blackwell), Chap. 10, 301–347.

Dumas, B., C. R. Harvey, and P. Ruiz. (1999). Are Common Swings in International Stock Returns Justified by Subsequent Changes in National Output? Working paper, HEC School of Business and Duke University.

Dumas, B., and B. Solnik. (1995). The World Price of Foreign Exchange Risk, *Journal of Finance, 50,* 445–479.

Elton, E. J., M. J. Gruber, and C. R. Blake. (1995). Fundamental Economic Variables, Expected Returns, and Bond Fund Performance, *Journal of Finance, 50,* 1229–1256.

Embrechts, P., A. McNeil, and D. Straumann. (1999). Correlation: Pitfalls and Alternatives, *Risk* (May), 69–71.

Engle, R. F., D. M. Lilien, and R. P. Robins. (1987). Estimating Time Varying Risk Premia in the Term Structure: The ARCH-M Model, *Econometrica, 55,* 391–407.

Erb, C. B., C. R. Harvey, and T. E. Viskanta. (1994). Forecasting International Equity Correlations, *Financial Analysts Journal* (November–December), 32–45.

Errunza, V., and E. Losq. (1985). International Asset Pricing under Mild Segmentation: Theory and Test, *Journal of Finance, 40,* 105–124.

Fama, E. (1965). The Behavior of Stock Market Prices, *Journal of Business, 38,* 34–105.

Fama, E., and K. French. (1988). Permanent and Temporary Components of Stock Prices, *Journal of Political Economy, 96,* 246–273.

Fama, E., and K. French. (1989). Business Conditions and Expected Returns on Stocks and Bonds, *Journal of Financial Economics, 25,* 23–49.

Fama, E. F., and A. Farber. (1979). Money, Bonds and Foreign Exchange, *American Economic Review, 69,* 639–649.

Fama, E. F., and K. R. French. (1992). The Cross-Section of Expected Stock Returns, *Journal of Finance, 47,* 427–465.

Fama, E. F., and K. R. French. (1993). Common Factors in the Returns on Stocks and Bonds, *Journal of Financial Economics, 33,* 3–56.

Fama, E. F., and K. R. French. (1996). Multifactor Explanations of Asset Pricing Anomalies, *Journal of Finance, 51,* 55–84.

Fama, E. F., and K. R. French. (1998). Value versus Growth: The International Evidence, *Journal of Finance, 53,* 1975–1999.

Ferson, W., and C. R. Harvey. (1993). The Risk and Predictability of International Equity Returns, *Review of Financial Studies, 6,* 527–577.

Ferson, W. E., and C. R. Harvey. (1994). Sources of Risk and Expected Returns in Global Equity Markets, *Journal of Banking and Finance, 18,* 775–803.

Ferson, W. E., and R. A. Korajczyk. (1995). Do Arbitrage Pricing Models Explain the Predictability of Stock Returns? *Journal of Business, 68,* 309–349.

Ferson, W., S. Foerster, and D. Keim. (1993). General Tests of Latent Variable Model and Mean-Variance Spanning, *Journal of Finance, 48,* 131–156.

Forbes, K., and R. Rigobon. (1999). No Contagion, Only Interdependence: Measuring Stock Market Comovement, NBER Working paper No. 7267 (July).

Frankel, J. A., Ed. (1994a). *The Internationalization of Equity Markets* (Chicago: NBER and University of Chicago Press).

Frankel, J. A. (1994b). Introduction, in J. A. Frankel (Ed.), *The Internationalization of Equity Markets* (Chicago: NBER).

Freimann, E. (1998). Economic Integration and Country Allocation in Europe, *Financial Analysts Journal* (September–October), 32–41.

French, K. R., G. W. Schwert, and R. F. Stambaugh. (1987). Expected Stock Returns and Volatility, *Journal of Financial Economics, 19,* 3–29.

Friend, I., and M. Blume. (1975). The Demand for Risky Assets, *American Economic Review, 65,* 900–922.

Furrer, B., and B. Herger. (1999). Struktur Europäischer Aktienrenditen: Bedeutung und Veränderung internationaler, nationaler und sektoraler Faktoren, *Finacial Markets and Portfolio Management, 2,* 194–206.

Gibbons, M., and W. Ferson. (1985). Testing Asset Pricing Models with Changing Expectations and an Unobservable Market Portfolio, *Journal of Financial Economics,* 217–236.

Giddy, I. (1994). *Global Financial Markets* (Lexington, MA: D.C., Heath & Co.).

Glosten, L. R., R. Jagannathan, and D. Runkle. (1993). On the Relation between the Expected Value and the Volatility of the Normal Excess Return on Stocks, *Journal of Finance, 48,* 1779–1801.

Goetzman, W., and P. Jorion. (1999). Re-emerging Markets, *Journal of Financial and Quantitative Analysis, 34,* 1–32.

Griffin, J. M., and G. A. Karolyi. (1998). Another Look at the Role of the Industrial Structure of Markets for International Diversification Strategies, *Journal of Financial Economics, 50,* S. 351–373.

Grinold, R., A. Rudd, and D. Stefek. (1989). Global Factors: Fact or Fiction? *Journal of Portfolio Management,* Autumn, 79–88.

Grossman, S., and R. Shiller. (1981). The Determinants of the Variability of Stock Market Prices, *American Economic Review, 71,* S. 222–227.

Grossman, S., and R. Shiller. (1982). Consumption Correlatedness and Risk Measurement in Economics with Non-Traded Assets and Heterogeneous Information, *Journal of Financial Economics, 10,* 195–210.

Grubel, H. G. (1968). Internationally Diversified Portfolios: Welfare Gains and Capital Flows, *American Economic Review,* 1299–1314.

Gultekin, M., B. Gultekin, and A. Penati. (1989). Capital Controls and International Capital Market Segmentation: The Evidence from the Japanese and American Stock Markets, *Journal of Finance, 44,* 849–869.

Gultekin, N. B. (1983). Stock Market Returns and Inflation: Evidence from Other Countries, *Journal of Finance, 37,* 49–64.

Gultekin, N. M., N. B. Gultekin, and A. Penati. (1989). Capital Controls and International Capital Market Segmentation: The Evidence from the Japanese and American Stock Markets, *Journal of Finance, 44,* 849–869.

Hamilton, J. (1994). *Time Series Analysis* (Princeton, NJ: Princeton University Press).

Hansen, L. P., and K. Singleton. (1982). Generalized Instrumental Variables Estimation of Nonlinear Rational Expectations Models, *Econometrica, 50,* 1269–1288.

Hansen, L. P. (1982). Large Sample Properties of Generalized Method of Moments Estimators, *Econometrica, 50,* 1029–1054.

Hansen, L. P., and R. Jagannathan. (1991). Implications of Security Market Data for Models of Dynamic Economics, *Journal of Political Economy, 99,* 225–262.

Harlow, W. V. III. (1991). Asset Allocation in a Downside Risk Framework, *Financial Analysts Journal* (September–October), 28–40.

Harvey, C. R. (1988). The Real Term Structure and Consumption Growth, *Journal of Financial Economics,* 305–333.

Harvey, C. R. (1991). The World Price of Covariance Risk, *Journal of Finance, 46,* 111–157.

Harvey, C. R. (1994). Conditional Asset Allocation in Emerging Markets, NBER working paper 4623.

Harvey, C. R. (1995a). Emerging Stock Markets and International Asset Pricing, *World Bank Economic Review, 9,* 19–50.

Harvey, C. R. (1995b). Predictable Risk and Returns in Emerging Markets, *Review of Financial Studies, 8,* 773–816.

Harvey, C. R., and A. Siddique. (2000). Conditional Skewness in Asset Pricing Tests, *Journal of Finance, 55,* 1263–1295.

Harvey, C. R., B. Solnik, and G. Zhou. (1994). What Determines Expected International Asset Returns? Working paper, Duke University.

Harvey, C. R., and C. Kirby. (1996). Instrumental Variables Estimation of Conditional Beta Pricing Models, in G. Maddala and C. Rao (Eds.), *Handbook of Statistics, 14* (Amsterdam: Elsevier), 35–60.

He, G., and R. Litterman. (1999). *The Intuition Behind Black-Litterman Model Portfolios,* Goldman Sachs Investment Management Research.

Heston, S., and G. Rouwenhorst. (1994). Industry and Country Effects in International Stock Return, *Journal of Portfolio Management,* 53–58.

Heston, S., and G. Rouwenhorst. (1995). Does Industrial Structure Explain the Benefits of International Diversification? *Journal of Financial Economics, 36,* 3–27.

Heston, S., G. Rouwenhorst, and R. Wessels. (1995). The Structure of International Stock Returns and the Integration of Capital Markets, *Journal of Empirical Finance, 2,* 173–197.

Huberman, G. (1982). A Simple Approach to Arbitrage Pricing, *Journal of Economic Theory, 28,* 183–191.

Huberman, G., and S. Kandel. (1987). Mean-Variance Spanning, *Journal of Finance, 42,* 873–888.

Ikeda, S. (1991). Arbitrage Asset Pricing under Exchange Risk, *Journal of Finance, 46,* 447–455.

Ilmanen, A. (1995). Time-Varying Expected Returns in International Bond Markets, *Journal of Finance, 50,* 481–506.

Ilmanen, A. (1996). When Do Bond Markets Reward Investors for Interest Rate Risk? *Journal of Portfolio Management,* Winter, 52–64.

Ingersoll, J. E. (1984). Some Results in the Theory of Arbitrage Pricing, *Journal of Finance, 39,* 1021–1039.

Jobson, J. D., and B. Korkie. (1981a). Performance Hypothesis Testing with the Sharpe and Treynor Measures, *Journal of Finance, 36,* 889–908.

Jobson, J. D., and B. Korkie. (1981b). Putting Markowitz Theory to Work, *Journal of Portfolio Management, 6,* 70–74.

Jorion, P. (1985). International Portfolio Diversification with Estimation Risk, *Journal of Business, 58,* 259–278.

Jorion, P. (1986). Bayes-Stein Estimation for Portfolio Analysis, *Journal of Financial and Quantitative Analysis, 21,* 279–292.

Jorion, P. (1991). Bayesian and CAPM Estimators of the Means: Implications for Portfolio Management, *Journal of Banking and Finance, 15,* 717–727.

Jorion, P. (1996). *Value at Risk: A New Benchmark for Measuring Derivatives Risk* (Homewood, IL: Irwin).

Jorion, P., and S. Khouri. (1995). *Financial Risk Management. Domestic and International Dimensions* (London: Blackwell), 273–322.

Jorion, P., and E. Schwartz. (1986). Integration vs. Segmentation in the Canadian Stock Market, *Journal of Finance, 41,* 603–617.

Kaplanis, E. C. (1988). Stability and Forecasting of the Comovement Measures of International Stock Market Returns, *Journal of International Money and Finance, 7,* 63–75.

Korajczyk, R. A., and C. J. Viallet. (1990). An Empirical Investigation of International Asset Pricing, *Review of Financial Studies, 2,* 553–585.

Lakonishok, J., A. Shleifer, and R. Vishny. (1994). Contrarian Investment, Extrapolation, and Risk, *Journal of Finance, 49,* 1541–1578.

Lakonishok, J., A. Shleifer, and R. W. Vishny. (1995). Contrarian Investment, Extrapolation, and Risk, *Journal of Finance, 49,* 1541–1578.

Ledermann, J., and R. Klein, Eds. (1994). *Global Asset Allocation: Techniques for Optimizing Portfolio Management* (New York: Wiley).

Lee, W. (2000). *Advanced Theory and Methodology of Tactical Asset Allocation* (Chicago: Frank J. Fabozzi Associates).

Levy, H., and M. Sarnat. (1970). International Diversification of Investment Portfolios, *American Economic Review,* 668–675.

Lewis, K. K. (1999). Trying to Explain Home Bias in Equities and Consumption, *Journal of Economic Literature, 37* (June), 571–608.

Liew, J., and M. Vassalou. (2000). Can Book-to-Market, Size and Momentum Be Risk Factors That Predict Economic Growth? *Journal of Financial Economics, 57,* 221–245.

Lo, A. W., and A. C. MacKinlay. (1990). Data-Snooping Biases in Tests of Financial Asset Pricing Models, *Review of Financial Studies, 3,* 431–468.

Longin, F., and B. Solnik. (1995). Is the Correlation in International Equity Returns Constant: 1960–1990? *Journal of International Money and Finance, 14,* 3–26.

Longin, F., and B. Solnik. (2001). Extreme Correlation of International Equity Markets, *Journal of Finance, 56,* 651–678.

Lucas, R. (1978). Asset Prices in an Exchange Economy, *Econometrica, 46,* 1429–1446.

Mandelbrot, B. (1963). The Variation of Certain Speculative Prices, *Journal of Business, 36,* 394–419.

Markowitz, H. (1952). Portfolio Selection, *Journal of Finance* (March), 77–91.

Mehra, R., and E. Prescott. (1985). The Equity Premium: A Puzzle, *Journal of Monetary Economics, 15,* 145–161.

Merton, R. (1971). Optimum Consumption and Portfolio Rules in a Continuous-Time Model, *Journal of Economic Theory, 3,* 373–413.

Merton, R. (1980). On Estimating the Expected Return on the Market: An Exploratory Investigation, *Journal of Financial Economics, 8,* 323–361.

Merton, R. C. (1973). An Intertemporal Capital Asset Pricing Model, *Econometrica, 41,* 867–887.

Michaud, R. (1989). The Markowitz Optimization Enigma: Is Optimized Optimal? *Financial Analysts Journal* (January–February), 31–42.

Müller, U. (2000). Managing Currencies in International Portfolios, Doctoral Dissertation, University of St. Gallen (HSG).

Nelson, D. B. (1991). Conditional Heteroskedasticity in Asset Returns: A New Approach, *Econometrica,* 347–370.

Newey, W. K., and K. D. West. (1987). A Simple, Positive Semi-Definite, Heteroskedasticity and Autocorrelation Consistent Covariance Matrix, *Econometrica, 55*, 703–708.

Oertmann, P. (1997). *Global Risk Premia on International Investments* (Wiesbaden: Gabler).

Oertmann, P., and H. Zimmermann. (1998). Global Economic Premia on Stocks and Bond Markets, Working Paper, Swiss Institute of Banking and Finance, University of St. Gallen (HSG).

Pitts, A. (1997a). Asset Allocation and Market Opinions: The Synthesis (Part 1), *Swiss Banking Corporations/Prospects, 4–5,* 14–23.

Pitts, A. (1997b). Asset Allocation and Market Opinions: The Synthesis (Part 2), *Swiss Banking Corporations/Prospects, 6,* 12–21.

Poterba, J., and L. Summers. (1986). Mean Reversion in Stock Returns: Evidence and Implications, *Journal of Financial Economics, 22,* 27–60.

Richardson, M., and T. Smith. (1993). A Test of Multivariate Normality of Stock Returns, *Journal of Business,* 295–321.

Roll, R. (1977). A Critique of the Asset Pricing Theory's Tests: Part I, *Journal of Financial Economics, 4,* 129–176.

Roll, R. (1992). Industrial Structure and the Comparative Behaviour of International Stock Market Indexes, *Journal of Finance, 47*(1), 3–42.

Ross, S. A. (1976). The Arbitrage Theory of Capital Asset Pricing, *Journal of Economic Theory, 13,* 341–360.

Ross, S. A. (1978). Mutual Fund Separation in Financial Theory—The Separating Distributions, *Journal of Economic Theory, 17,* 254–286.

Rudolf, M., and H. Zimmermann. (1998a). An Algorithm for International Portfolio Selection and Optimal Currency Hedging, in J. Mulvey and W. Ziemba (Eds.), *Worldwide Asset and Liability Modelling* (Cambridge: Cambridge University Press), 315–340.

Rudolf, M., and H. Zimmermann. (1998b). Diversifikationseffekte internationaler Branchenportfolios, in J. Kleeberg and H. Rehkugler (Eds.), *Handbuch Portfoliomanagement. Strukturierte Ansätze für ein Modernes Wertpapiermanagement* (Wiesbaden: Uhlenbruch Verlag), 913–929.

Schwert, G. W. (1989). Why does Stock Market Volatility Change Over Time? *Journal of Finance, 44,* No. 5 (December), 1115–1153.

Sercu, P. (1980). A Generalization of the International Asset Pricing Model, *Review of the French Association of Finance,* 91–135.

Smith, R., and I. Walter. (2000). *High Finance in the Euro-Zone: Competing in the New European Capital Market* (Upper Saddle River, NJ: Financial Times/Prentice Hall).

Solnik, B. (1974a). An Equilibrium Model of the International Capital Market, *Journal of Economic Theory, 8,* 500–524.

Solnik, B. (1974b). The International Pricing of Risk: An Empirical Investigation of the World Capital Structure, *Journal of Finance,* 365–378.

Solnik, B. (1974c). Why Not Diversify Internationally Rather Than Domestically? *Financial Analysts Journal* (July–August), 48–54.

Solnik, B. (1983a). International Arbitrage Pricing Theory, *Journal of Finance, 38,* 449–457.

Solnik, B. (1983b). The Relation between Stock Prices and Inflationary Expectations: The International Evidence, *Journal of Finance, 38,* 35–47.

Solnik, B. (1993a). The Performance of International Asset Allocation Strategies Using Conditioning Information, *Journal of Empirical Finance, 1,* 33–55.

Solnik, B. (1993b). Predictable Time-Varying Components of International Asset Returns, Working paper, HEC School of Management.

Solnik, B. (1994). Predictable Time-Varying Components of International Asset Returns, Working paper, HEC.

Solnik, B. (2000). *International Investments,* 4th ed. (Reading, MA: Addison-Wesley).

Solnik, B., C. Boucrelle, and Y. Le Fur. (1996). International Market Correlation and Volatility, *Financial Analysts Journal* (September–October), 17–34.

Solnik, B., and J. Roulet. (2000). Dispersion as Cross-Sectional Correlation, *Financial Analysts Journal* (January–February), 54–61.

Speidell, L. S., and R. Sappenfield. (1992). Global Diversification in a Shrinking World, *Journal of Portfolio Management, 19*, 57–67.

Stehle, R. (1977). An Empirical Test of the Alternative Hypothesis of National and International Pricing of Risky Assets, *Journal of Finance, 32*, 493–502.

Stein, C. (1955). Inadmissibility of the Usual Estimator for the Mean of a Multivariate Normal Distribution, *Proceedings of the 3rd Berkeley Symposium on Probability and Statistics* (Berkeley: University of California Press).

Stulz, R. (1995). The Cost of Capital in Internationally Integrated Markets: The Case of Nestlé, *European Financial Management, 1*, 11–22.

Stulz, R. (1999). Globalization, Corporate Finance, and the Cost of Capital, *Journal of Applied Corporate Finance, 12*, 8–25.

Stulz, R. M. (1981a). A Model of International Asset Pricing, *Journal of Financial Economics, 9*, 383–406.

Stulz, R. M. (1981b). On the Effects of Barriers to International Investment, *Journal of Finance, 36*, 923–934.

Stulz, R. M. (1984). Pricing Capital Assets in an International Setting: An Introduction, *Journal of International Business Studies*, 55–72.

Stulz, R. M. (1995). International Portfolio Choice and Asset Pricing: An Integrative Survey, in Jarrow et al. (Eds.), *Finance*, Handbooks in Economic Research and Management Science, 201–223.

Tesar, L. L., and I. M. Werner. (1995). Home Bias and High Turnover, *Journal of International Money and Finance, 14*, 467–492.

Uppal, R. (1993). A General Equilibrium Model of International Portfolio Choice, *Journal of Finance, 48*, 529–553.

Wheatley, S. (1988). Some Tests of International Equity Integration, *Journal of Financial Economics, 21*, 177–212.

Wheatley, S. (1989). A Critique of Latent Variable Tests of Asset Pricing Models, *Journal of Financial Economics, 23*, 325–338.

Zellner, A. (1962). An Efficient Method for Estimating Seemingly Unrelated Regressions and Tests for Aggregation Bias, *Journal of the American Statistical Association, 57*, 348–368.

Zimmermann, H. (1998). *State Preference Theorie und Asset Pricing* (Wiesbaden: Springer-Verlag).

notes

Chapter 2   International Asset Pricing, Portfolio Selection, and Currency Hedging: An Overview

1. See, for example, the discussion in Adler and Dumas (1983), pp. 931–932, or Solnik (1996), pp. 28–29.
2. The conditions for the existence of representative price indices are illustrated in Adler and Dumas (1983), pp. 975–976 (Appendix).
3. See Stulz (1984), pp. 56–59, or R. M. Stulz (1995), pp. 2–5. In the literature on international finance, the commonly used abbreviation for the International Capital Asset Pricing Model is "ICAPM" (see, e.g., Stulz, 1995, p. 5). But "ICAPM" is often also used as abbreviation for Merton's (1973) Intertemporal CAPM. Thus, in order to avoid confusion, we apply "IntCAPM" here.
4. Equivalently, it could be assumed that there is a consumption basket with consumption shares that are identical and constant across investors. PPP must hold then.
5. The formal derivation of the model is similar to that of the domestic CAPM.
6. See, for example, Stulz (1984), p. 58, or R. M. Stulz (1995), pp. 8–10.
7. See Solnik (1974a), p. 512 (Separation Theorem 2).
8. According to Adler and Dumas (1983), pp. 946–947, there is no reason to discriminate between Solnik's (1974a) first two funds since they are held in the same proportion by all investors. Adler and Dumas (1983) define international portfolio separation on the basis of just two funds: an internationally diversified stock-bond portfolio and a domestic risk-free asset.
9. "Domestic" refers to returns translated into the benchmark currency, that is, including currency risk ("unhedged"), while "local"

refs to returns measured in the foreign currency, for example, the U.S. stock market return measured in U.S. dollars.

10. See Solnik (1974a), p. 515 (Theorem 3).

11. See Sercu (1980), p. 104 (Equation 11).

12. See the discussion in Solnik (1974a), p. 515.

13. Of course, from the perspective of empirical testing, the market portfolio cannot be observed directly either. But it is observable in principle, that is, the market capitalization of the various markets and assets does not depend on preferences. This, however, is not true for the currency hedging portfolio.

14. See Adler and Dumas (1983), pp. 941–944. A similar separation result is derived by Stulz (1981a), pp. 390–393 (Proposition 1).

15. See Adler and Dumas (1983), p. 947 (Corollary).

16. See Adler and Dumas (1983), pp. 948–950. The condition is implied by their Equation (14).

17. Other than Adler and Dumas (1983), Stulz (1981a) allows for changes of the investment opportunity set. In addition, Stulz (1981a) includes more detailed assumptions on the evolution of the prices of goods.

18. See Stulz (1984), pp. 63–65. The derivation of the pricing condition is similar to the derivation of the domestic CAPM.

19. Proposition 2 in Uppal (1993), p. 544, includes the somewhat obscure notion that a more risk-averse investor will invest a larger portion in foreign assets.

20. The model can easily be extended to a world where there is more than one risky asset in each country. See the discussion in Ikeda (1991), p. 454.

21. As before with the discussion of the utility-based models, the superscript denotes the currency of denomination.

22. See Ikeda (1991), p. 451 (Theorem).

23. See Solnik (1983a), p. 453 (Equation 9).

24. Such factors might increase the residual variance in the factor model. This would lead to a deteriorated fit of the pricing restriction, as demonstrated by Huberman (1982) and Ingersoll (1984), among others.

Chapter 3   The Anatomy of Volatility and Stock Market Correlations

1. See Chapter 6 of this book for market integration tests.
2. See Bollerslev, Chou, and Kroner (1992) for an overview of the related literature.
3. To allow for time varying expected returns in response to time variation in risk, Engle, Lilien, and Robins (1987) introduced yet another approach, the GARCH-in-the-mean technique. Recently, De Santis and Gerard (1998) have used this methodology to estimate the time variation in currency risk premiums. An alternative way to incorporate asymmetries is the T-GARCH specification proposed by Glosten, Jagannathan, and Runkle (1993).
4. Of course, most points in the upper right-hand region of the graphs originate from a single event, the crash in October 1987. Due to the 36-month overlap, conclusions must be drawn with utmost care.
5. This notion was already presented by Fama and French (1989), international evidence has been provided by Solnik (1993a). For economic models that relate time variation in expected returns to the business cycle and the consumption-smoothing behavior of rational investors see Drobetz and Wegmann (1999) and Campbell and Cochrane (1999). For an overview of the related literature see Cochrane (1999b).
6. Assigning bad states a greater probability than their empirical frequency is the major property of risk-neutral pricing. We will briefly introduce this concept to price stock options later.
7. See the discussion in Embrechts, McNeil, and Strauman (1999) for this point.
8. See Jorion (1996) for a detailed overview.

Chapter 4   The Correlation Breakdown in International Stock Markets

1. See for example the studies by Freimann (1998) using a randomization procedure, or Solnik and Roulet (2000) using the concept of cross-sectional dispersion of stock market returns.

2. Note that the purpose of this section is neither to provide an explanation nor to give an overview of the existing literature of any particular episode of stock market behavior such as the October 1987 stock market crash, the recent Asia crisis or the oil crises in the early seventies, to name just the most impressives.
3. For a further discussion of the equity home bias puzzle, see the recent studies by Lewis (1999), Cooper and Kaplanis (1995), and Tesar and Werner (1995).

Chapter 5   Global Economic Risk Profiles: Analyzing Value and Volitility Drivers in Global Markets

1. Of course, the markets' beta coefficients could be estimated equation by equation in principle. Yet, the SUR method yields more efficient estimates if the residuals $\{\varepsilon_{it}, i = 1, \ldots, n\}$ are cross-sectionally correlated. Such correlations are likely to exist, since it is not assumed that the seven factors incorporated in the model fully explain the covariances between the market returns. Thus, the estimation technique used here is consistent with the assumption of an approximate factor structure.

Chapter 6   Testing Market Integration: The Case of Switzerland and Germany

1. See Stulz (1999) for the necessary conditions.
2. Given two random variables X and Y, the following relationship holds: $E[XY] = E[X]E[Y] + Cov[X,Y]$. Applying this relationship to the Euler equation, the pricing restriction falls out.
3. The prediction that different countries' consumption rates should be highly correlated, even if growth rates in output are not, fares miserably when confronted with actual data. The empirical observation that consumption rates are not highly correlated across countries is referred to as the "home bias" in consumption in the literature. A good reference that reviews the related literature is Lewis (1999).
4. For a more detailed discussion see Campbell, Lo, and MacKinlay (1997).

5. See Campbell (2001) for a comprehensive review of the related literature.

6. See Harvey and Kirby (1996) for an overview.

7. Following the discussion in Harvey (1988), consumption rates are lagged by two quarters.

Chapter 7 Emerging Market Investments: Myth or Reality?

1. Similarly, Global Depository Receipts (GDR) allow foreign firms to trade on the London Stock Exchange.

2. See Speidel and Sappenfield (1992) and Divecha, Drach, and Stefek (1992). It must also be noted that several of the emerging markets should be better regarded as re-emerging markets. In particular, the major Latin American countries had prosperous and well-functioning stock markets in the early 1900s. In the 1920s, Argentina had a higher market capitalization than the United Kingdom. For details see Goetzman and Jorion (1999).

3. The IFC also constructs investible indices. Although these indices would be more appropriate, data is only available starting in the late 1980s. For the period when both IFC series are available, the return correlations are typically well above 0.95.

4. In fact, there is evidence that emerging market stock returns are predictable on the basis of commonly used (local) information variables. Harvey (1995b) finds that the amount of predictable return volatility in IFC markets exceeds that of a typical MSCI market.

5. The correlation between the smaller IFC markets and the MSCI markets (not reported here) is usually considerably smaller than the entries in Table 7.2.

6. This procedure was originally suggested by Richardson and Smith (1993) and Harvey (1995b).

7. In an asset pricing context, assets that decrease a portfolio's skewness (i.e., make the portfolio returns more skewed to the left) should command higher expected returns (e.g., Harvey & Siddique, 2000).

8. Interestingly, imposing a short-selling constraint should not substantially change the analysis in Figure 7.1. Looking at the

portfolio weights along the efficient frontier, there is a substantial short position only in the Canadian market. Short positions in the emerging markets are modest.

9. See Ferson, Foerster and Keim (1993) for a derivation of these moment conditions on the basis of traditional beta pricing models. There is one restriction on the coefficients in the C matrix for each test asset.

10. However, note that ex post there is always some discount factor that prices both MSCI and IFC markets (see Hansen & Jagannathan, 1991).

11. In equilibrium, all market participants hold the tangency (market) portfolio. The choice of this strategy is also convenient from a computational point of view, because a closed-form solution is available for this portfolio (see Merton, 1971).

12. For example, see Rudolf and Zimmermann (1998a).

13. For an application of a strategy that applies conditioning information to emerging markets data see Harvey (1994).

14. See Stein (1955) for the original reference.

15. See Jorion (1986) for a derivation.

16. The general form of the Stein-estimator is well known from standard Bayesian analysis. Estimation risk is measured as the average loss of an investor's utility in repeated samples. Technically spoken, the Stein-estimator is admissible relative to a quadratic loss function. This implies that there is no alternative estimator with at least equal and sometimes lower estimation risk for any value of the true unknown mean return. The summation of the components of a quadratic loss function allows increased risk to some individual components of the expected returns vector and less to others.

17. Contrary to this view, Drobetz and Wegmann (1999) show that mean reversion is consistent with rational asset pricing.

18. Of course, weights have to sum to one and, hence, there are some markets in the sample that have to be sold short from time to time. It turns out that the high weights for Switzerland during the late 1980s imply negative weights for the Canadian stock market.

Chapter 8 The Structure of Sector and Market Returns: Implications for International Diversification

1. See Drummen and Zimmermann (1992), Heston and Rouwenhorst (1994, 1995), Furrer and Herger (1999), Beckers, Grinold, Rudd, and Stefek (1992), among others.

2. Detailed results are available from the authors upon request.

3. Notice, moreover, a small inconsistency in the calculation of the country and sector trends, which is caused by the successive inclusion of younger countries in the index universe (Poland or Turkey, for instance). Stocks of these countries constitute a new country index. These countries are also included in the respective sector indices. As constituents of the sector indices the stocks of "new" countries immediately enter the sector trend calculation. As the constituents of the new country index, however, they enter the country trend calculation with a time lag of 12 months, since each new index needs to have a 12-month history before its correlation/volatility can be calculated and, hence, before it can be included in the average trend. The same problem will arise in the calculation of the sector and country efficient frontiers in section 5.

4. The 7 countries that are excluded are Luxembourg, Poland, China, Argentine, Brazil, Columbia, and Brazil. As mentioned in the previous footnote, this partly distorts the comparability of country and sector performances: The 7 countries cannot be included in the country portfolios, but they enter the return calculation of the sector indices. However, the influence of these countries in the sector indices is negligible, because they only account for 1.77 percent of the market capitalization altogether.

5. These returns differ from the country and sector returns in Table 8.4, because the descriptive statistics are based on continuously compounded returns, whereas the portfolio calculations are based on simple returns.

Chapter 10 Integrating Tactical and Equilibrium Portfolio Management: Putting the Black-Litterman Model to Work

1. See Chan, Karceski, and Lakonishok (1999) for a recent attempt to condition the covariance matrix on macroeconomic variables.

2. Throughout the examples we assume a coefficient of relative risk aversion γ of 3.

3. See Drobetz (2000) for a discussion and empirical results of spanning tests using volatility bounds for stochastic discount factors.

4. See Black and Littermann (1992), p. 32.

5. See Black and Litterman (1992), p. 33.

6. See Black and Litterman (1992), p. 35 and the appendix, and Chapter 7 in Lee (2000).

7. See Lee (2000) for a more in-depth analysis.

8. See Pitts (1997b), p. 13.

9. See Lee (2000), p. 176 and the Appendix in Black and Litterman (1992), p. 42.

10. For a discussion of Bayes' Law see for example Hamilton (1994).

11. See point 8 in the Appendix in Black and Litterman (1992). They suggest that the solution can be derived by the "mixed estimation" of Theil (1971).

12. The parameter τ is set equal to 0.3. Larger values of τ indicate less confidence in the equilibrium returns, which seems nonintuitive.

index